D1608177

# Making Murder

# Making Murder: The Fiction of Thomas Harris

Philip L. Simpson

**PRAEGER**
*An Imprint of ABC-CLIO, LLC*

A B C ⬤ C L I O

Santa Barbara, California • Denver, Colorado • Oxford, England

**Library of Congress Cataloging-in-Publication Data**
Simpson, Philip L., 1964–
   Making murder : the fiction of Thomas Harris /
by Philip L. Simpson.
      p.   cm.
   Includes bibliographical references and index.
   ISBN 978-0-313-35624-7 (hard copy : alk. paper) — ISBN 978-0-313-35625-4 (ebook)
   1. Harris, Thomas, 1940—Criticism and interpretation. I. Title.
   PS3558.A6558Z88      2010
   813′.54—dc22           2009038536

ISBN:  978-0-313-35624-7
EISBN: 978-0-313-35625-4

14   13   12   11   10      1   2   3   4   5

This book is also available on the World Wide Web as an eBook.
Visit www.abc-clio.com for details.

Praeger
An Imprint of ABC-CLIO, LLC

ABC-CLIO, LLC
130 Cremona Drive, P.O. Box 1911
Santa Barbara, California 93116-1911

This book is printed on acid-free paper ∞

Manufactured in the United States of America

To the memory of my grandparents: Clarence and June
Simpson, and Emma and William Adams

# Contents

# Acknowledgments

I could not have completed this book without the support of many people. They have each earned my immense gratitude and appreciation. First, I would like to thank Suzanne Staszak-Silva, former senior editor at Greenwood Press, for contacting me in late 2007 with a query as to whether I would be interested in writing a book-length study of the fiction of Thomas Harris. I had already written one book on the subject of serial murder in fiction and film, but somehow I didn't feel I had paid proper scholarly attention to the man whose fiction started my interest in the subject in the first place. Nagged by persistent thoughts that I had something more to write about Thomas Harris, I found Ms. Staszak-Silva's e-mail to be serendipitous. I am also grateful to Daniel Harmon, arts editor at Greenwood, for overseeing the completion of the manuscript. He responded to my numerous e-mail queries quickly and professionally, which is all any anxious writer nearing deadline can ask. I thank Ruth Janson, Coordinator of Rights and Reproductions for the Brooklyn Museum, New York, for assisting me in securing permissions to reproduce the image of William Blake's *The Great Red Dragon and the Woman Clothed with the Sun*; Kathryn Charles-Wilson and Meghan Mazella of the British Museum for permissions to Blake's *The Ancient of Days Putting a Compass to the Earth*; and Jennifer Riley and Jennifer Marsh of the Museum of Fine Arts, Boston, for permissions to

Duccio di Buoninsegna's *Triptych: the Crucifixion; the Redeemer with Angels; Saint Nicholas; Saint Gregory.*

During the writing of this book, I have discussed its ideas with many colleagues, but a couple of them contributed immeasurably to its intellectual development. Gary Hoppenstand, my mentor in the Popular Culture Association, inspired me many years before to examine the fiction of Thomas Harris in a critical, scholarly way. Alone among the scholars I knew at that time, he encouraged me to explore my interest in popular culture, particularly the fiction of Thomas Harris. Though he may not remember this, in his capacity as Area Chair of Horror he accepted my presentation on "The Serial Killer as Postmodern Vampire" for the 1995 Popular Culture Association/American Culture Association Annual Conference— a fortuitous moment in my graduate student career that led more or less directly to the book you now hold in your hands. I thank him for his influence on my life and for his gracious praise of the first draft of this book. Tony Magistrale, one of the preeminent scholars on the work of Stephen King and a professor of English at the University of Vermont, suggested that I should look into Harris's treatment of race and class relations. I thank Tony for his insights and his generous praise of this book's first draft. I also thank Mary Findley, of Vermont Technical College, for her ideas about serial killer fiction and especially for her encouragement throughout the writing process. As a matter of fact, she persuaded me to say "yes" to this book when I had so many other writing projects already in the pipeline. Tony Williams, Professor of English and Film at my alma mater of Southern Illinois University, continues to earn my respect and gratitude for his never-flagging support of my scholarship. I thank David Tietge, Associate Professor of English and Associate Director of the Writing Center at Monmouth University, for not only being my friend, but also my sounding board for various theories. I thank Benjamin Szumskyj, editor of *Dissecting Hannibal Lecter*, a recent scholarly collection of essays on Thomas Harris's fiction. He graciously invited me to join the ranks of his contributors, a pleasurable task I had no sooner completed than the offer to write a book of my own on Thomas Harris came to me. I cite many of Benjamin's ideas, as well as those of his contributors, in these pages. I thank my two research librarians, Tracy Nectoux and Shelly Mudgett, both of whom spent many hours finding research on Thomas Harris for me. Tracy is a cataloger for the Illinois Newspaper Project at the University of Illinois-Champaign, and Shelly is a Library Services Specialist at Florida State University. I thank the faculty, staff, and administration at Brevard Community College for their professional support. Of course, this book would not exist without the patience, love, and support of my friends and family.

Finally, I am grateful to Thomas Harris for producing a remarkable series of books. They have entertained, thrilled, enlightened, challenged, and flat-out terrified readers for many years. I am proud to count myself among them, ever since I first read *Black Sunday* as a child in 1976. His work inspired me to write a dissertation, a first book, a couple of essays, and now this present study. Thank you, Mr. Harris.

# 1

# The Elements of Murder and Mercy: Thomas Harris and His Fiction

Investigator Will Graham, having been shot and stabbed by a madman, now lies in a hospital bed with an IV line feeding Demerol into his veins. Not unlike the serial killers he has confronted, he falls into a waking dream wherein the past collides with the present and memories have the power to recreate pain anew. Recalling an earlier springtime visit to Bloody Pond at Shiloh, he reflects on the tranquility of the place in ironic opposition to the bloody Civil War battle that once raged there and the small but lethal struggles that took place there when he visited. He witnessed predatory bream darting through the pond water and a snake mortally run down in the road by a passing car. Graham picked up the writhing snake and cracked it like a whip to end its suffering. His action combined both the tenderness of mercy and the violence of judgment. Lying in his hospital bed and thinking about Shiloh, he reaches an epiphany. Nature is indifferent to men. It is not nature that is haunted, but men. It is not nature that makes murder, but men. The one hope is that men also make mercy.

Thomas Harris, the best-selling novelist and creator of the character of Will Graham in the novel *Red Dragon*, attributes these words to Graham's consciousness: "There is no murder. We make murder, and it matters only to us."[1] In context, the passage suggests that while humans manufacture both mercy and murder, nature itself is blameless and outside of our fragile frameworks of morality. We cannot hold nature accountable for our own virtues or our own failings. Our minds make the kind of world in which we live, or as John Milton said in *Paradise Lost*: "The mind is its own place, and in itself, can make heaven of Hell, and a hell of Heaven." Following in the spiritual and literary tradition of John Milton, Thomas Harris shows us the worldly hell that human beings can forge from the molten heat of their interior anguish. The human plight, which Shiloh both witnesses and mocks, is to choose whether to dispense mercy or murder for wrongs both intended and unintended, real and imagined. The urge to murder translates all too easily into action when human beings are insulted. Mercy is harder to come by. Will Graham knows this dilemma as he lies in the multi-level prison of his mind and his hospital bed.

But Harris, a master of moral ambiguity, does not leave Graham, or the reading audience, helplessly pinned between the horns of this dilemma. Harris suggests the barest glimmer of hope to resolve or at least come to terms with this existential crisis when his fictional surrogate Graham wonders "if, in the great body of humankind, in the minds of men set on civilization, the vicious urges we control in ourselves and the dark instinctive knowledge of those urges function like the crippled virus the body arms against. . . . if old, awful urges are the virus that makes vaccine."[2]

Perhaps the very thing that haunts all of human history—our urge to murder one another—is what empowers us to resist it. Knowing we are capable of murdering those who have injured or offended us is the first step in refraining from acting upon it. Civilization is constructed upon this decision not to act in violence. However, Harris is very careful to phrase this as only a possibility. His selection of the word *if* is deliberate. The ambiguity in the hearts of humanity is a key aspect of Harris's work, both in this novel and his others.

While Graham is nominally the hero of *Red Dragon*, by far the center stage is taken by the savage serial killer of entire families, Francis Dolarhyde. The title of the book refers to Dolarhyde, not Graham. The dark fascination of the book lies in its excursion into the profound pain, loneliness, and rage that characterize Dolarhyde and lead him to kill to feel accepted and desired. Through Harris's skill in portraying the tortured landscape of Dolarhyde's consciousness, the reader is manipulated, almost seduced, into identifying with Dolarhyde. Graham, alienated from his family and peers by the awful burden of his own ability to sympathize with murderous points of view, succumbs to his own "old, awful urge" and sets up an annoying reporter for murder, or so the novel strongly implies. No one, not even the reader, is safe around Harris's serial killers, either physically or psychologically.

Within the pages of *Red Dragon*, Harris introduces the reader to yet another serial killer and an even more seductive symbol of the power of violence. Hannibal Lecter, MD, is now so well-known to the reading and film-going public, so much a part of our cultural consciousness, it is difficult to appreciate that in his first appearance he plays no more than a supporting role in the drama of Will Graham's pursuit of Francis Dolarhyde. Yet it is Lecter who manipulates much of the action within the story and ultimately sets Dolarhyde onto a direct collision course with the Graham family. Following his 1981 introduction, Lecter has grown into the character so well known to us now.

A small, sleek man with an extra finger and maroon eyes, Lecter combines polymath intellectualism with utter savagery. He is a lethal paradox, a study in binary oppositions. He embodies what is highest in the esteem of humanity and the lowest. He demands courtesy but does unspeakably discourteous things to his victims. His name, derived from the Latin *legere* (to read), designates him as a reader—a critical reader of other people. His skill in reading and thus manipulating other people is unmatched, enabling him to direct events on a large scale even while incarcerated. He is a criminal mastermind right out of the pages of noir. In effect, his portrayal is so compelling that he escapes the boundaries Harris sets for him in *Red Dragon* and steals the show. Since that auspicious debut, Lecter has returned in three more (to date) of Harris's novels, occupying a more central role in each one. The last, *Hannibal Rising*, takes the reading audience into the early development of the most famous literary serial killer and gives him an epic back story. Lecter has been very good to Thomas Harris. So far, Harris shows no sign of tiring of his creation.

The irony is that while Lecter has become a genuine cultural phenomenon, with a lot of people now knowing a lot about him, the reading public knows little about his creator, Thomas Harris. Nowhere is this distance between writer and public captured in more succinct form than the titles of a handful of published author profiles that just can't resist coming up with playful variations on Harris's own title *The Silence of the Lambs*, typically something like "The Silence of the Writer." From titles like these, it might be tempting to conclude that Harris is a literary, if not personal, recluse, a shut-in ranking up there with J. D. Salinger and Thomas Pynchon. The dark subject matter that Harris traffics in no doubt cements that conclusion in the minds of some.

Yet all those who personally know Harris insist that Harris is not reclusive, but rather that he's actually a sweet-natured Southern gentleman. He has a wide and loyal circle of friends, enjoying a reputation as an excellent cook. He has long been a fixture on the social scene in the Hamptons. He lives with his long-time girlfriend, the publishing editor Pace Barnes, in south Florida. Everyone in the media knows where to find him if they want to. According to writer Phoebe Hoban, he even takes the time to answer fan mail. One can hardly imagine Salinger or Pynchon being this accessible.

The one thing Harris consistently refuses to engage in is talk about his work, except in the broadest and most sweeping of terms. He explains to Hoban: "It's true I don't do interviews. And I haven't in fifteen years. I think it's better to try to put everything in books . . . I have to be fair to everybody. I think it's better to have a blanket policy about it. You can't favor one publication or another. So I just work and try to put things in my books that I want to say. And really that's about the size of it."[3]

It's hard to argue with the basic premise underlying Harris's policy statement. His fairness doctrine is practically unassailable in its integrity. Since he can't grant every media request that comes his way, he won't grant any of them. He won't play favorites or choose one interview forum over another based on arbitrary criteria.

Therefore, anyone approaching Harris's body of work in an effort to draw conclusions about it must do so without the benefit of Harris's own interpretations of his own novels. The work must speak for itself. Similarly, conclusions about Harris himself must be drawn from his novels, the testimony of others, and a handful of published statements about his craft. David Sexton says it best: "[Harris] can be profiled from the scenes of these crime books."[4] Let us endeavor to do just that, to the extent we can.

## THE LIFE AND CAREER OF THOMAS HARRIS

So what is known about Thomas Harris, the man? He was born in Jackson, Tennessee, in 1940 to William and

Polly Harris. At the time of Thomas's birth, William Thomas Harris Jr. worked as an electrical engineer for the Tennessee Valley Authority, and Polly as a high school teacher of chemistry and biology. Polly moved with her baby boy to Rich, Mississippi, to be close to family while the elder Thomas was away in World War II. Rich was a town of a few hundred people. Returning home after the war, William became a less-than-successful farmer of a small operation, while Polly taught biology at the local school. The Harris family suffered financially. This is the rural environment that Thomas Harris, an only child, grew up in. This type of southern rural, agrarian environment appears frequently in Harris's fiction.

Those who have spoken publicly about Harris's childhood in Rich speak consistently of his love of reading. His mother Polly reports that he was reading by the age of three years old. His uncle, Dr. James Arch Coleman, also speaks of Harris's love of reading and adds that he was "quiet" and "as plain as an ordinary shoe."[5] As Harris grew older, he often told his mother that he would be a writer when he grew up. Apparently one of his favorite writers, one whose influence is evident in the style of Harris's published prose, was Ernest Hemingway.

Reporter Meg Laughlin unearthed more information about Harris's formative years in Rich, the details of which explain a great deal about the various characters and themes populating Harris's novels. According to the various residents of Rich that she interviewed, Harris did not interact much with his peers. The boy's social ostracism may partially explain why Harris as an adult writes so convincingly about alienated loners. In particular, the childhood history of the character Michael Lander in *Black Sunday* and Harris's share some similarities, right down to the short, baggy pants. Occasionally, the young Harris joined his cousins to shoot snakes and turtles from the Yazoo Pass bridge but did not enjoy killing animals as much as his peers did.[6] If nothing else, this particular detail explains why Harris copyrights his books as Yazoo Fabrications.[7]

As an older boy, Harris attended Clarksdale High School and did not have a good experience there either. He did not often participate in sports and endured what is a fairly routine childhood rite of passage for many creative, sensitive males—not being picked for school sports teams. He moved to live with his aunt in Cleveland, Mississippi, leaving behind Clarksdale High and entering Cleveland High School. His experience at Cleveland High was much better. He interacted more with his peers, participated in chorus and drama, and cruised the town with his friend Stanley Gaines (who later grew up to be a wealthy oilman). For unknown reasons, Harris transferred to another high school in Clarksdale, Mississippi, to finish out his senior year.

Baylor University is a Baptist college in Waco, Texas. Established in 1845, the university has a long tradition of education with a strong Christian influence. This is the university environment that Harris chose for himself in 1961. Majoring in English, he also worked first part-time and then full-time at the city desk of the *Waco News Tribune*, writing about criminal cases. In addition to writing for the newspaper, he apparently wrote some gruesome short stories for now-defunct men's magazines *True* and *Argosy*.[8] Dallas Lee, one of Harris's student co-workers on the night shifts at the newspaper, said of Harris's trip to Mexico to investigate criminal trafficking in child prostitution: "[Harris] had an appetite to examine the horrors of existence . . . and a curiosity to know about these things."[9] Lee also shared other details about Harris's Mexican excursion, including the chilling story of a black-clad grandmother who gave gifts to families in order to take their children.[10] While in Mexico, Harris's exploration of the dark side of human nature led him to cross the path of another villainous character, this one a jailed Mexican doctor who was also a multiple murderer.

Harris apparently told publisher Helen Fraser that this doctor was the inspiration for the character of Dr. Hannibal Lecter.[11] The experience of working on such horrific real-life stories undoubtedly contributed to the verisimilitude of Harris's later crime thrillers. During these busy years, Harris also found time to marry a fellow undergraduate named Harriet, with whom he had a daughter named Anne. Harris graduated from Baylor in 1964.

The marriage did not last long, ending at some point in the sixties. Following his divorce, he left the United States for a period of time to travel throughout Europe. He secured a job as a reporter at the Associated Press (AP) in New York City from 1968 to 1974. He also worked as night editor and was remembered as "taking more time with each article than any of the other editors."[12] His generosity is remembered by Tom Goldstein, who was an AP writer at the time:

> I remember once I was covering the shooting of Joe Colombo in 1971 at Columbus Circle, and getting pushed around. When we filed, it always got dumped to a rewrite man. I remember when Tom got my story, he shook his head, and as soon as everybody left, he put my byline on it.[13]

Along with Nick Pileggi (future author of *Wise Guy*), Harris reported on numerous crime stories, most of them robberies and murders. In many ways, his work at the AP paralleled what he had been doing in Waco, except on a much larger, urban scale. However, Harris's world was on the verge of transforming dramatically.

One night in 1973, Harris and two other AP reporters, Sam Maull and Dick Riley, made the decision that they could write a thriller inspired by two recent high-profile acts of Middle Eastern terrorism: the 1972 massacres at the airport in Tel Aviv and the Munich Olympics. The three reporters met many times at Teacher's, a bar on the Upper West Side, to hash out their ideas. The resulting plot centered on a terrorist attack in the United States, specifically at the Super Bowl. The title of the book, *Black Sunday*, crowds a number of meanings into two simple words. It directly references the traditional game day of the Super Bowl, hints at an atrocity heinous enough to be deemed "black," and indirectly evokes the name of the infamous terrorist organization Black September. Of the novel's most striking plot device, Maull says, "Using the Goodyear blimp as the delivery vehicle for the explosives was Tom's idea."[14] The three co-writers researched the idea, sold it to Putnam, and divided the advance equally. At some point during this process, Harris took over solo authorship of the novel. The novel was published in hardback by G. P. Putnam's Sons in 1975 and achieved best-seller status. The Bantam paperback release, and many more reprintings, followed.

A film adaptation directed by John Frankenheimer premiered in 1977, starring Bruce Dern as American blimp pilot and would-be mass murderer Michael Lander, Marthe Keller as ruthless Black September operative Dahlia Iyad, and Robert Shaw as Israeli commando David Kabakov. Predicted to be a huge success, the film instead proved to be a box-office disappointment. Writer Daniel O'Brien attributes its financial failure to the release the year before of *Two Minute Warning*, a film from Universal about a sniper terrorizing the Super Bowl; the lack of bankable stars; a director and screenwriter past their primes; and a perhaps-too-sympathetic portrayal of the Palestinian cause.[15] The film release disappointment notwithstanding, the sale of the novel and the adaptation rights provided Harris with the financial wherewithal to become a full-time fiction writer. He left the AP behind forever.

Harris is not known for publishing novels in quick succession. It would be six years before he published a follow-up to *Black Sunday*. He was not idle during that time, however. A meticulous researcher who had honed his craft through years of crime reporting, he began to take note of what was just starting to happen at the FBI's

Behavioral Science Unit, or BSU, regarding the study of a "new" kind of murderer. The public would soon hear a great deal about the work of these FBI agents in analyzing the evidence of crime scenes to construct psychological profiles of the perpetrators, but Harris was researching the phenomenon before practically anyone else (outside of law enforcement). David Sexton writes of this period in Harris's career: "Although five or six years seems a long time to spend writing a thriller, Harris had actually identified a new trend extremely fast."[16] This brand of cultural prescience is typical of Harris, in that he wrote about an aerial terrorist attack against the United States more than two decades before it actually happened and anticipated what cultural critic Philip Jenkins calls the "serial killer panic" of the 1980s.[17] Arguably, Harris even helped create the panic with his second novel.

During the late 1970s, two FBI agents, John Douglas and Robert Ressler, began to conduct in-depth interviews with a number of convicted murderers, including multiple murderers. In particular, the agents were interested in determining what factors drove some men to murder again and again, with a certain period of "cooling off" between murders until the compulsion to kill seized them once more. Robert Ressler claimed a cultural immortality of sorts by coining the instantly memorable phrase "serial killer" to label this kind of murderer. While Douglas, Ressler, and other law enforcement agents were classifying these killers and sharing the results with their professional peers, Harris first showed up at the BSU in Quantico, Virginia, in 1978 or so, asking to see the facility and asking questions about criminal profiling and specific serial murder cases. Harris would return on a number of unspecified visits to the BSU, sitting in on classes and talking to agents. According to Douglas, Harris learned specific details about the *modus operandi* of serial killers such as Ted Bundy, Gary Heidnick, and Ed Gein— details later assigned to Harris's fictional characters. For example, Bundy sometimes wore a sling and cast on his arm to fool young women into helping him, at which point he would club them. Gary Heidnick kept women captive in a pit in his basement. Ed Gein wore female skins to make a "woman suit" for himself. All of these are behaviors exhibited by Jame Gumb, the serial killer in *The Silence of the Lambs*.[18]

We don't have to imagine what a seasoned FBI agent must have made of this quiet, bespectacled civilian writer's request to learn about serial killers and crime scene investigation, because Ressler tells us about it. According to Ressler, the FBI's public affairs office asked him to give Harris a tour of the BSU in the early 1980s. Harris told Ressler that he was writing a second novel, this one about a serial killer. Ressler's memory may be off by a few years here, since *Red Dragon* was published in 1981. It is more likely that Harris's first visit took place in the late 1970s. Be that as it may, Ressler explained to Harris how profiling worked and what role the FBI would play with local law enforcement in a serial murder investigation. Harris listened raptly, saying little, as Ressler shared details about the crimes of notorious serial killers such as Edmund Kemper, who murdered co-eds in and around Santa Cruz, California, and Richard Chase, "the Vampire of Sacramento," whose brutal crimes shocked even veteran police officers. Ressler mentioned that psychiatrists were being called in as consultants on these cases more and more. Harris most likely filed this fact away to re-emerge as the character of Hannibal Lecter, the serial-killing psychiatrist who helps the FBI develop profiles of unidentified killers, which later took shape in his mind. Ressler's final literary verdict on Harris, for what it's worth, is that his novels "are superb, though they are not truly realistic in their portrayals either of the serial killers or of the heroes and heroines inside the FBI."[19] Ressler mildly complains that Harris's killers display behaviors and traits not often found in one individual and that FBI profilers leave actual investigations to local law enforcement agencies. Certainly, Harris took dramatic license with what he learned from his visits to the BSU, as would be expected of a crafter of the most compelling story possible. It is also worth noting that Harris does not uncritically sing the praises of profiling, in spite of, or maybe because of, his time spent with the BSU.

While Harris was incorporating his research into drafting *Red Dragon* in 1979, his father became terminally ill. So Harris returned to Rich to be with his family and tend to his father. Harris ultimately spent eighteen months in Rich, working alone on the novel late into the night in an isolated shotgun-style house in the middle of a cotton field. The house belonged to a friend who let him use the house as a writer's studio. Harris informally adopted and fed a number of stray dogs of all types and temperaments that had gathered into a pack and whose range included the cotton fields. He sometimes took nocturnal breaks from writing to walk out into the flat field, accompanied by his canine friends. From far out in the field, he often looked back at the lighted house. By Harris's own account, this is the lonely rural setting in which Hannibal Lecter came to him as a fully realized character. It is easy to visualize Harris sitting at his writer's desk, or wandering into the cotton field in the dark of night, as the maroon eyes and imperially slim form of Dr. Lecter became ever more real to him in his writer's imagination. It was also here that Harris visualized the home of the Leeds family, the unfortunates who are murdered by serial killer Francis Dolarhyde, through the eyes of profiler Will Graham as he walks alone through the blood-soaked house at night to find clues. In many ways, *Red Dragon* is built upon this one primal scene. Harris says, "I pushed to find out, to see what came before and what came after. I went through the home, the crime scene, in the dark with Will and could see no more and no less than he could see."[20] Going through "the dark with Will" takes on added poignancy when Harris acknowledges sympathy for Graham as a result of Harris's own daily struggle at this time to accept the imminent death of his father. Harris's father died on May 1, 1980. Harris dedicated *Red Dragon* to him.

Harris's second novel was published in hardback by G. P. Putnam's Sons in 1981. The publication of *Red Dragon* brought him favorable reviews and much more money. The book became a best seller. The paperback rights sale to Bantam in the United States and Corgi in England brought in more than 1 million U.S. dollars and 115,000 British pounds, respectively. Additionally, it was a main selection of the Literary Guild and the Doubleday Book Club, and was serialized in *Crime Digest*.

Those familiar with Harris's writing from *Black Sunday* were in for a shock or a treat, depending on one's point of view. *Red Dragon*, a chilling depiction of a psychopath who murders entire families in the dead of night and an FBI relatively helpless to stop him, is both more finely crafted and much more frightening than the geopolitical melodrama and foiled mass murder plot of Harris's first novel. By all accounts, including the author's own, *Red Dragon* is the novel where Harris found his author's voice. And a terrifying voice it was. A friend of Harris named Lanford Wilson says that Harris reread the novel on the beach and "was horrified that he had written it. Because of the madness and violence. He said, 'My God, where did that come from?' He horrified himself."[21]

However horrified he actually was, Harris continued to explore the madness and violence during return visits to Quantico. There, he attended more classes, met again with Robert Ressler, and learned more about serial killer cases. Ressler says forthrightly that in the wake of publication of *Red Dragon*, he was "proud to have provided some facts on which [Harris's] fertile imagination could work."[22] Ressler takes issue with Harris's notion that Will Graham's mental disturbances after encountering Lecter would have disqualified him from returning to the FBI. Ressler elaborates, "I thought this was comical, given the weight losses, the pseudo heart attacks, and other problems that many of us in the BSU had experienced."[23] Whatever his reservations about Harris's artistic license, Ressler shared with him more details about killers such as Ed Gein. Ressler also says, none too subtly in light of the central female character of Harris's third novel, "I also introduced Harris to the lone female agent who was working with the BSU at the time."[24] Could this introduction indeed have been the genesis of Clarice Starling, the protagonist of Harris's third novel?

While Harris worked on his next project, the film rights to *Red Dragon* were purchased in 1983 by the maverick Italian producer, Dino de Laurentiis. It was not an especially promising development. Producer de Laurentiis had a spotty industry record at best, having left his native Italy in the late 1960s following a number of expensive failures. In the United States, he continued to bankroll notorious flops, such as the *Jaws*-derivative *Orca the Killer Whale* (1977). He was known for high-camp projects such as *Barbarella* (1968) and *Flash Gordon* (1980). Yet he had also accumulated successes, including *Serpico* (1973), *Death Wish* (1974), the much-reviled but financially lucrative remake of *King Kong* (1976), *Conan the Barbarian* (1981), and *The Dead Zone* (1983). If nothing else, he was savvy enough to legally lock in the rights to all future Thomas Harris novels. What this meant in practical terms was that whenever a new novel was published, de Laurentiis would be the first person allowed to bid on the book and, if he passed on it, to be given the last opportunity to match the bid.

The film version of *Red Dragon* was renamed *Manhunter*, directed by Michael Mann and released in August 1986. The film starred William Petersen as Will Graham, Brian Cox as Lecter (spelled "Lektor" in the film), Kim Greist as Molly Graham, Joan Allen as Reba McClane, and Tom Noonan as Francis Dolarhyde (spelled "Dollarhyde" in the film). While the film would later go on to achieve cult status on video and growing critical approval in retrospect, *Manhunter* earned only $8.62 million during its initial domestic run. Harris also reportedly disapproved of the film's changes to his storyline (although he may have liked Brian Cox's portrayal of Lecter). Given the disappointing performance of *Black Sunday*, the track record of Harris film adaptations was thus far not a good one.

Two years after *Manhunter*, seven years after *Red Dragon*, what many consider to be Harris's finest novel was published in hardback by St. Martin's Press in 1988. A sequel to *Red Dragon*, *The Silence of the Lambs* inverts the emphasis on its two serial killers, the returning Hannibal Lecter now in the feature role and Jame Gumb as the "guest" serial killer. Harris introduces young female FBI trainee, Clarice Starling, who now assumes the role that Will Graham previously occupied as FBI Special Agent Jack Crawford's protégé. The book became an instant best seller and secured praise from critics, including a glowing celebrity endorsement from famous horror writer Clive Barker. The Horror Writers Association (HWA) awarded *Silence* with the 1988 Bram Stoker Award for Superior Achievement in a Novel. Given this public and critical success, and in spite of the questionable financial performance of the earlier Harris-based movies, a film adaptation was inevitable.

Having been disappointed in *Manhunter*'s box office returns, Dino de Laurentiis did not pursue the rights to *The Silence of the Lambs* and reportedly gave them for free to Harris and Orion studios, a decision he would no doubt later bitterly rue. Hollywood star Gene Hackman was interested not only in the Lecter role, but in taking on the project for Orion Pictures as his first directing assignment. Screenwriter Ted Tally scripted the film, sticking fairly close to Harris's story. However, Hackman eventually passed on the film. The director's role went to Jonathan Demme. A veteran of Roger Corman's New World production company, Demme set about crafting the film on a relatively modest budget. Michelle Pfeiffer declined to play the role of Starling, so Jodie Foster took her place. Brian Cox, the "Lektor" of Mann's film, was replaced by Anthony Hopkins. Like Harris before them, Foster, Hopkins, and actor Scott Glenn (who played Crawford) visited Quantico and spent time with John Douglas. Some of the scenes were shot at the FBI facility, adding to the movie's verisimilitude.

The film was released on February 13, 1991—surely a unique Valentine's Day present to the film-going public and decidedly not the typical "date movie." The third time proved the charm for a Harris adaptation, as *Silence* grossed $130 million in the United States and Canada to become the third-highest grossing film of 1991. Before its run was over, the film had grossed over $250 million worldwide (none of which saved financially strapped Orion Pictures from filing for bankruptcy in December 1991). It won five major Academy Awards in 1992, including Best Picture, Best Actor for Hopkins, Best Actress for Jodie Foster, Best Director for Demme, and Best Adapted Screenplay for Tally. Flush with success, Demme announced backstage at the awards ceremony that he couldn't wait to make a sequel to *Silence*. The critical reaction to *Silence*'s Oscar triumph was by no means universally laudatory, and many gay-rights advocates objected to the film's perceived derogatory portrayal of transsexualism/transvestitism. In any event, cinematic history had been made. Anthony Hopkins was the first actor since Marlon Brando in *The Godfather* (1972) to win the major acting award for playing a villain, and the first actor since Fredric March in *Dr. Jekyll and Mr. Hyde* (1932) to win it for a horror film. Only two other films, *It Happened One Night* (1934) and *One Flew Over the Cuckoo's Nest* (1975), had won in all five major awards categories.

Cashing in on the phenomenal success of *Silence*, studios scrambled to make other "respectable" or upscale serial killer movies, like *Seven* (1994) and the ironically named *Copycat* (1995), marketed to mainstream audiences. Director Spike Lee turned to the genre with his film *Summer of Sam* (1999), based on the "Son of Sam" murders that terrorized New York City during the 1970s. Several television series appeared that were obviously indebted to *Silence*, including *The X-Files*, *Millennium*, and *Profiler*. The lead female character in *The X-Files*, FBI Agent Dana Scully, exists only because Starling existed before her. Other strong female leads appeared in Hollywood serial killer films, including *Copycat*, *Kiss the Girls* (1997), and *The Bone Collector* (1999). The publishing industry also followed suit, with the crime novels of Patricia Cornwell in particular focusing on a strong female character, medical examiner Kay Scarpetta, who bore the genre influence of Clarice Starling. The serial killer trend lasted throughout the remainder of the decade and endures well into the next. In effect, Harris could now claim responsibility for a new multimedia subgenre of psychological horror centered on preternaturally cunning serial killers, often engaged in lethal courtship with strong professional women. Yet none of his numerous emulators came close to matching either his artistic achievement or his cultural impact.

As the 1990s progressed, fans of Starling and Lecter called for more. Rumors of publication dates of 1994, 1995, and 1996 came and went. Yet Harris himself remained serenely distant from the clamor, presumably indulging his love for fast cars and gourmet cooking while plotting the next novel. He spent time in Paris, attending Le Cordon Bleu cooking school while there. If he ever felt pressure to produce another novel quickly, he never acknowledged it. His literary agent, Morton Janklow, auctioned off the bidding rights for Harris's next two novels, at which time, his publisher at St. Martin's Press, Thomas McCormack, dropped out. McCormack based his decision on the track record of the lengthy spans between each

Harris novel and later reported that Harris said of his writing pace, "I can't write it until I believe it."[25] The rights were sold to Delacorte for $5.2 million.

Meanwhile, Harris continued his research into forensics by attending a homicide detectives' conference in Orlando for three consecutive years and meeting (in some cases, even socializing) with renowned serial-murder researchers such as Ron Holmes. Public speculation ran wild when it became known that Harris attended the 1994 trial of Pietro Pacciani, who had been charged with the murders committed by the so-called "Il Mostro," or the Monster of Florence. Over a period stretching from 1968 to 1985, Il Mostro killed young couples in the hills surrounding Florence and sexually mutilated the female victims. A task force led by Chief Inspector Ruggero Perugini eventually zeroed in on Pacciani, who had already served time for murder and sexual assault against his daughters at the time of his arrest in January 1993. The trial began on April 14, 1994, amid much public and media clamor. Chief Inspector Perugini personally accompanied Harris into the crowded courtroom. Like Harris, Perugini was quite a student of the FBI's profiling techniques and had used computer technology and his own version of profiling to narrow down the suspect list to Pacciani. Through attending the trial, was Harris signaling that Lecter would indeed seek post-captivity exile in his beloved Florence? In any event, Pacciani was convicted of the crimes in 1995, but was later acquitted on all charges by the Corte d'Aissise d'Appello in 1996.

Harris's research into the Il Mostro case does find its way into his next novel *Hannibal*, but primarily as atmospheric background for the Florentine scenes and the novel's thematic insistence upon human nature as fundamentally corrupt, cruel, and depraved. Some details of the Il Mostro investigation are used for authenticity, such as the deployment of police officers posing as parking couples in the lovers' lanes during the nights favored by the Monster to strike. After attending Pacciani's trial as a guest of Perugini, Harris "repaid" the courtesy by modeling *Hannibal*'s fictional Chief Inspector Pazzi after Perugini, which reportedly displeased Perugini once he read the book.[26] Given that Pazzi's professional disgrace in arresting the wrong man in the Il Mostro case leads him into making a deal with an evil pedophile for illicit reward money and ends with him both eviscerated and hanged, one can perhaps understand Perugini's alleged sense of grievance against Harris.

Many other aspects of Harris's time in Florence also lend verisimilitude to the book. The island of Sardinia, famous for its trade of kidnapping for ransom, provided the home for Carlo Deogracias, the kidnapper enlisted by Mason Verger in the plot to abduct Lecter from Florence. Even one of *Hannibal*'s most baroque and striking elements, its central plot to feed Lecter to man-eating boars, was no invention, but rather was inspired by the story of three Sardinian criminals who during their kidnapping activities during the sixties and seventies fed a kidnapped count's body to pigs.[27] Additionally, *Il Porcellino*, a large bronze statue of a pig whose nose has been rubbed shiny by countless tourists over the years, may have done its part in inspiring Harris. Certainly, Harris was enamored of the statue, later commissioning a replica of it for his own garden back home.[28]

Florence's rich history gave Harris any number of historical anecdotes to lace throughout the book's narrative, but one used to great effect is the hanging of Francesco de' Pazzi from the windows of the Palazzo Vecchio following the murder of Giuliano de' Medici in 1478. This act provides the template for Lecter's murder of Chief Inspector Pazzi. Invited during the trial by Count Niccolo Capponi to the Palazzo Capponi, Harris later made the Palazzo the setting for Hannibal Lecter to serve as curator of its archives. Before installing Lecter there in fiction, Harris called the count, the actual curator, to seek his and his family's permission to do so. The family agreed to do so "on one condition—that the family would not be the main course."[29] In this, at least, Harris repaid the courtesy extended him.

Returning home, Harris began integrating his research into his plans for his next novel. Harris had by this point purchased two homes, one in Sag Harbor, New York, and another in Miami, Florida. When not traveling abroad, he divided his time between the two residences and composed what would become *Hannibal* in both. The writing process, reportedly a source of angst for Harris at the best of times, was especially painful for Harris this time. He says he "dreaded doing *Hannibal*, dreaded the wear and tear, dreaded the choices I would have to watch, feared for Starling."[30] This kind of comment is indicative of why, combined with Harris's penchant for research, it takes so long for a new Harris novel to appear in the bookstores. Unlike many popular writers, who write at a clip fast enough to turn out two or three novels a year, Harris clearly does not place a premium on speed.

Eleven years after the 1988 publication of *Silence*, long after many had quietly resigned themselves to never seeing a follow-up and Delacorte had undoubtedly gotten very nervous about the multimillion dollar deal it had inked for two no-show books, Harris set the publishing industry and the general public afire by delivering a lengthy manuscript to his agent, Morton Janklow, and publisher, Carole Baron, on March 23, 1999. The title for this manuscript remained secret, but speculation ran amok, with titles such as *Morbidity of the Soul* being floated. While Hollywood mobilized to pounce upon this hottest of properties, a handful of individuals at Delacorte Press signed confidentiality agreements and began reviewing the manuscript. Harris is reportedly loathe to accept editorial changes, however, so the novel was set for bookstore delivery on June 8, 1999. Publishers immediately got their own imminent, highest-profile releases out of the book's way. Advance word of the storyline began leaking out. The word on the street was that the book was far more violent and sadistic than its predecessors.

Manuscript copies were also sent to the following key Hollywood figures: actors Jodie Foster and Anthony Hopkins, screenwriter Ted Tally, director Jonathan Demme, and producer Dino de Laurentiis. De Laurentiis, of course, had the first opportunity to bid, but MGM Studios, now the legal owner of bankrupt Orion Studio's film library, also showed keen interest in making the sequel to *Silence*. Universal, sporting production deals with both de Laurentiis and Demme, also prepared to enter the fray. The starring principals of the previous film, Jodie Foster and Anthony Hopkins, were unknown quantities. Foster had stated publicly on many occasions she'd love the chance to make the sequel, but Hopkins wavered at times over the years, reportedly disturbed by Lecter's heroic status among some impressionable youth. In May 1999, the media began reporting that de Laurentiis was closing in on the prize of a history-making $9 million for the film rights. Between this cost and the price of bringing Hopkins, Foster, and Demme back together, the proposed budget of the movie was already approaching the $100 million mark. The book had not even been published yet, let alone a production crew assembled on a sound stage. The success of *Silence* had changed everything from that film's rather modest $23 million budget.

When all the business deals had been made, de Laurentiis in association with Universal Pictures would distribute the new movie overseas, while MGM would distribute it in the North American markets. So while the co-producers were now in place, the stars and the film's director were not. Jonathan Demme announced in mid-May, following preliminary discussions with de Laurentiis, that he would not helm the picture. He stated that he was unhappy with the book's storyline and violence levels.

The book itself, titled *Hannibal*, hit the bookstores and the review pages in early June and, as expected, became an immediate best seller. Ultimately, the novel spent over fifteen weeks on the *New York Times* best seller list in hardcover and thirty weeks in paperback. In paperback alone, 4 million copies of the book existed. The novel was also a finalist for the Horror Writers Association's 1999 Bram Stoker Award.

However, in spite of the novel's guaranteed financial success and the production of the now-inevitable movie full steam ahead, a number of vocal readers and critics, echoing Demme's comments, were not happy with the novel's unexpected twists and turns, its sadism, and the dalliance between Starling and Lecter. So "controversy" quickly became the mood surrounding *Hannibal*. Various media accounts suggested that Jodie Foster was not happy with her character's fate in the book, she was unhappy with Demme not being part of the project, de Laurentiis was unhappy with her asking price of $20 million, and so forth. She did reserve judgment, however, until she read a finished script. Screenwriter Ted Tally, who had adapted Harris's work so successfully for *Silence*, also had no interest in adapting *Hannibal*, for the same reasons Demme cited. Hopkins seemed more likely to commit, and indeed his participation was deemed critical for the project.

In Demme's place, Ridley Scott, the high-profile director of *Alien* (1979) and *Gladiator* (2000), was hired. Renowned playwright David Mamet was hired to script a first draft. Harris, for his part, resisted initial efforts to provide a different, presumably more "uplifting" ending to his original storyline. Mamet's script was ultimately rejected, so screenwriter Steven Zaillian, winner of the Academy Award for *Schindler's List* (1993), was hired. Harris met with Zaillian in Los Angeles for a couple of days in an effort to come up with an ending that, in Scott's view, still respected the "love story" between Lecter and Starling without fatally compromising Starling's character. In fact, Scott insisted that Lecter himself would not want Starling to join his world, that part of what Lecter admired about Starling was her "straight arrow" integrity. As he explained to Harris, Scott just didn't believe that Starling would join Lecter, even under the influence of drugs and hypnosis. From all accounts, Harris agreed to the logic and helped Zaillian craft a new, still-secret ending.

In spite of all the collaborative efforts to revise the ending, Jodie Foster finally passed on reprising her role as Starling. There is plenty of speculation that Foster's reasons were not just artistic dissatisfaction with the portrayal of the character in the script. Perhaps, as the rumors had it, she was unhappy with the proposed salary, or she didn't like the new focus on Lecter's character, or maybe she just didn't believe Starling would have the same impact on an audience the second time around. Reportedly, Universal and Hopkins were not pleased with this development. In any event, Julianne Moore, best known for *Boogie Nights* (1997), was eventually cast as the new Starling. Hopkins finally signed on as Lecter. Rounding out the headliners in the cast were Ray Liotta as Starling's nemesis, Paul Krendler; an uncredited Gary Oldman as Mason Verger, the faceless villain with a vendetta against Lecter; and Giancarlo Giannini as Pazzi.

Production began on the film in May 2000. Five weeks were filmed on location in Florence, with the production paying the city for the privilege of shooting in certain key locations. At a press conference in the city, producer de Laurentiis spoke not only of the current film but also his next project, a remake of *Red Dragon* in partnership with Universal. For the most part, with the exception of some protests mounted by the Green Party and the Popular Party, the city welcomed the *Hannibal* production and the

dollars they brought with them. Count Capponi, curator
of the Palazzo Capponi, played host to the film crew as
he did for Harris before them. According to Capponi,
director Scott was obsessed with fake smoke (which is
certainly prevalent in many of Scott's films) and was
delighted when Capponi brought out a number of family
busts from storage to decorate the grand saloon of the
Palazzo for the film shoot.[31] The crew filmed at many
other famous Florence locations, including the Palazzo
Vecchio, the Piazza del Duomo, and the Uffizi Galleria.
Harris, in the city on other business, visited the set. At
that time, he finally met Hopkins in person, which must
have been an indelible moment for those who witnessed
it. Back in the United States, other scenes were shot at the
Biltmore estate in North Carolina, the Montpelier estate
in Virginia, and Union Station in Washington, DC. The
production wrapped in September 2000.

Following postproduction and the typical dizzying
Hollywood publicity buildup, the film was released with
an "R" rating on February 9, 2001. The film grossed $58
million domestically on its opening weekend, at its time
the best "R"-rated opening ever recorded. By February
20, the film was a certified blockbuster, having grossed
$140 million worldwide. While the film may have been a
success in Hollywood business terms, its critical reception
was mixed at best. Many blamed the source novel, calling
it a less-than-sturdy foundation upon which to build a
strong film. Others cast the blame upon Ridley Scott,
others upon Hopkins's mannered and campy interpretation of Lecter, others upon the gore . . . the list went on
and on.

None of this critical carping bothered de Laurentiis,
who proceeded with his plan to remake *Red Dragon* in
order to, presumably, put the bitter memory of *Manhunter*'s commercial failure behind him once and for all.
In the wake of *Hannibal*'s financial success, *Red Dragon*
must have looked like as sure a thing as there was in

Hollywood. Ted Tally agreed to write a screenplay that began with Graham's near-fatal first confrontation with Lecter, expanded Lecter's role in relationship to jailhouse consultations with Graham, slightly updated the technological means by which Dolarhyde selects his victims, and stuck to the novel's original twist ending. Tally's first draft was completed in early 2001. While *Hannibal* was still enjoying its recent box-office success, the ever-tenacious de Laurentiis courted Anthony Hopkins to play the role once more and publicly panned the merits of Michael Mann's 1986 film. The press whimsically reported that computer-generated imagery (CGI) would reverse time on Hopkins to make him look younger than he did in *Silence*.

When Hopkins did indeed sign on to the remake (or prequel or reinterpretation, depending on whom was asked), no such CGI magic was employed. Rather, the actor engaged in a diet and physical training regimen that, for the most part, did the trick. Opposite Hopkins, Edward Norton, an actor known for edgy work in films such as *Fight Club* (1999), was cast in the role of Graham. Also cast were Harvey Keitel as Jack Crawford, Philip Seymour Hoffman as Freddy Lounds, Ralph Fiennes as Dolarhyde, and Emily Watson as Reba McClane. Earning himself a permanent place in Harris-related trivia, Frankie Faison reprised his role as Barney Matthews, Lecter's former orderly, thus appearing in all four "Lecter" adaptations, going back to Mann's *Manhunter* in 1986, where Faison played a police officer.

After Michael Bay turned down an offer to direct, Brett Ratner, best known for *Rush Hour* (1998), was chosen to lead the production. The budget was set at $90 million. Universal Pictures was the distributor of the film domestically and worldwide. However, in the complicated world of legal rights surrounding Harris adaptations, MGM became a co-distributor in exchange for an establishing exterior shot of Lecter's hospital, which according to Ratner was needed from *Silence* footage because the hospital no longer existed. Rumors of friction on the set began to circulate. For example, Ratner allegedly clashed with Norton during filming.

As the shoot progressed, de Laurentiis moderated his tone toward Mann's original, but still slammed some of the performances and delivered his bottom-line verdict: "I wasn't disappointed [with *Manhunter*], because the picture was very good. But box office—no work. No work because, number one, Hannibal Lecter no come out the way he's supposed to be. And number two, the casting for the FBI agent was not the best choice."[32]

Brett Ratner was equally blunt: "No one saw the movie. It was at the box office for, like, one weekend. . . . [*Manhunter*] stays in the *Miami Vice* '80s thing. It's very stylized. I made *Red Dragon* to be more a timeless movie."[33]

One cannot help but wonder what the original cast and crew of *Manhunter* thought of all this. Brian Cox, who played "Lektor" in *Manhunter* and in the eyes of many was just as good, if not preferable, to Hopkins's interpretation of the character, was apparently never asked to reprise Lecter at any point. The actor told *USA Today*, in an indirect swipe at the new film, that *Manhunter* "stands as a classic . . . a remake will always be a remake. . . . The irony of it is, Dino wouldn't let us use the title *Red Dragon*. He said it sounded like a kung-fu movie."[34] William Petersen, who portrayed Graham and went on to fame in a similar role in television's *CSI* series, was publicly silent about the remake. Not so was Tom Noonan, who played "Dollarhyde" in *Manhunter*: "It doesn't feel great that they're remaking it. But I've quit being surprised by the greed of Hollywood. We made a great movie, with real characters and no gratuitous violence. But that usually doesn't mean that much in this business."[35] Fans of *Manhunter*, which had achieved a second life through video, posted online their complaints that the remake was unnecessary, mostly a product of corporate greed.

Heedless of the debate, or perhaps even spurring it on for commercial ends, the Hollywood hype machine geared up to position *Red Dragon* as a blockbuster. The stars did their obligatory interviews and magazine covers. The latest "Lecter" film was released on October 4, 2002. Its opening weekend earned the number one spot, at $36 million. While its reviews, too, were mixed, it generally fared better with the critics than did *Hannibal*. According to Tally, Harris told de Laurentiis that the film was the best adaptation of any of his books.[36] All seemed primed for another *Hannibal*-sized success.

Then something odd happened. The film slowed in its revenues, its $93 million by December not quite clearing the $100 million mark to be called a "blockbuster." Certainly a disappointment next to *Hannibal*'s earnings, the film nevertheless did well enough that when the time came, another Lecter movie would be inevitable. Given Harris's record of significant lags between publications, no one seemed to think that time would be soon. Producer de Laurentiis mused aloud that perhaps he didn't have to wait for Harris: "Another book may take another ten years. But we can ask Thomas Harris if he'd give some cooperation for the storyline, because if you have the right storyline and then there's a script, then you can have Hannibal Lecter."[37]

As things turned out, it wasn't ten years, but only (!) seven before the next novel appeared. It had been a wild few years for the Lecter franchise, but with *Red Dragon* the remake a part of history, Harris turned to the thought of where to take the character next, or whether to go in a new direction altogether, away from Lecter and serial killer melodramas. The decision was made relatively quickly and may well have been due in part to a not-so-gentle verbal prod from Dino de Laurentiis. The producer told *Entertainment Weekly*: "I own the [movie rights to the] character Hannibal Lecter . . . I say to Thomas, 'If you don't do [the prequel], I will do it with someone else . . . I don't want to lose this franchise. And the audience wants it . . .' He said, 'No. I'm sorry.' And I said, 'I will do it with someone else.' And then he said, 'Let me think about it. I will come up with an idea.'"[38] Whether this exchange, or a version of it, is what motivated Harris or not, and exactly when this dialogue might have happened, is strictly a matter of conjecture.

In any event, two years after the release of the remake of *Red Dragon*, on October 28, 2004, came the joint announcement from William Heinemann of the Random House Group in the United Kingdom and Bantam Press in the United States that there would indeed be a fourth Lecter novel. Delacorte, an imprint of Bantam, would publish the book in hardcover. Harris's agent, Morton Janklow, announced that Bantam had signed Harris to a two-book, eight-figure contract. Anticipating the inevitable question of "when" the new novel would see print, Janklow said, "[Harris's] books are very, very complex, and I think he thinks about them for a long time before he puts a pen to paper . . . [he] lives a full life."[39]

Over the next year, various working titles were publicized, including *The Lecter Variations*, *The Adventures of Young Hannibal* (!), *The Blooding of Hannibal Lecter*, and the rather uninspired *Hannibal IV*. The "official" title, announced in the fall of 2005, was *Behind the Mask*. The book and the film version would be released nearly simultaneously, with the book appearing first by a few months, on December 5, 2006. The hope was that the public excitement from the book publication would carry over into the film release in February 2007, thus creating a lucrative multimedia spectacle. Once again, the Dino de Laurentiis Company produced the film, with the Weinstein Company handling the marketing. Peter Webber, the director of *Girl with a Pearl Earring* (2003), was signed as director. The relatively unknown actor Gaspard

Ulliel was cast as the young Lecter. For the first time, Harris also signed on to be the screenwriter for the adaptation of one of his novels. With this latest complex business deal, then, Harris had entered new territory. As was the case more often than not for him when it came to the world of cinema, the outcome proved to be a mixed bag.

While researching the novel, Harris spent some time with the Paris police, specifically the Brigade Criminelle, who showed him the police station at 36 Quai des Orfevres, also the titular subject of a 1947 film directed by Henri-Georges Clouzot. The manuscript, now titled *Hannibal Rising*, was delivered to Bantam in August 2006. The usual secrecy shrouded the novel's details, with reviewers receiving their copies only one day prior to the public. The press planned to run at least 1.5 million hardcover copies, in spite of stiff competition from the latest novels by Michael Crichton, John Grisham, and Stephen King. Chapter 6 of the novel was made available online on November 15 in order to whet the public appetite for the main course a few weeks later. Harris recorded an unabridged audio version of the book, taking seven hours and six CDs, to be released by Random House Audio.[40] By this time, principal photography on the film had been completed, with the project now in postproduction.

On December 5, 2006, the novel was delivered to bookstores worldwide as planned, and debuted sixth on the *New York Times* best seller list. Critics were not terribly friendly to the book. In business terms, the novel performed solidly but not spectacularly. By the middle of February 2007, Nielsen BookScan in its nationwide survey of booksellers reported that only 270,000 copies out of the 1.5 million had been sold.[41] By March 5, however, the novel was still registering in the top 10 on the *Publishers Weekly* best seller list. The book's performance, however modest it may have been, still looked pretty good in comparison to how the feature film did. The movie, released on February 9, finished its opening weekend in the number-two slot with $13.4 million, a distant second behind *Norbit*'s $33.7 million opening. The following week, the movie dropped to number seven with $5.5 million, a 59 percent drop from the previous week. Its third week, the film stood at number thirteen with not quite $2 million. By the time *Hannibal Rising* finished its three-month domestic U.S. run, its gross was about $27 million, which was less than either *Hannibal* or *Red Dragon* in their opening weekends.

The film's commercial disappointment was no doubt attributable to a number of factors, but the fact that no major Hollywood stars were associated with it may have been one of the primary ones. Perhaps the decision to humanize or even redeem Lecter through depicting the root cause of his pathology was ill-advised and people truly did prefer Lecter as a symbol of transcendent evil. Some critics even speculated that perhaps, just perhaps, the Lecter character had outlived his cultural moment. In the post-9/11 age of global anxiety over rising prices, environmental degradation, dwindling resources, and seemingly never-ending war or the threat of it, had Lecter as a lone serial killer lost his ability to frighten and fascinate? All told, one of the few bright spots for Harris that spring was being awarded the Horror Writers Association's Lifetime Achievement Award for profound, positive impact in the horror field over the course of a career. Previous writers so honored by the HWA included Stephen King, Peter Straub, Joyce Carol Oates, and Ray Bradbury—august company indeed.

As of this writing, Thomas Harris stands at a crossroads in his literary career. As the Horror Writers Association so justly affirmed by giving him its Lifetime Achievement Award, Harris has already left his mark on literary history with some of the most unforgettable stories and characters in fiction. If he wrote not one more word, his influence has been and will remain profound in what he did to enshrine the serial killer as a popular culture demon.

However, it must not be forgotten that only one book in his reported two-book deal with Bantam has thus far been delivered, so it seems highly likely we shall see at least one more novel in the next decade or so. No definitive word has come from Harris or those close to him as to what that next book might be. As some have suggested, will he continue with the adventures of Hannibal Lecter, showing his audience the early years of Lecter's serial killings in the United States? Will he go against expectations and return to the story of Lecter and Starling, the star-crossed lovers on the lam in South America? Will Lecter face his own mortality in any upcoming novel? Will Harris's literary future not include Lecter? Will Harris surprise everyone and move away from tales of serial murder altogether? Might Harris decide after this next book and the completion of his contract that he's done with writing? Whatever the answers to these questions may be, Harris will reveal them to us in his own way.

## LITERARY HERITAGE

Thomas Harris draws upon many genres and literary traditions to create his distinctive style of serial killer fiction. His stories are genre hybrids of crime and detective fiction, police procedurals, psycho thrillers, melodramas, and horror. As Davide Mana aptly puts it, the publication of *Red Dragon* in 1981 essentially defined the emerging serial killer character as one "straddling the line that separates mystery and horror fiction, crossing *Black Mask* with *Weird Tales*."[42] The influence of literary movements such as Gothic and its cousin Southern Gothic also shapes Harris's fiction. His modernist, even elitist, love of referencing classics of literature, poetry, drama, and art is on proud display, particularly from *Red Dragon* on. Yet he appeals to the mainstream as well. He has even dabbled in screenwriting with the adaptation of *Hannibal Rising*.

While his career is most likely not over, Harris already is ensured of a continued place in the history of U.S. popular literature through the resounding impact of his iconic creation, Dr. Lecter.

Each writer dealing with Harris's literary significance tries to place him within various traditions. In my own work *Psycho Paths*, for one, I made the case he is working within the Gothic romance tradition, mainly because the world he creates in each story is ambiguous in meaning, shadowy, and dangerous.[43] Its characters are often Gothic archetypes: the monstrous villain, the threatened innocent girl, and the heroic knight. Look, for example, at the fictional world of *Red Dragon*. It is strewn with corpses and full of clues that frustrate all attempts to decipher them, even when left in plain sight. The threat of even more murders hangs in the near future. A profoundly gifted clue reader is the only hope for reading the clues well enough to save the blind woman who has fallen into the thrall of the evil villain. To get close to the villain, the clue reader must consult an oracle just as dangerous as the villain. Or look at *The Silence of the Lambs*. A young female apprentice must consult this same dangerous oracle to find another villain who skins other young women to make clothes from them. In both worlds, the oracle is a shadow reflection or companion to the heroes, and the villains reflect some deep fear or undesirable character trait of the heroes. All of these aspects are derived from the Gothic tradition.

Peter Messent concurs that Harris both uses and interrogates the Gothic genre to break many boundaries, for example, normality and monstrosity, low and high culture, sanity and madness, logic and instinct, and so forth. The point in doing so is to undermine or subvert our standard ways of looking at rigidly defined categories to produce new, even shocking realizations about life. Messent further observes that Harris self-consciously cannibalizes, so to speak, the lexicon of the nineteenth-century Gothic by working in *National Tattler* headlines calling Starling the "Bride of Dracula" and so forth. The prevalence of "doubling" or twinning of key characters, another marker of the Gothic influence, is pervasive. Characters in Harris's fiction are always looking in metaphoric mirrors. For example, Messent points to the mirroring between Mason Verger and his abusive relationship with his sister and Lecter's protective, nurturing relationship with his. Messent concludes, "What the Gothic does, in its use of the literalisation of metaphor and of doubling . . . is to set up a liminal fictional space where each side of this equation—inner and outer, subject and society—can be brought together in a kind of 'third space'—and there explored at one and the same time. In this liminal space, the Gothic can do what it does best, challenge our fixed preconceptions."[44] In other words, by setting up a fictional scenario in which the ordinary categories by which we make sense of the world are wiped out, we (hopefully) emerge from the story with fresh perceptions.

Tony Magistrale agrees that Harris is a modern-day practitioner of Gothic literature in that Harris's fiction returns again and again to the theme of identity in transformation (also a staple feature in horror literature). Magistrale notes that Harris repeatedly cites the poetry of William Blake, the early English Romantic poet and another writer obsessed with transformation and the breaking of ordinary human boundaries. Blake and his fellow Romantics believed it was not only possible, but necessary, to violently recreate one's identity by shattering social codes in order to achieve divinity. Harris, according to Magistrale, takes this logic to its extreme in characters like Francis Dolarhyde or Jame Gumb, who seek to create newly transcendent selves through the slaughter of others. For Magistrale, Harris expresses the clearest difference between Gothicism and Romanticism: "Whereas Blake and other romantics understood that freedom from social, political, and ethical codes of conduct would produce true individuals capable of realizing their divine potential, the Gothic romance marked a shift from faith in human nature to moral skepticism."[45]

Harris's fiction illustrates just this kind of moral skepticism in portraying human nature always wavering between the dualities of civilized conduct and murderous impulse. His killer characters thirst for violent transformation while, as Magistrale puts it, "Harris's detectives are poised in a counter struggle of their own: how does one enter the world of madness . . . and emerge with sanity and humanity intact?"[46] Magistrale concludes with the observation that, far from radically breaking boundaries, Harris tends to reinforce conservative worldviews simply because the reader is so relieved to re-embrace their relative normality after experiencing the frightening world of a Dolarhyde, a Gumb, or a Lecter.

Taking us in a slightly different direction in understanding Harris's literary influences, David Sexton argues that Harris is a practitioner of melodrama, as opposed to high literature. Melodrama is defined as fiction that uses sensational events and strong emotional appeals to stir the audience, certainly an apt description of Harris's effect on his readership. Sexton goes on: "Thomas Harris easily stands comparison with the great melodramatists of the past: Bram Stoker, Conan Doyle, Wilkie Collins or Edgar Allen Poe, say, perhaps even Robert Louis Stevenson. He will last as they have lasted."[47] Sexton places Harris within the Southern Gothic, or Grotesque, tradition, in which Flannery O'Connor, another Southern writer, is often categorized.[48] Other famous Southern Gothic writers include Tennessee Williams, William Faulkner, Erskine Caldwell, Truman Capote, Katherine Ann Porter, John Kennedy Toole, and Cormac McCarthy. Plots in Southern Gothic fiction typically hinge upon extraordinary or violent incidents. Additionally, its characters or settings are often grotesque in nature—corrupt or even depraved in one or more ways, but also virtuous enough to allow for at least the possibility of redemption. Outsiders or social exiles of one type or another are all throughout Southern Gothic literature. These violent incidents, grotesques, and outsiders are used as commentary on society, usually Southern society.

All of these aspects are prominent in Harris's work. The plots center on sensational murders: a mass murder plot to blow up the Super Bowl, entire families slaughtered, a man glued to a wooden wheelchair and set on fire, young women skinned, an Italian detective eviscerated and hanged from a window, a man decapitated with a rope pulled behind a horse, and the like. The settings are often rural, and thus far from civilization: Starling's West Virginia, Lecter's boyhood hunting lodge, or Dolarhyde's decadent Southern mansion. The characters are outsiders or exiled. Starling and Graham are outsiders from the law enforcement mainstream. Starling's helper Ardelia Mapp is black, an outsider to the white establishment. Dolarhyde, Gumb, and Lecter are killers many times over, which exiles them from the society of men and women. Harris comments slyly on certain social realities, such as Lander's victimization by the Southern code of manhood, Dolarhyde's and Gumb's suffering at the hands of crazed Southern ladies, sexual terrorism inflicted upon women by jealous men, and so forth.

Davide Mana locates Harris's fiction within the noir tradition or, more precisely, the neo-noir. Noir is a term that critics have long struggled to define; it is slippery at best. Is it a specific genre? Or a literary movement? For our general purposes here, noir can be best defined as a bleak, pessimistic, paranoid, cynical, alienated mood running throughout a given narrative. Characters in noir fiction have no external moral base upon which to base decisions. Left to their own devices in this fundamental way, these antihero characters often operate in the realm of criminality and invariably meet with tragedy. Usually critics identify this kind of narrative mood as a mid-twentieth-century phenomenon, born from the tragic cultural consequences and profound disillusionments of two devastating world wars. However, noir's origins can be traced back much further, back through the tales of "hard-boiled" detectives of the 1920s and 1930s to lurid tales of psychotic criminals popular in the nineteenth century.

Mana claims Harris's novels are neo-noir, meaning that Harris crosses genre lines to produce not just a hybrid, "but a true merger, with old rules respected, and new rules established."[49] For example, Will Graham is a psychologically damaged character on the fringes of his own profession and the larger society who reluctantly, but willingly, strikes a deal with a criminal (Lecter) to track down another criminal—a classic noir theme of pervasive corruption in a meaningless world. Graham's struggle with his own inner darkness is, as Mana says, the essence of the novel, and that is all there is to say about noir, if you will—set in a corrupt world and facing his own dark side, the hero must strive not to succumb. From this simple core, one can derive any noir plot—and Harris himself uses this device as the unifying core of his three Lecter novels.[50] In other words, Harris sets all of his characters at odds with their own basest emotions and then propels the plot forward to see how far they fall—another trope of noir fiction.

S. T. Joshi explores the legacy of mystery and horror tales within Harris's work. Both the mystery and horror tale, according to Joshi, are more or less indistinguishable from each other in structure, with the difference being mostly in that of emphasis on a sliding scale between intellectual problem-solving and horrific emotions. The mystery/horror tale is best understood as containing elements of suspense, the attempt on the part of the protagonist to uncover something that is hidden, and a climactic revelation of that formerly hidden thing. It is tempting to say that the horror or "weird" tale (as writer H. P. Lovecraft prefers to deem it) involves a supernatural explanation, but Joshi quickly points out many weird tales involve non-supernatural agencies behind the central mystery under investigation. Of the meeting ground between mystery and horror, a subset of psychological horror has evolved, wherein certain works, according to Joshi, "can virtually be considered weird in their acute depiction of madness and their cumulative atmosphere of foreboding."[51] Having established all these parameters, Joshi locates Harris's fiction within the suspense or mystery camp, although certainly there are some horrific elements in the stories. However, Joshi insists, the emphasis is more on forensic analysis than the level of psychological terror required to classify these novels as "weird" or "horror."

Charles Gramlich is not so concerned with classifying Harris's fiction by genre as he is with emphasizing Harris's role as modern American mythmaker. In particular, Gramlich says, Harris "is one of the major architects" of the contemporary myth of the serial killer or "super predator."[52] Gramlich elaborates, "Thomas Harris is not the only writer who helped create the myth of the modern serial killer. . . . But no one has done it as well as Harris, and no serial killer has been so thoroughly transformed into a cultural icon as has Hannibal Lecter. Particularly, no one but Harris has yet dared turn a serial killer into a hero."[53] This last statement was not entirely accurate at the time of Gramlich's essay's publication in 2008, in that the *Dexter* novels by Jeff Lindsay and the *Showtime* cable television series loosely based on them do feature a serial killer as hero, but certainly Harris's work went there first.

The essence of Gramlich's argument is that Hannibal Lecter is the *ur* serial killer, a reworked mythic archetype for our postmodern irrational age who has almost no relation to the reality of serial murder. Harris may have researched real serial killers with the help of the FBI, but the killers who stalk his pages, Lecter in particular, are exaggerated far beyond any recognizable real-life inspiration. In turn, the success of Harris's work has lent an aura of malevolent genius to actual serial killers past and present ever since. Whereas the Ted Bundys, the John Wayne Gacys, and the Jeffrey Dahmers are in actuality a rather shabby collection of sad individuals notable only for the depravity of their crimes, Lecter is anything but average. He is extraordinary in ways "ordinary" serial killers could never hope to match. From his origin as a sadistic villain in *Red Dragon* to his fully rehabilitated status as sympathetic tragic hero in *Hannibal Rising*, Lecter's progress through our cultural awareness is a case study of how a myth transmutes over time to reflect the desires of its cultural audience. American myth-making has tended to transform its real-life rogues and scoundrels (Billy the Kid for one) into legendary folk heroes over time; Harris's character arc for Lecter replicates that tendency in fiction.

Another way to read Harris is from a psychoanalytic perspective. In fact, his fiction practically cries out for it. In every novel to date, repressed and internalized early childhood trauma is the real villain, the primary catalyst for the murderous actions of Michael Lander, Dahlia Iyad, Francis Dolarhyde, Jame Gumb, and Hannibal Lecter. Even the protagonists suffer from unresolved childhood issues, most notably Starling. Of course, one of the central insights of the field of psychoanalysis as pioneered by Sigmund Freud and carried on by practitioners such as Jacques Lacan is that painful memories are repressed within the unconscious mind. These memories create unconscious conflicts that then manifest themselves within the waking mind, causing what is often called "the return of the repressed." Additionally, Freud theorized that children form sexual attachments during their normal stages of development, sublimating these desires to various objects. In particular, the sexual attachment to the parent of the opposite sex, with a corresponding resentment of the parent of the same sex, is so taboo that the mind buries it down deep. Any trauma during any of these stages could create any number of lasting psychic warps or kinks, resulting in sexual fetishes, unhealthy attachments to parents, and the like. Psychoanalytic therapy, in a very general sense, thus attempts to recover and articulate what has been heretofore repressed or unacknowledged in order to relieve inner conflict. Freud's theories have been both roundly criticized and defended over the years, but popular culture continues to resonate to them. Specifically, Harris's fiction both depends upon and complicates the psychoanalytic approach.

Consider, for example, the relationship between Lecter and Starling. As countless observers have noticed, these two initially have what amounts to a therapist/patient dynamic. Starling suffers from traumatic childhood memories and an unresolved attachment to her father, all of which Lecter walks her through by getting her to verbalize and confront them. Slavoj Zizek, for one, calls Lecter a Lacanian analyst, albeit "a desperate, ultimately failed attempt of the popular imagination to represent to itself the idea of a Lacanian analyst."[54] In *Hannibal*, Starling returns the favor by bringing Lecter out from his unresolved psychic tension in dealing with the loss of his sister and unconscious resentment toward her for taking their mother's attention away from him. Pietra Palazzolo makes the case that Lecter and Starling's exchange of knowledge or "Quid pro Quo enables them to be analysts, detectives, interpreters and patients at the same time."[55] Harris's other characters lend themselves to psychoanalytic interpretations as well. Francis Dolarhyde and Michael Lander suffer from feelings of inadequacy and inferiority rooted in childhood, while Jame Gumb acts upon a mother fixation in the grandest Norman Bates tradition. This reading of Harris's fiction is so obvious, in fact, that one can't help but wonder if Harris, ever the literary trickster, is mocking the whole psychoanalytic tradition by making Lecter its representative practitioner.

Harris's fiction has also been keenly scrutinized through a feminist lens. Undoubtedly the strong central character of Clarice Starling, both in *Silence* and the film adaptation, is the primary reason for the feminist subtext often attributed to Harris's work. Much of this attention has been favorable. Phillip A. Ellis calls Starling a "feminist role model,"[56] in part because of a widespread tendency to look to literary characters as examples of how to live our lives. Starling's earnest dedication to duty and drive to save the innocent fits that bill for many readers, both male and female (at least until the end of the fourth novel). Harriett Hawkins adds that in Harris's third novel "the professional ambition of the heroine is unselfconsciously portrayed with unqualified approval, admiration and sympathy. . . . The portrayal of Starling's ambition . . . seems remarkably positive in a post-feminist, even post-sexist way."[57] Greg Garrett argues that the book is remarkable for being written by a man while emphasizing "from the very outset the trials of an intelligent and capable woman in a patriarchal system."[58] In the opening chapters, Starling is "harassed, humiliated, emotionally raped, and both physically and symbolically imposed upon by males,"[59] so that Miggs's vile act of throwing semen on her becomes a literalization of the way men treat her. That particular scene marks a turning point in the narrative—from that point forward, Starling wins over the alliance of intelligent men who "recognize a woman's worth and let her do her job."[60] Garrett lists Starling's primary male allies and mentors: Jack Crawford, Hannibal Lecter, attorney Yow, gunnery instructor John Brigham, entomologist Noble Pilcher, and orderly Barney. From this critical point of view, then, Harris is portraying an enlightened, supportive network of men and women working together as equal partners to achieve a noble goal. Even the darker, more defeatist version of this utopia in *Hannibal*, where Starling's career has flamed out because of patriarchal obstructionism and her male allies are almost extinct, honors the ideal all the more for its fading into the past like Camelot.

Others are a little more dubious of Harris's alleged feminism. Thomas A. Van says pretty bluntly that for all of *Silence*'s "agents of virtue," its primary audience fascination is "the killing and flaying of young women,"[61] surely a disturbing aspect of the book for those who celebrate its postfeminist approach to gender. From this perspective, Harris's feminist-themed agenda throughout his novels is complicated and ambiguous. In the first three novels, consider the female characters on display. There is Dahlia, the lethal seductress of *Black Sunday*. *Red Dragon* shows us Mrs. Leeds and Mrs. Jacobi, the slaughtered and violated wives; Molly the dutiful, but resentful, wife of the hero; Marian Dolarhyde and Grandmother Dolarhyde who in tandem create a monster through their abuse; and Reba, the blind woman seduced and terrorized by Dolarhyde. As Ellis points out, the majority of these women in *Red Dragon* are mothers, who are either "good" mothers like Molly and Mrs. Leeds and Mrs. Jacobi, or "bad" mothers like Marian and Grandmother.[62] In *Silence*, many overweight young women are abducted, starved, killed, and flayed to make a coat for a wanna-be transsexual, who himself aspires to be a woman only out of self-hatred. Ellis concludes that Harris's female characters are "either victims or villains."[63]

Perhaps by way of literary atonement, Harris brings the full brunt of his vividly gruesome imagination down upon his male characters in his fourth and fifth novels. Nevertheless, let us not forget the remarkable fashion by which Lecter violently penetrates his pupil Starling's mind through shock therapy in order to exploit her for his own selfish desires in *Hannibal*, or the function of Lady Murasaki in *Hannibal Rising* as little more than a clichéd exotic enticement for the young Hannibal to change his ways. Nor should we forget the way in which many of the male characters are rendered passive or "feminized," literalized most obviously in Dolarhyde's raging castration anxiety and Gumb's frustrated desire to have himself surgically castrated. In context, then, femininity as a social construct becomes identified with positions of weakness. All told, it's difficult to maintain that Harris delivers an entirely positive view of postfeminism. Typically, his vision is more ambiguous.

Equally open to debate is Harris's depiction of other diversity-related issues, such as race and sexual orientation. Not a great deal has been written about Harris's treatment of race, nor is it typically a central thematic concern of his. Nevertheless, the portrayal of Arabs as villains in *Black Sunday* has been commented upon by Stephanie Reich: "The Palestinian characters . . . are all commando fanatics and egomaniacs. . . . Harris [is] careful to make sure that [his] Israeli characters distinguish between fighting for the security of Israel and hating the Arab people, in contrast to the Arab characters, who always vent their hatred on the Jews collectively, rather than on the Zionists or on the Israeli army."[64] The net effect of this distinction, Reich argues, is to persuade the American audience to identify with Israel rather than the Palestinian plight. Harris leaves himself open to a charge of oversimplifying the Palestinian-Israeli conflict for the purposes of crafting an exciting thriller with good guys and bad guys.

Additionally, African American characters are few and far between in Harris's fiction. When they do appear, they are sympathetically depicted but typically relegated to service positions in relation to whites.[65] The Dolarhyde family cook, Queen Mother Bailey, shows genuine affection to young Francis but is still little more than a slave carted to and from work in no less than a mule-drawn wagon. Undoubtedly the most important African American character is Ardelia Mapp, Starling's roommate first introduced in *Silence*. She remains a bulwark of loyalty for Starling even during Starling's professional disgrace as shown in *Hannibal*.[66] Even Mapp, however, functions primarily in a subordinate position, to lend moral support to Starling. Furthermore, her street-smart sass and cynical view of "The Man," that is, the white establishment, treads perilously close to the clichéd image of an "urban" black as the white main character's sidekick. Arguably, Harris's fiction is racist in these depictions.

The most controversial aspect of Harris's work, largely due to some negative critical attention given to the film version of *Silence*, is its alleged homophobia. This accusation centers on Harris's portrayal of gay, lesbian, and transgendered characters. In *Red Dragon*, Graham enters what appears to be a rough-trade gay bar named The Hateful Snake to question Niles Jacobi and his presumably gay companion, an ex-convict named Randy. Graham is afraid of Randy, ostensibly because the man is a knife fighter, but in context Graham's fear reads as homophobic. Similarly, Dolarhyde fears being labeled as homosexual and reacts explosively when portrayed as such in the *Tattler*. However, ground zero of this controversy is Jame Gumb, the villain of *Silence*. It should be noted again that the main target of the gay backlash against *Silence* was the film. Gay-rights advocates protested bitterly and publicly that the film was homophobic and Gumb's transsexualism was used to render him monstrous. To be fair, Harris is more explicit in the book that Gumb is not a transsexual, but rather a man who hates his own masculine identity so much that he wants to transcend it by becoming a female as beautiful as his idealized beauty-queen mother. Admittedly, the nuance is easy to miss.

Harris is on even shakier ground in *Hannibal*, where Margot Verger is presented as a decidedly "butch" lesbian built like a masculine bodybuilder and looking to start a family with her partner. Robert Plunket in his review of *Hannibal* in *The Advocate* isn't sure whether gay

readers should be "insulted or amused" by all this, while
noting that even Lecter's personal style comes across in
the novel as "piss elegant."[67] Certainly, characters like
Gumb and Margot represent Harris's ongoing theme of
physical and psychological transformation, but they also
put Harris at great risk of being accused of casting homosexuals and the transgendered as villainous caricatures.

## A WORD BEFORE PROCEEDING

This book's purpose is to serve as a rounded introduction
to Harris's fiction, discussing such elements as plot structure, characters, writing style, allusions, symbols, and
themes. Over the span of five books, Harris constructs an
elaborate moral cosmology, or what we may rather
whimsically call the "Harrisverse," with due acknowledg-
ment to the term "Buffyverse" as adopted by the fans and
creators of the popular television series *Buffy the Vampire
Slayer* (1997–2003). As Harris does in *Hannibal* by taking
us by the hand to lead us through the streets of Florence
up to Lecter's ancient library, I ask you to come with me
on a similar guided tour through the Harrisverse.

I make no claims that what follows is in any way an
exhaustive or encyclopedic treatment of all that is important in Harris's fiction. To attempt such a feat would be
beyond the scope of this study. Nor do I analyze the film
adaptations of his novels. A great deal of academic and
public attention has been dedicated to these films ever
since the breakthrough success of Demme's version of
*The Silence of the Lambs*, but in-depth critical discussion of
the novels has lagged far behind. That is a gap I hope to
address here. Finally, I do not endeavor to supply a com-
prehensive listing of all of Harris's literary and cultural
allusions. I leave that to Web sites such as *Dissecting
Hannibal*, *The Hannibal Lecter Studiolo*, and *Loving Lecter*.
Rather, I have been guided as much as by what I find
fascinating about the books as any objective set of

"literary" criteria or what other people have to say about them. I am hopeful, however, that you will find this journey, in its dark way, both educational and enjoyable. With that being said, let us descend, like Virgil and Dante, into the depths of the inferno as re-envisioned by Thomas Harris.

# 2

# "The Pumping Heart of Rage": *Black Sunday*

An aerial assault against an American institution using civilian aircraft, financed and carried out by a known Middle Eastern terrorist organization. An intended death toll in the tens of thousands. Happening in full view of a horrified national audience on television. That's an apt summary of the terrorist attacks against the World Trade Center in New York City and the Pentagon in Washington, DC, on a beautiful fall morning on September 11, 2001. It's also an accurate description of the climactic event in Thomas Harris's first novel, *Black Sunday* (1975), twenty-six years before the terrorist attacks in 2001 that killed 3,000 people. So not only did Harris anticipate the serial-killer panic of the 1980s, but he forecast in general terms what would happen to the United States on the dawn of the new millennium. Certain incidents in *Black Sunday* also foreshadow the national debate over the efficacy of torture as a tool in the war against terrorism. In that the plastique used in the terrorist attack is brought to the country in the hold of a foreign freighter, the book heralds the widespread concern about the safety of ports and incoming cargo in the wake of 9/11. If one wants to push the point, it can even be argued that the novel's domestic terrorist, Michael Lander, eerily resembles the perpetrator of the 1995 Oklahoma City bombing, Timothy McVeigh. Harris has a pretty impressive record as a cultural prognosticator.

Of course, Middle Eastern terrorism was very much on the minds of the American people during the mid-1970s as well, when Harris and his fellow Associated Press reporters Sam Maull and Dick Riley conceived of the central idea of the novel and researched it. Two major terrorist events dominated world attention in 1972: the attack on the Tel Aviv airport and the massacre of the Israeli athletes at the Munich Olympics. Both attacks were linked to the Palestinian Liberation Organization (PLO). The Olympic Village atrocity was carried out by Black September, the terrorist arm of the PLO. If the Olympics were targeted by terrorists, Harris and his colleagues reasoned, why not extend that idea into a fictional scenario in which Black September plans a strike on the Super Bowl to create a thriller that was, as the standard jacket-blurb cliché has it, "ripped from today's headlines?" Add to the mix a psychotic Vietnam veteran who seeks out Black September to help him carry out an airborne act of mass murder, and the result is Harris's first novel, *Black Sunday*.

As a work of fiction, the novel is structured around one bankable high-concept idea, a terrorist attack on the Super Bowl.[1] The plot built around this idea takes the reader from the moment where operative Dahlia Iyad meets in Beirut with key Black September and Al-Fatah leaders to the climactic explosion of the blimp in the skies over New Orleans on Super Bowl Sunday. Favored by many thriller writers for the mass market, this kind of linear progression is easy to follow and, at first glance, simplistic. Harris's voice as a writer at this early stage tends toward the journalistic reportage of time, place, action, and person, as indeed one would expect, given Harris's immediate past employment. The influence of another writer/journalist, Ernest Hemingway, is obvious in the brevity of the sentences and the reliance upon the well-chosen image. Harris does not often get in the way of his own storyline with rhetorical extravagance or showmanship. He remains transparent, if not invisible, to the reader's eye. The words serve the thumping beat of the plot's relentless forward momentum. It is a minimalist style, sparing of words but rich in poetic imagery and turn of phrase—the foundation of what will become the Harris stylistic signature.

However, the narrative simplicity is deceptive. For one thing, the structure is divided into two complementary, converging storylines. One story arc follows the Michael Lander/Dahlia Iyad relationship and the murderous plot they conceive. The other story arc focuses on a manhunt, led by Mossad agent David Kabakov, to apprehend or kill the would-be mass murderers. At key points, natural in the organic flow of the twin story lines, flashbacks relevant to character development are also introduced. Harris interweaves these two story lines across an international stage and then brings them to conclusion. It's the same binary structure Harris will replicate and perfect in *Red Dragon* and *The Silence of the Lambs*. The bifurcated structure is tailor-made for a thriller. The antagonistic dynamic between the manhunter and the criminal provides enough conflict with enough high points to sustain reader interest.

Another complexity hidden within the minimalist narrative is the character development. The primary characters are given nuanced personalities and back stories that take them beyond the cartoon figures often found in mainstream action thrillers. While it would be tempting to paint Lander and Dahlia as irredeemably villainous and Kabakov as unquestioningly virtuous in order to create a stronger binary opposition between these enemies, Harris instead invests his characters with motivations that grow out of the memories of deep wounds and social injustice. These wounds create a lasting murderous anger, or what Harris memorably calls the "pumping heart of rage." The dramatic payoff for this strategy is not only to set the characters on collision courses based on conflicting self-interest, but to create layered depths of characterization not often found in popular thrillers. Lander and Dahlia become, if not sympathetic, at least understandable. Kabakov as the hero is nevertheless morally compromised in his adoption of the methods of torture and the bitter embrace of his own violent nature. As is typical of all of Harris's work thus far, *Black Sunday* is a book about violent men and women, some on one side of the law and some on the other.

## CRITICAL RECEPTION

The critics were, for the most part, favorable to the book. In a representative positive review, Christopher Lehmann-Haupt compares the novel favorably to the fiction of Frederick Forsyth and Richard Condon, this in spite of what he calls the plot's absurdity. For Lehmann-Haupt, it's Harris's "resourcefulness" that saves the novel: "Given Mr. Harris's ability to keep the plot boiling, he could have thrown Godzilla and King Kong into the Super Bowl and I still would have bought it."[2]

A few critics didn't buy it, however. Newgate Callendar can't suspend disbelief long enough to buy the plot and blames it on Harris's lack of literary ability: "'Black Sunday' is written in a stolid, expository, unimaginative style in which dialogue is stilted and characterizations are as interesting as an old wad of chewing gum. There is no relieving touch, and Harris grimly plows on to the end with conventional last-moment heroics."[3]

Stephanie Reich goes even further, saying that this novel and a crop of similarly themed popular novels about Arab terrorism in the wake of the energy crisis of the early 1970s do not have enough literary merit to "warrant extensive discussion of plot and character development. Rather, they must be exposed as sources of political misinformation and reflections and reinforcers of anti-Arab racism."[4]

After Harris became famous for his later work, this introductory novel was viewed by some as a curiosity or anomaly for the writer who had created Hannibal Lecter and Clarice Starling. In fact, *Black Sunday* is dismissed as a serious work by some of these later critics. S. T. Joshi, for one, calls the novel "a mere potboiler with a preposterous premise"[5] and takes it to task for its stereotypical characters. Others regard the novel as a respectable but flawed freshman effort, such as David Sexton, who calls it "an efficient thriller, not much more."[6] Stephen King, generally a reliable advocate of Harris's talent, says Harris did not yet know what he was up to in his fiction.[7]

Alex Diaz-Granados, on the other hand, lauds Harris for the masterful way his plot flashes backward and forward through time: "The pace is fast and furious, giving the reader an excellent example of a well-crafted suspense novel that not only never loses focus or goes into unnecessary tangents, but is also grounded in the reality of the mid-1970's."[8] Scott D. Briggs praises the novel for "characters, dialogue, and action sequences, as well as psychological conflicts, that are often unforgettable," and in particular for the character of Major David Kabakov as "easily one of his most complex heroes, perhaps even more so than Clarice Starling."[9] Briggs is further impressed by the novel's prediction of the next generation of large-scale terrorist attacks against American high-profile targets: "It is startling to realize that the allegedly 'outlandish' and far-fetched plot posited by [the] novel was actually, to a frighteningly accurate degree, prescient of events to come."[10] Overall, it seems fair to say, particularly in light of the 9/11 terrorist attacks, that *Black Sunday* holds up reasonably well for a first novel by a soon-to-be major American author making the transition from journalism to fiction.

## PLOT DEVELOPMENT

Though not formally divided into sections, the novel has a basic three-act structure. Act 1 covers Chapters 1–5 and performs the essential function of introducing all of the major characters and their backgrounds, as well as setting the converging plot threads in motion. The Lander/Dahlia/Black September thread is one, and the Kabakov/Mossad/FBI thread the other. The novel begins in Beirut, with Dahlia Iyad explaining to an Al-Fatah/Black September tribunal her progress with an American named Michael Lander in planning a suicide bombing attack on 80,000 Americans at the Super Bowl in New Orleans. Lander is an embittered Vietnam veteran and former prisoner of war, now an Aldrich blimp pilot. His plan is to place the bomb in the blimp, fly to the stadium as usual, and detonate the bomb over midfield at low altitude. Later that night, an Israeli commando force led by Major David Kabakov leads a raid against the terrorist stronghold, killing many there. Dahlia escapes, however, to return to Lander's home in New Jersey. Kabakov flies to the States to brief Washington on the outcome of the raid, during which he collected evidence pointing to a massive attack on the United States. The specific target remains unknown.

Act 2 covers Chapters 6–16. This act begins with Lander and Dahlia taking his boat to an offshore freighter to retrieve the plastique needed for his plot. They also pick up from the freighter Muhammad Fasil, an ambitious confederate of Dahlia's. With the explosives in the country, the plot's clock begins ticking.

As the plotters fashion the plastique into the deadly bomb, Kabakov tracks down a series of leads related to the importation of the explosive. Fasil places a bomb in the refrigerator of the importer who arranged the initial meeting between Lander and Black September so as to remove any links to the terrorist plot. The resulting explosion kills the importer and injures Kabakov, who learned one of the plotters was American before the bomb went off. Dahlia attempts to kill Kabakov while he recovers in a New York hospital, but is unsuccessful. Kabakov decides to convalesce at the New York apartment of Rachel Bauman, a doctor whom he fell in love with while she was in Israel. They now resume their relationship, becoming lovers. Once Kabakov is strong enough, he begins tracking down more leads, one of which suggests the mysterious American is a pilot.

Act 3, Chapters 17–26, sees Lander complete the construction of the bomb, but nearly die from pneumonia following a drinking binge set off by news of the death of a fellow POW. Fasil, attempting to initiate an alternate plan to deliver the bomb into the stadium by cargo helicopter, is captured by Kabakov. Lander bounces back from the brink of death. Aided by Dahlia, he manages to attach the bomb to the blimp and fly to the Super Bowl on game day. Kabakov, relentless to the end, commandeers the cargo helicopter to chase the blimp. He fatally shoots Dahlia, but Lander is still able to dive the blimp into the stadium. Kabakov shimmies down a cable in midair to hook the blimp's tail fin. The pilot of the cargo helicopter pulls the blimp back out of the stadium and out over the river. The wounded Lander finally manages to detonate the bomb. The blimp and helicopter are utterly destroyed, killing Lander, Kabakov, an FBI agent, and the pilot. Thousands of others, however, have been saved.

## CHARACTERS

### Michael Lander

Michael Lander is the prototype, or "pupa" if you will, of Harris's tormented killers. In Briggs's words, Lander "gives the other more celebrated Harris psychotic villains . . . a run for their money."[11] Lander is by turns obsessed, psychotic, methodical, and cunning. His moods and behaviors are often uncontrollable, threatening to blow apart his mission before it can be completed. He often seems at the mercy of his programming, ritually collecting clippings of bombings and other acts of terrorism. Yet, in most respects, he is able to function as a capable human being. The contradiction between Lander's sense of pride and the ritualistic nature of his behavior is typical of Harris's villains. Lander is a complex character and not entirely unlikable. Harris creates for him a past history of bad parental role models, isolation, ostracism by peers, traumatic formative experiences, physical scarring, and adult humiliations to explain, if not justify, his pathology.

The cumulative effect on the reader is to create a certain bond of sympathy, however reluctant, for a tortured man who is plotting the deaths of 80,000 people. At times Lander seems like nothing more than a desperately needy child with a longing for love and acceptance doomed never to be realized. Thwarted in this goal, he lashes out in rage. Unlike the Middle Eastern terrorists he allies himself with as a matter of convenience, his motivations to murder are apolitical, entirely self-directed. The tragedy of Lander is how gifted he is in terms of intelligence, technical expertise, and skill in machine operation. How sad that his gifts have been warped into the service of mass murder!

Much of what drives Lander to murder is a childhood characterized by self-loathing so profound that to call it "low self-esteem" is laughable. As an only child in the home of a repressed Baptist minister and a fiercely overprotective mother, Lander develops deep anger, directed at his parents and himself, from an early age. He also believes himself to be physically unattractive, which makes him even angrier. At some level, no matter what his chronological age or his social achievements, Lander always sees himself as an unappealing child in the grip of compensatory rage about the injustices he has suffered.

The corrosive effect of physical or psychological abuse upon innocent children, especially when inflicted by

parents or those in the parental role, is a dominant thematic concern of Harris's. More specifically, the identity
confusion afflicting many of Harris's characters stems
from parents who reverse traditional gender roles. Lander's parents are the first examples of this trend in Harris's
fiction. In a character dangerously bordering on misogynistic caricature, Lander's mother is a 200-pound force
of nature who has beaten her husband into passive sub-
mission and is now in the process of breaking Lander's
sensitive spirit. She follows Lander to school and snatches
him from the football practice field in his one attempt to
engage in the game that means so much as a marker of
manhood in his culture. The football coach, watching
Lander being marched off the field, says to his snickering
team, "We don't need no mama's boys no way."[12] The
humiliating scene is a symbolic emasculation of the adolescent Lander by an aggressive, masculinized mother.

Lander's father is not a suitable masculine role model
for young Lander. The Reverend Lander is rendered symbolically impotent and/or feminized, both by virtue of
his marriage to a domineering woman and his choice of a
profession considered effeminate by Southern males. He
is a pathetic, laughable figure who not only preaches
uninspired sermons but writes secret letters to a long-lost
high school love and never mails them. Michael Lander
feels nothing but contempt for his father, maybe because
the scorn heaped upon the Reverend is all too close to
that directed at Michael by his own peers.

In addition to parental influence, Lander's social environment plays a significant role in shaping him. He is
born in rural South Carolina, growing up as a sensitive,
intellectual boy among male peers who first play "cow-
boys" and then move on to playing football as a manly
rite of passage. In a very real sense, the promising man
that Lander could have grown into is killed by the fists
and jeers of his male peers. Promoted into an older grade
as a result of his scholarly prowess, Lander is beaten by

older classmates for reciting his paper to his class and subjected to the humiliation of not being chosen for football games during recess. What Harris calls "The Code" of Southern manhood may not literally kill Lander, but it certainly kills his self-esteem and leads to the rage dominating his entire life.

As Lander enters his teen years, he finds some degree of self-confidence by, paradoxically, acts of losing—shedding his physical awkwardness, his virginity, and his high grade point average, all in the name of conformity. But part of his mind stands distant from all of his newfound achievements. He cannot bear to participate in any kind of games or personal competition because his new image is so shaky, so he does not experience what Harris calls "the gradients of controlled aggression that allow most of us to survive."[13] He cannot shake his religious training, instead engaging in surreptitious prayers interspersed with hateful desires to harm others and then praying more out of remorse for his negative thoughts. Through this portrait of the psychopath as a young man, Harris shows us that early childhood training is a cruel schoolmaster that one never truly leaves behind. Because the young psychopath knows that he must fit in, he learns to avoid situations that bring out the inner child's rage. Like Harris's other killers, he is learning to avoid detection and to disguise himself as a normal man.

Lander's campaign to live some kind of normal life lasts several more years. Joining the Navy at sixteen to escape his parents, he flourishes in an environment in which he capitalizes on his love of machinery. For Lander, machines are powerful extensions of his body, and he blissfully loses his troubled identity while working with them. For Lander, interacting with a machine provides a transcendent experience in which he can escape the ugliness of everyday life. Blimps in particular, soaring above the earth like great silver whales, have affected Lander in this way since his first sight of one at the age of eight. By gravitating toward an environment in which his gifted touch with machinery is rewarded, Lander enjoys a brief period of happiness in which his defects lay dormant. In flight training, he even manages to court and then marry a lovely young woman from West Virginia (the home state of Clarice Starling) named Margaret. They have two children together. But while it may seem that Lander has an ordinary family existence, he still endures periods of blackness in which he becomes cold, even cruel. The child's rage is not extinct, only slumbering.

The beginning of the end for Lander occurs when he is shot down on an air-sea rescue mission in Vietnam and taken prisoner. The pain from his wounded hand is so bad he agrees to record a confession to war crimes against the North Vietnamese in exchange for repair of his hand. As a result of the confession, Lander is ostracized by his fellow American prisoners, his only friend a kindly prisoner named Jergens. When finally released, Lander is brought up on charges of collaborating with the enemy. He is allowed to resign, but it is an ignominious ending to his military career. Humiliation has once more become the governing theme in his life. His excruciating experience in the Vietnam War, when combined with his history of childhood humiliation, is the catalyst for his transformation into a homicidal adult. Though by now the concept of the psychologically damaged Vietnam veteran is rather old hat, the character type was relatively fresh in 1975.[14]

Lander's readjustment to civilian life is superficially smooth to outside observers, given that Lander signs on with the Aldrich Company to fly their blimps. No one knew, however, that Lander was under constant attack by another half of his mind whispering to him, feeding on his insecurity, and stoking his rage. Obsessed by thoughts of his wife's infidelity since his captivity, he finally explodes at her one day by shoving her kitten down an active garbage disposal. Stricken with remorse the next day, Lander embarks on a campaign to win her back, but his hopes are dashed when he discovers Margaret having sex with a stranger in their bed. This fateful discovery kills most of what is left of Lander's humanity. Harris describes the transition from man to murderer: "Lander smiled an awful smile, a bloody rictus smile, when he felt his will die. . . . The relief came to him then. It was over. Oh, it was over. For half of him. . . . What was left could live with rage because it was made in rage and rage was its element and it thrived there as a mammal lives in air."[15] One of the central themes in Harris's work is the dual nature of the psyche, and this passage illustrates what happens when the civilized half of the mind succumbs to the primal urge to kill.

Like Harris's other villains, Lander is intellectually gifted. He is blessed with the ability to manipulate machinery to carry out his commands. He is, according to Briggs, a "mechanically gifted obsessive genius."[16] While he bastardizes this talent into the service of murder, the skill itself is pure. Even in the midst of his madness, he finds poetry when guiding boats over the waves and blimps through the air. In moments like this, the reader senses the kind of man that Lander might have been had not loneliness, rage, and too many humiliations overthrown him.

The ability of Lander to merge with machinery, to lose himself behind the controls of an airship or a boat, is linked to his desire for mass murder/suicide through transcendence, a theme Harris visits often in his fiction. Almost always, this urge is most strongly associated with Harris's criminals, who lash out like children to gain relief from the torment of their identities by obliterating others. Lander wishes to transcend the bounds of earth, something he has felt since he was a child. He literally does so through flying, especially the dirigibles and blimps that float on the air and take him to a great height, where he can look down on such wonders as whales sounding into the icy depths of the Arctic Sea. Looking into Dahlia's fathomless eyes reminds him of his childhood experience of transcendence: "He remembered as a child lying in the grass on clear summer nights, looking into heavens suddenly dimensional and deep. Looking up until there was no up and he was falling out into the stars."[17] Compare that to his adult urge to sit atop his bomb and detonate it so he can "ride the mighty firebloom into the face of God."[18] Lander's explosive murder fantasies empower him to feel like a god floating above humanity, able to dispense death with the fire of his wrath: "Sometimes, as he lay awake, the upturned faces of the crowd filled his midnight ceiling, mouths open, shifting like a field of flowers in the wind. . . . Then the great fireball lifted off the heat of his face and rose to them, swirling like the Crab Nebula, searing them to charcoal, soothing him to sleep."[19]

Passages such as these suggest that Lander's wish for personal transcendence through death has been fused with an apocalyptic urge to silence others through the act of mass murder. Thus, once he cleverly finds a way to link up with the Black September movement in the form of Dahlia Iyad in a marriage of lethal convenience, the end is near. Having given in to his primitive urge to murder, it is inevitable that Lander will die in the act of killing as many others as he can.

## Dahlia Iyad

In some strange way, Dahlia Iyad is Clarice Starling in prototype.[20] She is a beautiful and intelligent woman fiercely devoted to a cause, but also angry because of childhood loss. For Starling, that loss was of her father when she was ten years old. For Dahlia, the loss is of her family, also at a young age. At the age of eight, she and her mother were forced into a Palestinian refugee camp in Tyre. For the most part, Dahlia represses her memories of that time, but they stoke her righteous fury against Israel and the United States, whom she believes to be the authors of her family's demise.

These memories can also be brought to the surface by certain emotional triggers, such as when her half-hour interrogation by Black September leader Abu Ali about the sexual habits of Michael Lander leads her to think of her past in a Palestinian refugee camp, when her mother slept with the man who brought food to them. This scene not only reinforces the association between sexuality and terrorism literally embodied in Dahlia, but introduces the primary/primal motivator for her adult commitment to terrorism: the loss of family. Dahlia's mother died when Dahlia was ten years old. Thus, on the eve of the Super Bowl and her own death, Dahlia summons the memories of her mother's painful death in the refugee camp. So steeled by her memories of childhood trauma, she can commit murder/suicide, just like Lander. Both are avenging past injustices against a nation and a culture they loathe, albeit for much different reasons.

Above any other characteristics, the adult Dahlia is dangerous. She is fully capable of taking human life without hesitation or remorse. For example, she once executed a Japanese terrorist who lost his nerve while being trained for an attack on Lod Airport in Tel Aviv. She methodically calculates odds, anticipates threats, and devises strategies to counter opposition. Even when acting on matters of great emotion, such as her improvised attempt on the hospitalized Kabakov's life, she coolly enacts a plan to infiltrate the hospital in nurse's garb, outwit inquisitive security guards, and locate Kabakov's room. When a New York City policeman tries to arrest her in the hospital, she calmly injects him with a near-lethal dose of potassium so she can make good on her escape. When the bomb plot seems in danger of failure following Lander's life-threatening case of pneumonia, she decides that she can eliminate her comrade of many years, Muhammad Fasil, if his alternate plan does not meet her standards. In light of these actions, Harris's comparison of her to a puma seems an apt enough animal metaphor to capture her essence of grace and danger.

Dahlia uses her attractiveness and her sexuality as tools in her professional life as terrorist. Much of her relationship with Lander is built upon manipulating him through sex. She is a sexually expressive woman overall, ironically quite Westernized in her attitudes. But her sexuality is also linked in some pathological way to violence, another favorite theme for Harris. Just as Francis Dolarhyde early in life learns to associate violence and blood with sex, so too has Dahlia learned about sex from her mother's liaisons in the refugee camp—a debased setting that forever forges the association between sexuality and political violence in her mind.

In the book's opening scenes, she uses the taping of her post–Super Bowl message to the American people about the suffering of the Palestinian people as a kind of foreplay before she sleeps with Hafez Najeer, the head of Al Fatah's intelligence unit. Upon her return to the States, she soothes Lander's shattered psyche following a traumatic visit to the Veterans Affairs office by seducing him in a candlelit bedroom. Her sexual attention to Lander is not based on love or even desire, but rather on a calculated political move to keep him stable long enough to carry out his attack on the Super Bowl. As she explains to Abu Ali, she uses her body to control Lander, but if a gun worked better, she would use that. Lander and Dahlia's sexual relationship is a type of shared madness, as Dahlia's reaction to Lander's first announcement of his intent to detonate 1,200 pounds of plastique in the Super Bowl demonstrates: "She looked at him as though he had admitted a sexual aberration that she particularly enjoyed. Calm and kindly compassion, suppressed excitement. Welcome home."[21] The equation of violence to sexual fetish unites the two in a common purpose.

However, Dahlia clearly dominates and controls her partner. Once Lander accepts her, he opens up to her and reveals many painful secrets of his past. Therefore, she is able to manipulate his emotions and direct his actions. Her skill in controlling situations and people, especially a man bewitched by her beauty, is aided by her ability to dispassionately observe behavior and then act decisively on her judgments.

Dahlia skillfully manipulates Lander many times. When she realizes that Lander is about to spoil the bomb plot by losing his control and killing a clerk during his routine meeting at the Veteran's Affairs office, she deliberately reminds him of two excruciatingly painful memories of his time in captivity with the North Vietnamese. Once Lander is incapacitated by the memories, she soothes him by saying he doesn't have to kill them (other Americans) one at a time. She re-establishes in his mind the importance of the mission and the necessity of him holding it together long enough to complete it.

Another way she controls Lander is to drug him repeatedly, without his knowledge. After Lander's nerve-wracking meeting at the VA, she drugs him with opium on the ride home so he can sleep. When she worries that Fasil's rudeness toward Lander will drive Lander over the edge, she ensures her hold over Lander by drugging him again. Her combination of sexual therapy and drug-induced moods of relaxation foreshadow the Starling/Lecter relationship in *Hannibal*.

As a therapist and nurse, Dahlia is capable of both kindness and murder. Literally dressed in nurse's garb, she enters a hospital to kill a man. However, when Lander becomes deathly sick and lies in a hospital bed, she stays by his side in an act of genuine nurturing that could at any moment turn to murder if Lander begins to rave about the bomb plot to anyone other than Dahlia. Harris describes her this way: "No man ever had a kinder, deadlier nurse than Dahlia Iyad."[22] She is simultaneously a lethal seductress and a caring nurse.

On occasion, she displays moments of vulnerability that render her more sympathetic and create a more effective character for us to identify with. Probably her most dramatic vulnerability is the moment when she is showering and Kabakov bursts in upon her, machine gun leveled at her breast. Mistaking her for a "whore," Kabakov spares her life. We are not given access to Dahlia's thoughts at this moment. We see her as Kabakov sees her—a naked, beautiful woman seemingly frozen in horror. This literally naked vulnerability gives us a very different picture of Dahlia than we would otherwise have. When in her fright and desperation she vows to Fasil that the Americans and the Israelis will pay for the raid on the terrorist stronghold by 10,000 to 1, we can understand her emotional state, if not condone her actions.

When Dahlia next sees Kabakov on television following the explosion at Muzi's house, the terror of the raid comes back at her full force. She goes pale as she remembers Kabakov's machine gun leveled at her. Lander, seeing this reaction, does not understand that she, as a Palestinian, is reacting with conditioned cultural hatred, not the type of personal hatred that motivates Lander. As readers with insight into Dahlia's refugee past and her recent encounter with Kabakov, however, we understand why she would risk her own bombing mission to attempt to kill Kabakov in the hospital.

Underscoring the point that Dahlia's past in some way explains, if not justifies, her terrorist agenda, Dahlia's escape from the hospital is made possible when she embraces a crying Puerto Rican mother in the emergency room and walks with her through the police lines. The scene is evocative of Dahlia's embrace of her own dying mother in the refugee camp and moves Dahlia to a rare moment of introspection as she leans back in the taxi cab whisking her away from the place where she just tried to kill a policeman. "I really do care about her, you know,"[23] she says to herself.

Within the precise economy of these eight words, Harris implies a certain fracture within Dahlia's mind, as if she were constructing a separate conscience, almost a tribunal, against which she can defend the morality of her own actions. She wasn't just using the Puerto Rican mother as a means to walk past the cops, she is saying. She cares about this woman. The most likely reason she cares about this woman, as opposed to any others in the emergency room she might have used for the same ruse, is because something about her plight as a mother touches Dahlia in the deepest part of her memory. Like Lander, Dahlia's past injuries direct her adult life. Unlike Lander, however, she embraces a cause larger than herself, ostensibly for the deliverance of her people from the cruelties of the Israelis and Americans.

## David Kabakov

Major David Kabakov of the Mossad Aliyah Beth is first described as a hunter. Locked in a dynamic of ancient hatred in which there has been no mercy granted, Kabakov has adopted the ruthless methods of those terrorists he hunts. He will torture and kill to achieve his goal of protecting Israel, though he takes no pleasure in doing so. At times of relaxation a gregarious and good-humored man, his bitter experiences have nevertheless turned him into an avowed enemy of the Palestinians. Ironically, in many key ways he resembles Dahlia Iyad, his mortal enemy. Like Dahlia, he too has devoted his life to a political cause, one that puts him on the other side of the ideological divide between Israeli and Palestinian. Like Dahlia, he is willing to die for his cause and his people, which ultimately he does, in the skies above New Orleans.

Also like Dahlia, his childhood is scarred by war. His family had to flee Latvia during the German invasion of World War II. His father was killed in the extermination camp of Treblinka. His mother, dying from an unspecified disease, took him and his sister to Trieste, Italy, to turn them over to the Zionist underground. She died immediately thereafter. One of Kabakov's strongest memories of his mother is on the road to Trieste. This memory of a lost mother compares and contrasts with Dahlia's. Both memories represent the mother as physically fallen due to the ravages of war. However, Kabakov remembers his mother as glowing, an archetype of purity or holiness. Dahlia's memory debases the mother, associating her with the sexual ugliness and moral compromises of the refugee camp. In this way, through the contrasting comparisons of the suffering mothers, Harris sets up his schema of good and evil. The saintly mother gives rise to the heroic Mossad agent, and the corrupt mother gives rise to the terrorist harlot.

Kabakov, formed in the crucible of the Eastern front of World War II (like a certain cannibal psychiatrist of Harris's creation), becomes a warrior by the age of ten. Ten seems to be a pretty significant age in the Harrisverse, an age at which the die is cast irrevocably for the characters' destinies. Kabakov grows into an adult who, while not hating his enemies, certainly doesn't negotiate with them either. In fact, he becomes such a proficient killer that behind his back Mossad agents call him "the final solution." Newspapers call him "The Tiger of Mitla Pass." His future lover, Rachel, tired of the never-ending hostilities in the Middle East, tells him she overheard a secretary from one of the foreign missions saying if real peace ever came, Kabakov would have to be gassed like a war dog. The fact that one of the man's drinking buddies slapped him for insulting Kabakov's name does not negate the essential truth of the statement. Kabakov is a warrior who has never known peacetime.

As a warrior, Kabakov becomes quite versed in weaponry, military and guerilla tactics, personal combat, and the psychology of his enemy. He speaks the language of his enemy, able to pass among them on the streets of Beirut. In a crisis, he thinks clearly and ingeniously, ultimately improvising the strategy that saves the Super Bowl crowd from the blimp explosion at the novel's climax. He is so good at what he does that he scares even himself. He fears his acts of murder have scarred his mind as much as his body. Ever since observing an eagle flying over a herd of sheep in Galilee, he has also known he is by nature a hunter: "And then he realized that he loved the eagle better than the sheep and that he always would and that, because he did, because it was in him to do it, he could never be perfect in the sight of God."[24] This personal epiphany makes him glad he will never have any real power, because for Kabakov, the mentality of a man completely given over to murder, with the power of an entire society behind him to carry out his will, wears the face of Hitler. While not usually a reflective man, Kabakov has the presence of mind to recognize his own predispositions to evil committed in the name of some cause. He is a man who hates torture even if he grudgingly accepts its utility.

While not a mindless brute, he certainly employs brutal force when needed. A large man with the graceful movements of a warrior, he radiates menace to others. Eddie Stiles, a street-smart ex-addict known to Rachel from her volunteer work at a halfway house, notices that Kabakov and his fellow agent Moshevsky move like predators. Rachel, familiar with both men, is nevertheless unsettled by them: "Size and silence are a sinister combination in nature."[25] Even hardened policemen fear Kabakov instinctively.

He is indeed a stealthy predator, hardened by many years of combat to hurt others if necessary to track down clues. By creating this character, Harris proves to be a forecaster of national mood once again, anticipating today's debate in the United States over the efficacy of torture to avert terrorist disaster. Kabakov creeps silently into Mustapha Fawzi's cabin in the middle of the night, awakens the man, and threatens him with torture if he does not reveal what he knows about the ship's cargo. Stealing his way onto another boat, Kabakov tortures Jerry Sapp into divulging vital information by ramming an ice pick into the man's ear. Upon capturing Fasil, he flexes the man's broken collarbones in a vain effort to torture the man into confessing the whereabouts of the plastique. Kabakov's extra-legal methods of obtaining information, while frowned upon by the bureaucratic and rules-constrained FBI men like Corley, are part and parcel of his predatory nature.

Kabakov has little patience with timidity on the part of others to engage the enemy. The FBI's procedures to ensure some modicum of civil rights for suspects are anathema to him. Even Sam Corley, Kabakov's closest ally in the FBI, will not tolerate violations of civil rights. However, Kabakov, who has not been as sheltered as his American law-enforcement counterparts, realizes the threat posed by Dahlia and the Arab terrorists. His hands tied by the FBI's regulations, Kabakov grows ever more contemptuous of such safeguards, and indeed believes they are a hindrance to the safety of the citizenry. The haste he feels is not only because of the imminent terrorist strike and the potentially staggering death toll; the fact that he did not kill Dahlia in Beirut also weighs heavily on his mind.

Kabakov's regard, even need, for women in general is a paradox in an otherwise ruthlessly expedient, predatory nature. It could perhaps be argued that his purely sexual relationships with any number of women in Israel are one more example of his hunter's-eye view of the world. Certainly, he enjoys sex, but he does not choose anyone who isn't after the same thing. A bigger problem for Kabakov is his lack of intimacy. He remains guarded around women, out of professional necessity to keep state secrets. At the same time, he recognizes that his loneliness compels him to seek out female companionship. The subplot of his tender relationship with Rachel fully demonstrates both the extent of his romantic nature and his respect for Rachel as a professional peer.

Their relationship is years in the making. After Rachel tends to Kabakov in post-op in Galilee in 1967, he is smitten by her. Though she initially rebuffs him, he persists in his attentions to her, wearing down her resistance with his characteristically loud, outgoing, humorous nature when he is not at war. At a party in Israel, he dances with her all night, pressing up against her, desiring her with all of his being, inviting her to come to Haifa with him. When their relationship resumes in the States seven years later, Kabakov and Rachel finally become lovers. Contrary to what one might expect from Kabakov, their encounters are gentle. They are unafraid to be silly around each other, as when Kabakov offers her a cigar after one particularly intense love-making session.

This romantic relationship contrasts with the manipulative, self-centered relationship between Lander and Dahlia, establishing Kabakov and Rachel as considerate of each other as they are passionate. While recuperating in her apartment, Kabakov treats her like a fellow professional, telling her in detail about the Black September plot. Admittedly, he does so in part so that he can use her knowledge of psychology and American culture, but also because he recognizes that she has helped him. Their relationship quickly resumes, progressing to the point that the night before the Super Bowl, Kabakov asks her to return to Israel with him.

She almost certainly would have done so, but the injuries of Kabakov's past and the urgency of the threat to others decree that he take to the skies above New Orleans to confront Lander and Dahlia as the only man capable of handling the situation. He does not survive the confrontation, so one can only wonder, given his predatory nature and the sheer quantity of blood on his hands, if he could have actually enjoyed a loving domestic relationship with Rachel.

### Rachel Bauman

Rachel is a psychiatrist whose dedication to her profession has taken her to many war zones to repair the physical and psychological damage that human beings all too will-ingly inflict on one another. Beginning her career as a resi-dent at Mt. Sinai Hospital in New York, she has served in volunteer capacities both as a battlefield surgeon in Galilee and a rehabilitation counselor at a halfway house in the South Bronx. Her volunteerism speaks to her humani-tarianism, contrasting her definition of dedication against that of Dahlia or even Kabakov. She does not view the world as a binary split between Arab versus Israeli. She sees only human suffering inflicted in the name of "duty."

Thus, it is ironic that she falls in love with Kabakov, whose willingness to kill and maim in the name of duty at first repels her. She is conflicted by her attraction to the man and her knowledge that he is a killer. As a result, she often gets angry at him. After losing a brain-damaged young Arab solider in the operating room, Rachel con-fronts Kabakov that night: "I'm thinking that in some Cairo hospital they're working just as hard to clean up the messes you make. Even in peacetime you do it, don't you?"[26] When rejecting his offer to take her to Haifa with him, she tells him that the war will never be over for him. War is an interruption in the trajectory of her life; she fears becoming involved with a man engaged in a perpet-ual war. She is also leery of a relationship with Kabakov because she has her own career and duty to consider. Her career is every bit as important to her as his is to him. For all of these reasons, Rachel turns Kabakov away in Israel. When she does decide to marry another man years later, it is primarily because he does not interfere with her life. She is obviously dissatisfied with her fiancé and the bor-ing professional and personal life he promises. However, his dullness makes him a safe counterpoint to the larger-than-life Kabakov. Her calling remains her top priority.

What can't be denied, however, is how much she is attracted to Kabakov. Even after her first angry confronta-tion with Kabakov about his duty, she comes to find him at the café party outside Tel Aviv the night before she returns to New York to complete her residency. Many years later, when Moshevsky interrupts her vacation with her fiancé in the Pocono Mountains, she first asks him if Kabakov is all right. Leaving her fiancé alone at the lodge bar symbolizes the sudden end to their engagement and whatever life they had been planning together. Kabakov and Rachel's proximity to each other in her apartment while he recuperates from his injuries resembles a type of marriage (the only kind they are destined to share together). Still obviously conflicted by the imperatives of Kabakov's duty, she tells him that she loves him to a certain extent. Even if that is not quite a confession of undying love, nevertheless, on what turns out to be their last night together, she first brings up the topic of what will happen after the Super Bowl. She seems interested in a shared life with Kabakov once the danger passes.

Just as the relationship between the two grows, Rachel's rigid opposition to Kabakov's chosen profession eventually softens to the point where she actively helps his investigation into the source of the plastique. Her participation in the investigation only goes so far. Her questions to her former rehab client Eddie about his knowledge of smugglers' boats constitute a compromise of her ethics, which disturbs her greatly. Eddie's loyalty to Rachel for her helping him break a heroin addiction finally leads him to speak to Kabakov about the smuggler Jerry Sapp, but Rachel resents Kabakov for putting her in this position. When Kabakov asks her to convince Eddie to make contact with Sapp, Rachel flatly refuses. She accepts that she and Kabakov use each other, because they also have a loving relationship, but she will not use Eddie in this way. Kabakov, far from being offended, finds her stance admirable and respects her enough not to push it any further.

Because Rachel and Kabakov do use each other, the two bear a resemblance to Lander and Dahlia. Unlike the psychopath and the terrorist, however, Kabakov and Rachel share a much more affirmative kind of loving relationship. While the relationship is ultimately doomed, it stands as one of the most positive romantic partnerships in Harris's fiction, with the long-lived marriage between Jack and Bella Crawford being the other. Rachel, as the most nurturing and life-affirming of all the four main characters, earns her status as the only one left alive by the story's end.

## STYLE

Harris's background as a journalist is evident in his writing style in *Black Sunday*. His language in this first novel is nowhere near as colorful or baroque as it will become in, say, *Hannibal*. Rather, his style here is expository or even "stolid," as we've already heard Callendar disparagingly say. His style is an objective, "just-the-facts" approach much of the time. His descriptions are usually spare, to say the least. This passage, for instance, is stripped of any rhetorical flourishes almost to the bone: "Leaning his weight on the door. Cold air in their faces. The sidewalk and the street lit in red flashes by the squadcar lights. No running, police around."[27] In this brief sketch, we are given only sentence fragments and the broadest of details. We must fill in the rest.

In other places, his sentences are typically simple declarative, with the occasional compound sentence for variety. Here's a representative passage to illustrate: "She was telling the truth. Lander could always tell. His eyes opened wide again, and in a moment he could no longer hear his heart."[28] The novel does not lack complex sentence constructions, not at all. However, the cumulative effect is a relatively unembellished journalistic style, somewhat in the style of Ernest Hemingway, but without his degree of precise control. Clearly, reporter Harris in career transition endeavors to find his own voice. True to one of his favorite themes, he begins transforming from one identity into another.

Throughout his career, Harris has been able to captivate general audiences with high-concept plots, interesting (to say the least) characters, and intense action scenes. *Black Sunday* is no exception, even if not as masterful as some of the later work. While acknowledging the novel's tendency to bog down between action sequences, Briggs says that "Harris does demonstrate his gift for plot, action, and well-developed character histories."[29] Taking Briggs's observation as cue, let's examine how Harris writes his action sequences. These sequences are key to demonstrating Harris's control of language to produce certain literary effects.

One of the most exciting scenes shows Kabakov sliding down the helicopter cable to hook the blimp's tail fin. The scene is described from Moshevsky's point of view on the ground:

> The fin was rising, swinging. It hit Kabakov and knocked him away, he was swinging back, passing the length of rope between the rudder and the fin, beneath the top rudder hinge, snapping it in a loop through the hook, one arm waving, and the helicopter strained upward, the cable hardening against Kabakov's body like a steel bar.[30]

Harris's language here speeds as breathlessly as the spectacle of a man trying to hook the tail of a blimp while suspended in midair from a helicopter. All of this action is conveyed in exactly two sentences, the last one practically a gallop, taking the reader with it. The "no!" at the end of the first run-on sentence emphasizes the suddenness of the tail fin swatting Kabakov away. It captures, without explicitly stating it, Moshevsky's dismay in seeing it happen. By cutting his teeth on such scenes in *Black Sunday*, Harris perfects his sense of timing in later intense action sequences, such as Lecter's escape from Memphis.

Another stylistic technique Harris frequently utilizes is to step out from behind the story, so to speak, and speak directly to the reader. Rather than being the invisible narrator typical of many popular thrillers, he temporarily stops (while remaining in the third person) to pass on an observation, make a comment, call attention to a significant idea, or highlight a metaphor or simile. At these moments, he's shedding the objective journalistic voice of his past life to "out" his creative voice. When he does this, the verb tense shifts from the past to the present. Through this device, he directs our attention to metaphoric language early in the story. Here is one example: "Black September lives within Al Fatah as desire lives in the body."[31]

He editorializes, or coaches us, to view the story in a certain way by using the present tense. Put another way, at key moments he forces an interpretation for his audience. For example, in regard to the Dahlia/Lander relationship, he says: "It is true that she learned Lander in order to use him, but who will ever listen for free?"[32] Through this truism, he places Dahlia's manipulative actions on a continuum of behavior more understandable to us. Occasionally, that intervening authorial voice just wants to share a personal feeling, as if Harris suddenly scoots back from his writing desk to speak to us as friends. Consider this authorial aside: "Hospitals threaten us all with the old disasters of childhood, the uncontrolled bowel, the need to weep."[33] Such comments call attention to Harris's narrative persona as a character of its own.

The present verb tense has one more use. A couple of scenes critical to Lander's early development are written in the present tense, the first being his classroom humiliation in grade school, and the second his football-field humiliation in high school. The effect is a kind of "you are there" feeling as we witness the formation of a psychopath. Harris's omniscient third-person narrator examines in a present-tense voice the contents of selected documents forming part of Lander's official service record. We learn some details from the transcript of his closed hearing in the Judge Advocate General's office and how he was forced to resign following Colonel DeJong's testimony. The present tense for Harris signifies breaking the temporal frame of the narrative to let us know more about Lander's past so that we may understand more about his deeds.

## SYMBOLS

Harris begins to develop his ear for metaphor and figurative language in this book. He's not as skilled at doing it in this early work as he will become, but nevertheless he shows real flair. Many different images are used in support of the themes. Scars, for example, appear throughout the story. Generally speaking, the characters' physical scars are not only the literal remnants of wounds but also metaphors for the psychic wounds of the past. The more physically scarred a Harris character is, the more psychologically damaged he or she is—as Fasil says, "are we not all marked with our wounds?"[34] In another context, Mark Seltzer has written of America's wound culture, which he defines as "the public fascination with torn and open bodies and torn and opened persons, a collective gathering around shock, trauma, and the wound."[35] Certainly, this concept applies to Harris's best-selling fiction, where readers gather around any number of torn and scarred individuals seeking to inflict wounds upon others in a type of free-floating payback against personal injustices.

Lander, as primary villain, is the character most often described in terms of his scars. Lander's hand, mangled by a bullet in Vietnam and then left untreated for a number of days, heals into a scarred claw, most often referred to as "ugly." Lander is hypersensitive about its appearance but, like a monster showing his ugliness to an audience for shock effect, displays it to Dahlia to test her reaction to him. The ugly hand represents the corruption of Lander's character. To save his hand, Lander sells his soul to his North Vietnamese captors in exchange for surgery and completes the long process of alienation from

American society that began when he was a lonely boy. The hand that facilitates Lander's transcendental merging with flying machines is also the hand that has now been corrupted into the means by which Lander constructs his killing device.

Other characters bear their scars as well. Fasil, his face scarred by a bullet during Kabakov's commando raid in Beirut, is described as a monster. Though less monstrous, Kabakov is also a mass of scar tissue as a result of bullet wounds, bomb explosions, hand-to-hand combat, and who knows what kind of other injuries inflicted over a lifetime of war. Though not a man given over to random death like Lander, Kabakov too is morally compromised, since he will use torture and other violent means despite his distaste for them.

Harris initiates his career-long fondness for animal imagery in this book. He draws upon a veritable menagerie of animal metaphors: civet cats, cows, praying mantises, whales, snakes, pumas, rats, wolves, mice, horses, sheep, eagles, and sharks, among others. The animal images establish for us an awareness of the predator/prey dynamic, which complements the novel's insistence that while most of us are sheep, eagles and wolves prowl among us.

Certain characters are given animal-like qualities to establish their station within the food chain. Abu Ali has small, neat gestures like a civet cat. The unsuspecting Veterans' Affairs bureaucrat Pugh is likened to a cow, while Lander is compared to a predator in the bush watching him from downwind. Dahlia has puma eyes and mannerisms to match. Fasil's soul is populated with savage undersea creatures. Lander's quick temper compares to a serpent with a capacity for lethal strikes. Kabakov is probably the most complicated of the characters, compared to both predator and prey. His thigh is as hard and warm against Rachel's thigh as a horse's neck, yet the animal he identifies with most (his totem animal, if you will) is the eagle. He has spent his adult life killing. Even his "herbivore" self (the horse) is hard, vital, solid, and swift—anything but soft. So while he possesses the capacity for life and love, he really comes out on the balance sheet as a predator.

In other instances, the animal image illustrates a certain philosophical concept, such as Harris's poetic description of the state of Lander's soul: "What was left could live with rage because it was made in rage and rage was its element and it thrived there as a mammal thrives in air."[36] In other words, Lander's rage takes on its own self-sustaining life. In another image remarkably evocative of Hannibal Lecter's "roller pigeon" discussion with Barney in *Hannibal*, Lander's friend Jergens compares his North Vietnamese guard to creeper fowl and the yellow mouse. His rants about lethal genetic malformation occur after a prolonged period in solitary confinement as a prisoner of war. Since the creeper fowl and the yellow mouse are doomed by genetic "lethal factors," the clear implication is that certain human beings are equally cursed. They are haywire genetic machines that break down and, in the breaking down, murder other human beings.

## THEMES

The novel is carried aloft by several themes that inform Harris's later work as well. First, the novel keys in on the theme of transformation. In the story, Lander changes from a sensitive, intellectual boy in short pants into a man twisted by rage to plot an act of murder on an unimagined scale. Dahlia changes from a scared little girl in a Palestinian refugee camp into a battle-hardened and ruthless terrorist operative. Kabakov changes from an orphaned boy into a fierce warrior, albeit one somewhat tempered by self-doubts about the savagery of his own nature and his embrace of torture in the pursuit of the Israeli cause. The politics of the Israeli/Palestinian conflict, while semi-realistically presented, are secondary to Harris's real agenda, which is to examine what injuries and injustices change men and women into murderers. This theme is what bridges the gap between Harris's first novel of political intrigue and his later novels of serial murder.

Another theme is the linkage of epiphany to the pleasure of the hunt. For Lander, a chain of epiphanies sets him on the hunt to kill thousands at the Super Bowl. The first of these epiphanies saves him from suicide after his resignation from the Navy. He sees the Aldrich blimp, crossing behind the Washington Monument, as if the tall structure were a rifle sight aimed at the blimp. The sight gives him hope that he may have a second career as a commercial blimp pilot, but also foreshadows the direction this career move will take him. His ordinary routine as blimp pilot suddenly reveals itself to be the inspired answer to his rage. Only later do the practical problems in carrying out his epiphany manifest. He realizes he cannot obtain the explosives on his own. However, another epiphany comes to Lander's rescue. While watching a news special on Arab terrorism, he suddenly realizes he can find the plastique he needs by contacting Arab terrorists. The details remain to be worked out, but all of the ideas Lander needs fall into place so he can carry out his destructive farewell to a world he hates.

The other important epiphanies in the story belong to Kabakov, the investigative foil to Lander's criminal psychopath. We've already noted Kabakov's discovery of his true hunter's nature while he watches the eagle soar over the sheep in Syria. A second epiphany comes to Kabakov while he examines a box full of Abu Ali's personal effects taken from Beirut. His hunter's mind, intently focused on all of the particulars of his investigation into the Black September plot in America, has at this point still not discovered the terrorists' intended target. However, when he finds a coffee-stained copy of a recent *Sports Illustrated* magazine amid Ali's effects, he is puzzled enough by its presence to flip through it. Then it

hits him: A pattern suddenly leaps out from heretofore random facts. He solves the puzzle in a flash. Analysis and
intuition merge perfectly to provide the answer to the investigation: the terrorists are going to strike the Super Bowl.
Similar epiphanies happen for Will Graham, Clarice
Starling, and Rinaldo Pazzi in the later novels. That both
Kabakov and Lander are prone to these quasi-mystical leaps
of intuition lends support to the notion that their predatory
natures are similar, though set in different directions.

The world of *Black Sunday* is indeed full of predators,
ceaselessly circling one another, preying on sheep when
it suits them and waiting for opportune moments to take
out the other predators as threats. These predators are
exiles or outsiders from the mainstream society. For
Harris, the outsider is a threatening figure, susceptible to
surrender to violent urges at best and lethal at worst.
Here, the outsider is a kind of political metaphor, a way
to criticize American society and the toxic milieu of the
Israeli/Palestinian conflict.

Lander's type of predator—the sick, lone "rogue"
exiled by his kind and existing on the fringes of his pack
as best as he can until he can find his opportunity to
strike—is a metaphor for how the tendency of American
social codes to ostracize those who differ from the norm
can result in the worst kind of blowback. When Lander
establishes a connection to Black September, he enters
into another kind of predatory dynamic altogether. Black
September operates as a pack or "cell," independent of
and unacknowledged by Al Fatah, the guerilla arm of the
Palestinian Liberation Organization. The fanatical but
methodical terrorists within this cell are absolutely ruthless in the service of their cause to liberate the Palestinian
homeland. They collectively believe themselves to have
been victimized by an even larger pack of predators, the
joint U.S./Israeli alliance. Their lives given meaning by
this ideology, the terrorists cautiously accept Lander as a
means to an end. Harris sets up Lander and the Black

September terrorists as the predatory villains of his political melodrama. He casts them as outsiders personally and politically for the purpose of making it easier for a large American audience (the kind that buys hardback books and turns them into best sellers) to root against the success of their plot.

Lander is the prototypical outsider in Harris's fiction—an alienated Southerner who escapes his cruel home and heritage through military service. However, his gambit is destined to turn him into an even bigger loser. He is first exploited by the military for his skills and then abandoned when he becomes a burden as a POW and an embarrassment because of his coerced confession of war crimes against the North Vietnamese. Harris is more interested in writing an action thriller than he is a political screed, but it's still impossible to miss the critique of American culture. For example, when Lander pilots a blimp over a football game, he does not see people below him, but rather a screaming mob easy to kill. He works for a rubber company that makes not only tires but body bags, an irony not lost upon Lander. When one of his crewmates asks what a body bag is, Lander explains in a politically charged double entendre that it's a big "rubber" used by Uncle Sam. The bitter joke, rooted in Lander's wartime experience of seeing corpses bundled into body bags, is Harris's comment upon the foolishness of the Vietnam War. Significantly, the joke also emphasizes Aldrich's role in manufacturing products not only for domestic civilian use (tires) but military purposes (body bags), suggesting the extent to which the military war machine and domestic industry are intertwined. Nor are the returning veterans given their due, as Lander's periodic ritual humiliation at the VA illustrates. The United States has much to answer for, Harris implies. Lander is its own homegrown lethal product retaliating against it. On the international scale, Black September is the whirlwind the country must reap for its imperialistic excesses.

Harris's focus on the extremist group Black September brings with it the charge that he is trafficking in racist portrayals of Arabs for the sake of a best seller. While *Black Sunday* as a first novel is clearly the least sophisticated of Harris's novels, Harris does take a few proactive steps to mitigate the critical accusation that he demonizes Arabs. In terms of character development, for example, he gives Dahlia, the most developed of the terrorists as a character, a background that makes her at least somewhat sympathetic to audiences. By contrast, he shades Kabakov (and to some extent Moshevsky) just enough to make the Israeli's methodology, and even his motives, not that far removed from those of the terrorists. In terms of the then-recent history of the Arab/Israeli conflict, Harris attempts to convey something of the convoluted sociohistorical background leading up to his fictional terrorist strike, particularly the very-real 1972 Olympic Village massacre. The Black September movement is given something of a justification for its actions, although it's a little hard to swallow. The terrorists seem naïve in hoping the horrific death toll of its atrocity will lead to the United States re-evaluating its investment in the Middle East, deciding the cost is just not worth it, ceasing its arms sales to Israel, and pulling out of the region to let the Arabs and Israelis battle it out on their own.

Granting Harris all this, the case can still be made that Harris oversimplifies the Middle Eastern conflict. Stephanie Reich argues forcefully that "not a word is written about the history of the Palestinian situation, or even about who the Palestinians are," and the Palestinian characters who are depicted are members of a fringe terrorist group. She concludes that the melodrama of the bomb plot ignores "real political developments in the movement."[37] Examining the book's Arab characters, who are set up as unattractive, fanatical, small-minded, lustful, and/or evil, bears out some of what Reich says. Thus, Harris arguably reinforces an ancient prejudice, which is the view of the Arab world (and the Orient in general) as a locus of irrationality, mysticism, religious zealotry, and savagery in contrast to the supposedly enlightened and civilized West.

Consider, for example, the novel's first scene, where Dahlia is taken by taxi ride from the airport to the dark inner heart of Beirut where the organizers of Black September wait for her in an inner sanctum. Since the Westernized Dahlia is coming from the United States, this journey represents her literal and psychological movement from the enlightened Western world to some hidden evil room populated by dangerous Arab fanatics from the mysterious Eastern world. In the time Dahlia spends in this building in Beirut, the term most often used to describe it is "dark." In this building, the plot against the United States is finalized by Najeer, the fear-inspiring commander of Black September who prefers the purity of holocaust over reasoned political solutions. The sex act that follows between Dahlia and Najeer represents the lustful side of the evil concentrated within the dark setting. Kabakov's subsequent raid is too late, and his sparing of Dahlia too merciful, to prevent the specific evil birthed between Dahlia and Najeer from returning to poison the comparative tranquility of the United States. The Black September terrorist cell, embodying the stereotypical traits of the Oriental world, infiltrates the country to plan a sneak attack even worse than the Japanese bombing of Pearl Harbor. Of course, Lander's North Vietnamese captors, depicted as faceless ciphers, also factor into the novel's demonization of the Eastern world.

From this "Orientalist" perspective, if we examine all of the Arab characters in *Black Sunday*, we find a rogue's gallery of villains, each one representing a particular facet of the American fear of the Arab other. Najeer, the commander of Black September, is known behind his back as "The Praying Mantis," a name suggestive of cannibalism, which implies he will not hesitate to kill even those of his own kind if they displease. Loyalty has no meaning to him, only the cause. We have already discussed how Dahlia's open use of sexuality is one of her weapons. In this context, her sexuality marks her as lustful or oversexed, another trait ascribed to the exotic/erotic Eastern world. Fasil, the planner of the Munich massacre and accomplice in the Super Bowl strike, is known as the "Technician" or the "Architect." His knowledge of weapons, strategies, tactics, and technology (as opposed to any real insight into people) in the service of murder designate him as a killing machine, devoid of sympathy for the enemy.

At times, Harris lampoons the Arab villains, making them as laughable as they are lethal. The best example is the crooked importer Benjamin Muzi. He is a grotesquely fat man—a fleshly caricature of gluttony, avarice, and treachery reminiscent of Sydney Greenstreet or Jabba the Hutt. His attempt to sneak into his house to retrieve his passport while dressed as a woman makes him appear even more ridiculous. These characters in their totality both demean and demonize the Arabs for the presumed American readership, a readership increasingly anxious about foreign terrorists and looking for the opportunity to defeat them vicariously in a spectacular action thriller.

Of course, given Harris's selective misanthropy, the Americans in the story come off little better, particularly those working in federal law enforcement. In what some would call reactionary fashion, the plot presents the various police and governmental agencies as hamstrung by regulation and liberal civil rights, enfeebled by their immensity, and ill-served by their overly cautious leaders. FBI Special Agent Sam Corley, as the most important of these federal law enforcement representatives, is competent but definitely plays second fiddle to the fierce individualism of the Kabakov and Moshevsky show, which would not be out of place in a typical episode of the Fox television series *24*. Corley is mostly ineffectual, unable to convince the FBI to move quickly on an obvious imminent threat. Without the two Israeli agents on scene to help Corley, Lander's strike would have succeeded in racking up a fearsome casualty list.

Nor are other American agencies any better at detecting, or even believing, the threat. Fowler, the CIA agent present in the first briefing about the terrorist plot, shows open antagonism toward Kabakov. After the briefing, Fowler makes an anti-Semitic joke to Corley about Kabakov's dire predictions and says he is tired of working with the Israelis because of their tendency to kill Arab terrorists rather than turn them into useful informants. Fowler's personal experiences blind him to the evidence in front of him. In a follow-up meeting, Corley confirms Kabakov's suspicion that U.S. intelligence believes the Arabs wouldn't dare to attack the United States. The State Department later officially expels Kabakov from the country when there is some sticky newspaper publicity over Kabakov's brutal questioning of the *Leticia*'s first mate, although he is allowed to covertly return as long as he remains beneath public notice. This kind of timid action on the part of the U.S. government compels the reader to root for Kabakov as the sole person who can combat the terrorists, using their own methods against them. The preference for forceful individual action over sluggish institutional response is one of Harris's most reliable themes, no doubt one that appeals to his more reactionary readers.

In Harris's fiction, human beings, like other animals, behave according to a complex mix of genetics and environment. But the predatory instinct that restlessly circles within all of us is always on the verge of manifesting itself, thus overwhelming our civilized selves and driving us to murder. Harris has spent his career elaborating upon this theme, beginning with *Black Sunday*. If *Black Sunday* were Harris's primary contribution to American popular culture, we would no doubt look back on it now as an interesting curiosity in light of the 9/11 attacks and a minor entry in the history of the political action-thriller genre. However, much bigger things were just ahead on the horizon for Harris.

# 3

# "The Price of Imagination": *Red Dragon*

Home. Home sweet home. Home is where the heart is. A man's home is his castle. You can't go home again. All these well-known aphorisms point to one overwhelming sentiment: that in our homes, we feel safe, secure, and somehow invulnerable to the hostility of the world at large. When we venture out into that world and it changes us through bitter experience so that indeed we can't go home again, nevertheless home remains in our minds as a sacred memory of innocence—or so the sentimental vision of home has it.

Thomas Harris's second novel, *Red Dragon* (1981), assaults this sentiment like a gloved, gun-wielding intruder in the dark of night. In fact, the novel begins with two competing visions of home: one as literally a safe harbor, and another as a blood-smeared slaughter-house. Even Will Graham's apparently safe subtropical retreat where he lives with his wife and stepson is ultimately invaded by the killer. The killer's law-enforcement nickname, "the Tooth Fairy," plays on the notion of home as a place of safety. The nickname is a bit of black humor derived from the story told to children that the Tooth Fairy will visit them while they are sleeping in their homes and leave behind money for their extracted baby teeth left under their pillows. This Tooth Fairy, however, is no benign nocturnal presence and would never be knowingly welcomed into any home.

*Red Dragon* is a novel as frightening as no other Harris novel has ever been, at least in the judgment of many who had never read anything like it before. Back in 1981, serial killers were by no means as large a part of the national consciousness as they are now. In fact, the term "serial killer" had not even really entered the national vocabulary then. Harris's novel presented the reading public with a twin set of villains like none most of them had encountered before: Francis Dolarhyde, murderer of entire families, and Dr. Hannibal Lecter, incarcerated cannibalistic psychiatrist.

Equally unique was the emphasis on criminal profiling, or at least that practiced by the FBI, in a work of popular fiction. Through the character of Will Graham, Harris creates the template of the criminal profiler who, through an act of projective imagination, enters the fantasy life of a serial killer in order to make sensible otherwise incomprehensible clues left behind at crime scenes. To use this gift of imagination, however, Graham risks his own sanity by coming into contact with the thoughts and desires of the human monsters he chases. "It's the price of imagination," as one character says. Such uncomfortable proximity to savagery threatens to unleash Graham's own buried resentments, fears, and murderous impulses. He may even set up, consciously or unconsciously, a loathed tabloid reporter to be murdered by Dolarhyde. Graham's involvement in the investigation leads to alienation from his family, a drinking problem, and finally an ambush by Dolarhyde in which Graham is stabbed in the face and his wife and stepson are nearly killed. Ultimately, Graham is a tragic character, wounded and on the verge of abandonment by his family. Through creating a sympathetic but fatally flawed character in what many readers experienced as a genuinely terrifying novel, Harris sets the stage for generations of such troubled fictional profilers to come.

## CRITICAL RECEPTION

The novel was greeted enthusiastically by its first reviewers. Probably the most effusive is fellow novelist Stephen King, who calls it "the best popular novel to be published in America since *The Godfather*." He goes on to explain his reasons for this claim, including a prose style that "ticks in such perfect time that the reader is amazed with delight." He also lauds the novel's "raw, grisly power" to leave the reader "shaken and sober and afraid on a deeper level than simple 'thrills' alone furnish."[1] Joseph Amiel deems it a "chilling, tautly written, and well-realized psychological thriller."[2] Christopher Lehmann-Haupt is slightly more circumspect in his evaluation, but concludes by saying, "I have to acknowledge my gut response to Mr. Harris's thriller. It hits us in our outrage, and titillates the part of us all that would like to get rid of evil with a gun."[3]

A couple of reviewers center on the villain and the combination of fear and pity he elicits. Jean Strouse points out Harris's narrative sympathy for Dolarhyde: "Astonishingly enough, Thomas Harris . . . manages to make you sympathize with both Graham and Dolarhyde as he brings them inexorably to confrontation. Poor old D. fights hard against the hideous monster he becomes, and isn't that the ultimate scare—fear of our own monstrously negative capabilities?"[4]

Thomas Fleming pens a phrase undoubtedly beloved by the publishers when he says the book "is an engine designed for one purpose—to make the pulses pound, the heart palpitate, the fear glands secrete." He is somewhat skeptical of Harris's philosophical subtext as expressed in Dolarhyde's love of William Blake. Fleming views this as a potential story hindrance when he says it is "about as pertinent as Joseph Wambaugh's attempts at constructing a Weltanschauung from the cop on the beat, but it does not do any significant damage to Mr. Harris's engine."[5]

In the years following the novel's first visceral impact on its reviewers, later critics still speak rather highly of it. David Sexton characterizes the book in superlatives: "Nor had any previous crime book presented a crime scene with such detailed horror as that uncovered at the start of *Red Dragon*. Nor had the thought-processes of a monster been made so intimately plausible to the reader as they are in the scenes in which Dolarhyde is taken over by the Dragon."[6]

Daniel O'Brien writes: "An astute combination of detective fiction and character study, *Red Dragon* is taut, well-paced, scrupulously researched and persuasively detailed."[7] So certainly the novel has aged well in terms of its overall critical estimation. But what are some of the specifics that critics analyze?

Some focus on character dynamics. John Goodrich, for one, focuses on the introduction of Hannibal Lecter, the sort of character he is, and how he became so wildly popular. Goodrich concludes that Lecter serves both as a mentor and teacher to Graham.[8] The teacher/student archetype is a powerful one, thus suggesting one reason for Lecter's immense popularity. Robert H. Waugh analyzes another dynamic prevalent throughout the book—that of master/slave. Waugh argues that within the context of the book, "the slave" is a term for the residual energy of past trauma. For example, Dolarhyde as an aspiring master seeks a truly independent consciousness (the "Red Dragon") but "draws his energy from the castration traumas of his childhood."[9] Tony Williams examines how the book's characters must confront their traumatic pasts, with their souls hanging in the balance. Because they suffer from fractured psyches, Graham and Dolarhyde are doubles of the other. They share what Williams calls a "symbiotic relationship between the searcher and his prey."[10]

Other critics focus on the book's place in literary and genre history. Davide Mana explores how the noir literary movement is redirected by *Red Dragon*, in particular how it "recalls, re-uses, and updates the classical themes of noir, heralding the birth of what will be called, at the end of the twentieth century, neo-noir."[11] One of the reasons the book had such an impact on its initial readers, Mana argues, is its introduction of the modern serial killer into the classical mystery or detective story to add a new layer of horror. In another study, I argue that Graham's moral complicity in Freddy Lounds's murder places the book in the Gothic genre, one "to which Harris's serial killer novels owe much."[12] S. T. Joshi maintains that Harris doesn't do anything really all that new. For Joshi, the book is decisively within the detective story tradition. He argues that for all of the narrative emphasis placed on Graham's so-called ability to enter the mind of a killer, what Graham really does is "simply to interpret the physical evidence more thoroughly, sensitively, and keenly than others have."[13] Joshi concludes that the book is as much psychological case study and thriller as it is a detective story. Tony Magistrale tracks the influence of William Blake's poetry and Romantic philosophies throughout *Red Dragon*, arguing that it is likely Harris intends for Dolarhyde's co-opting of Blake's positive visionary work to stand in for a bleak, Gothic view of the human capacity for evil. In other words, humans whose impulses remain unchecked are "more likely to perform acts of perversity than poetry."[14]

Phillip A. Ellis examines the role of gender in the book. He discovers that a complex web of character interactions develops that makes it difficult to assign hard-and-fast gender attributes to anybody. The blurred gender lines bear out Ellis's contention that "it is, in a sense, impossible to totally isolate aspects of either [masculinity or femininity],

without addressing aspects of the other."[15] Nicholas M.
Williams focuses on the scene where Dolarhyde, having
gained access to the archives of the Brooklyn Museum, eats
William Blake's watercolor of *The Great Red Dragon and the
Woman Clothed with the Sun*. For Williams, this scene serves
"as a figure for the reception, the incorporation, of high-art
culture in mass-market media and, by extension, for the
trope of consumption itself."[16] Put another way, Williams is
interested in exploring how Harris's novel combines
characteristics of both popular fiction and elite, modernist
culture such as that represented by Blake's *Great Red
Dragon* painting. The range of these critical responses demonstrates vividly the increase in quality and complexity
between Harris's first and second novels.

## PLOT DEVELOPMENT

Like *Black Sunday* before it, *Red Dragon* is not divided
formally into sections. However, it too can be divided
into three acts for convenience's sake. Act 1, covering
Chapters 1–12, takes us through Will Graham's investigations of the first two "Tooth Fairy" crime scenes and
Graham's preliminary interview with Lecter. Act 2, covering Chapters 13–24, intensifies the FBI manhunt once a
vital clue is discovered in Lecter's cell. The act concludes
with the murder of reporter Freddy Lounds. Act 3, covering Chapters 25–54, describes killer Francis Dolarhyde's
brief affair with Reba McClane and his resulting identity
crisis. The federal manhunt closes in on Dolarhyde,
finally leaving Dolarhyde dead and Graham wounded in
the hospital.

   In Act 1, FBI Special Agent Jack Crawford persuades
Will Graham, retired after a near-fatal attack by serial
killer Hannibal Lecter, to return to federal service to profile the "Tooth Fairy," a serial killer who has murdered
two entire families during the past two full moons. The
Leeds family in Atlanta has just been murdered, leaving

a month before the next homicides. Reluctantly, Graham leaves his wife Molly and stepson Willy in the Florida Keys to investigate the crime scene at the Leedses' house. Based on the bloody evidence left behind, Graham concludes that the killer may have taken off his gloves to touch Mrs. Leeds's body and to open the eyes of the dead family to "watch" his defilement of her. Vital fingerprint clues, formerly overlooked by the police, are discovered based on Graham's "hunch." To regain familiarity with the killing mindset, Graham interviews Lecter, incarcerated in a Baltimore hospital for the criminally insane, about his insights on the Leeds case. The encounter upsets Graham and ultimately ends up as a tabloid story, written by reporter Freddy Lounds, in the *National Tattler*. Graham flies to Birmingham, Alabama, to visit another crime scene. He discovers two more overlooked clues, a high branch trimmed away from a tree in the backyard and a symbol representing the "red dragon" in Mah-Jongg carved into the trunk. Though Graham does not know it, the Red Dragon is the personal avatar of Francis Dolarhyde, aka the "Tooth Fairy." Dolarhyde works at Gateway Labs in St. Louis, Missouri. He chooses his victims from the films sent to the lab for developing.

Act 2 begins with the discovery of a coded message between the Tooth Fairy and Lecter in Lecter's cell. The Tooth Fairy was motivated to contact Lecter by the *Tattler* story about Graham. Lecter does not know that the note has been discovered, and Crawford wants to keep it that way. In the short amount of time the note is available to the FBI before it must be returned to Lecter's cell, forensics specialists subject the note to a battery of tests. Analysis reveals Lecter is to communicate with the Tooth Fairy in a coded reply in the personals section of the *Tattler*, but no one knows what the code means. Graham decides to run the ad. When breaking the code reveals that Lecter gave the Tooth Fairy Graham's home address, Graham's family must go into hiding. The FBI's next move is to use the *Tattler* and Freddy Lounds to write an exclusive interview with Graham in order to bait the Tooth Fairy into a trap in Washington, DC. While Graham is under police protection, Lounds in Chicago is not. Angered by the ad, Dolarhyde abducts Lounds back to his home in Missouri. Dolarhyde forces him to read a taped message to Graham. He next returns Lounds to Chicago, sets him on fire in front of the *Tattler* office, and escapes back to Missouri. Lounds dies in the hospital shortly thereafter.

In Act 3, Dolarhyde meets and begins an affair with Reba McClane, a blind worker in the lab next-door to Gateway. A vestige of his humanity restored by his romance with Reba, Dolarhyde struggles to regain power over the Red Dragon part of his personality that has taken him over and compelled him to murder. Meanwhile, Graham begins to review the home movies of the Jacobi and Leeds families. He reaches a startling epiphany—the Tooth Fairy must have seen these same movies. A quick search reveals that the film was developed by Gateway. The manhunt converges on Gateway and Dolarhyde. To elude Graham and the police, Dolarhyde fools Reba into thinking he killed himself. He sets a fire in his house, which apparently consumes his body. Graham and his family return home, believing the danger is over. However, they are attacked by Dolarhyde on the beach. Graham is stabbed in the face, leaving Molly to kill Dolarhyde. Graham recovers in the hospital. However, he realizes his marriage is probably over now. His is the last family to fall victim to the Tooth Fairy.

## CHARACTERS

### Will Graham

Will Graham was a poor child. His father worked in boatyards from the Deep South to the Great Lakes, taking the young Graham with him on a nomadic existence. As an adult, he began his law enforcement career in the New Orleans homicide division. He attended graduate school in forensics at George Washington University. From there, he worked in the FBI crime lab and went out into the field as a "special investigator," though never a special agent.

Eventually, he became a forensics instructor and criminal profiler at the FBI Academy. He identified a Minnesota serial killer as Garrett Jacob Hobbs, fatally shooting him before Hobbs could be arrested. Shortly afterward, Graham was hospitalized for four weeks in the psychiatric wing of Bethesda Naval Hospital. He returned to federal service in time to catch another serial killer, Dr. Hannibal Lecter, who nearly killed him with a knife. Following his recovery, Graham resigned from the FBI to work as a diesel mechanic at a boatyard in Marathon in the Florida Keys. He met Molly a year after his nearly fatal encounter with Lecter and eventually married her. He lives with her and her son, Willy, in the Keys. As the novel opens, he is in his late thirties and just starting to feel the weight of accumulated years.

Certainly, Graham's skill level as a detective and criminal profiler is superb. His intellectual capacity is matched by few, his command of crime scene evidentiary procedure is superb, and his intuitive leaps are unparalleled. He enjoys the thrill of the hunt. Indeed, when he realizes how the Tooth Fairy chooses his victims, he experiences a savage burst of joy that is the happiest moment of his life. As an investigator, he finds satisfaction in the professionalism of his colleagues.[17]

The problem is, Will Graham is man who mistrusts himself. His gift of super-charged empathy, combined with his hunter's zeal to chase down human predators, leads him into extremely dangerous mindsets and situations from which he finds it difficult to disengage. He is disturbed by how easily he enters the minds of the killers he hunts. His ability to do this happens at some preverbal, sensory-driven level that places him in danger of losing his learned values. Because he cannot easily shake his imagination's wanderings into forbidden territory, he finds it difficult to cultivate and nurture loving relationships. All too often, he numbs his acute perceptions with booze. His thought processes, contaminated by proximity to human beings damaged by their horrible family histories, lead him to resent those closest to him. As a result, he finds himself increasingly estranged from both his wife and his stepson, even before Francis Dolarhyde shows up to finalize the disintegration of the Graham family unit, if not their actual murder. If Graham is a hero, he is a tragic one, laid low by his own flaw of imagination applied too closely in the service of bringing murderers to heel.[18]

Graham is introduced as a man with thought patterns unlike those of other people. His mentor, Jack Crawford, understands Graham has a gift for insights into criminal minds and so seeks to reinstate his profiling career specifically for this reason. Crawford explains to Molly that Graham's bad luck is to be the best at what he does. Graham's gift consists of two closely linked skills: visualization and empathy. With enormous recall of visual details, Graham reconstructs the movements of the murderer based on what he leaves behind at a crime scene. In the second chapter of the novel, Graham eventually visualizes exactly how the killer murdered the Leeds family, in what order, and what he did with the victims postmortem. He demonstrates this ability again at the Jacobi crime scene, even though it's a month old now—the house cleaned, the trail gone cold. Graham experiences his moments of visualization as a type of bonding with the killer. At the Leeds house, the moment of imaginative connection between Graham and the killer is described as the itch of a leech. As Graham gets ever deeper into the case, he feels the crime scenes trying to reveal their secrets to him. He attempts to visualize the killer himself while examining forensic evidence (saliva, hair, and semen) in the lab. Drunk after the murder of Lounds, he tries to imagine the face of the killer but sees only a faceless silhouette in his mind's eye. These details incubating away in Graham's skull come together in a flash of epiphany when he realizes the killer saw the Leeds and Jacobi home movies.

Empathy is the other aspect of Graham's gift. Crawford has long been aware of Graham's empathy, particularly in the way Graham mimics the speech patterns of others. Others also recognize how unique Graham's abilities are, such as the faculty at Duke University who want to test him for any psychic abilities. Dr. Alan Bloom realizes Graham is no psychic, but rather an *eideteker*, or a person with what is sometimes called "a photographic memory." Bloom tells Crawford that Graham's ability to assume other points of view scares and sickens him. Graham's empathetic skills are so good they create a paradox. Some people feel discomfort or even fear around him. Dr. Bloom won't be alone with Graham, in case Graham picks up on Bloom's professional curiosity. Graham's abilities to read a crime scene and find clues unseen by everyone else unsettle even professional detectives, such as Springfield, the Atlanta detective who reacts with incredulity to the discovery of a partial fingerprint on the cornea of the oldest Leeds child's eye. Graham's spooky professional reputation follows him into the pages of the *National Tattler* when Freddy Lounds quotes a police officer as comparing Graham to a king snake that lives under the house and eats moccasins. Even Francis Dolarhyde, realizing Graham is hot on his trail, ascribes supernatural powers to Graham, cursing him as a "son of a bitch" and a "monster."

Graham not too convincingly tries to cut through what he dismisses as "a lot of bullshit about the way I think."[19] He explains his method to Molly as a process of extrapolating from evidence to find patterns and thus reconstruct the killer's thinking. However, because he is justifying his leaving early retirement, he minimizes the extent to which he immerses himself in the psyches of killers. Sitting out on the roof of the Leeds house at night to escape the blood-soaked desolation within, Graham is a little more honest with himself in a moment of reflection: "Graham had a lot of trouble with taste. Often his thoughts were not tasty. There were no effective partitions in his mind. What he saw and learned touched everything else he knew. . . . His associations came at the speed of light. His value judgments were at the pace of a responsive reading. . . . He viewed his own mentality as grotesque but useful, like a chair made of antlers."[20]

Put another way, Graham cannot compartmentalize or separate his thought processes. He can make breathtaking intuitive leaps and pull together patterns based on his near-perfect recall of seemingly unconnected facts, images, and memories. But he can't stop the ugliness of his professional life from contaminating the sanctity of what he holds dear in his personal life. The imbalance had led him to mental collapse and confinement to a mental hospital once before.

Graham has much to lose besides his life. His identity and sanity are at risk. He has found a fulfilling family relationship, albeit troubled, and a safe harbor in the Florida Keys far from the madness of his earlier life. Now nearly forty years old, still young enough to have many happy years ahead of him but old enough to feel tired, his fear robs him of any joy in his experiences. For example, in the brief flashback scene where Graham is meeting Molly for the first time, he fears the future loss of the relationship before it even begins. Bloom claims that Graham suffers from fear as the price he pays for having imagination—a reasonable conclusion, given that Graham spends much of his time imagining all the things that can go wrong. If Molly has taught him to relish every moment, without her he has no system of checks and balances to keep him from dwelling on disastrous possibilities.

Graham's fear renders him both defensive and angry. For example, when Molly in a phone conversation makes a seemingly innocent joke about him having a criminal mind as a boy because he stole a watermelon from a neighbor, he reacts quite defensively. His fear of losing his family sometimes translates into resentment of them, as illustrated in the scene where Graham silently fumes about justifying his actions to Willy. He resents Molly's parents, whom he perceives as a threat to his family, especially when Molly takes Willy to stay with them. As the stress of the investigation mounts, his resentment intensifies, and he is so fatigued that he often becomes childish. At times he feels hostility for the murdered Leeds and Jacobi families for their affluence and materialism in life. Of course, he hates Freddy Lounds for publicizing his greatest moments of vulnerability—his hospitalizations after encounters with Hobbs and Lecter—to the world. His often hostile attitude toward the world parallels him in many ways to Dolarhyde, a rather morally compromised place for a hero to be.

In fact, Graham is no traditional hero, for all of his gifts as a profiler. He is not very handsome or stylish; in fact, Detective Springfield thinks he looks like a rumpled house painter. Graham is slightly built, no match for the hulking body-builder Dolarhyde. He drinks alone too much under stress, as when he gets drunk following the death of Freddy Lounds and Molly's leaving for Oregon. He may even have subconsciously set up Lounds for murder by placing his hand on Lounds in the newspaper photograph as if Lounds were a pet (a sure-fire trigger for the pet- and family slaying Tooth Fairy). Graham compounds this tactical error by not providing police protection for the reporter, a serious omission for a trained detective. Graham's not much of an action hero either. When Dolarhyde attacks his family and injures Graham, Graham hightails it down the beach as fast as he can, although admittedly he may not be thinking too clearly since Dolarhyde just shoved a knife halfway through his head. All of these less-than-flattering details serve to humanize Graham, to render him that much more accessible (if not always admirable) to us. In short, Graham behaves like many of us probably would in the same circumstances. He tries to do the right thing, but he's hindered by a tense family dynamic and any number of character flaws aggravated by extreme stress.

That's a good thing to remember about Graham. In spite of those flaws, for all of his petty resentments, Graham faces his fears squarely in order to track down the Red Dragon and save lives. He risks his family and sanity in the pursuit. He endures the psychological torments inflicted upon him by the imprisoned serial killer who nearly killed him because Lecter holds the key to re-entering a type of mindset Graham had long since left behind for the sake of his own sanity. Even after his family is all but lost to him because of the intolerable stress of the investigation, he consoles Reba by telling her nothing is wrong with her and that Dolarhyde was actually trying to stop killing because of her. One can't help but think that Graham deserves better than to have his face rearranged by a madman's knife and his wife and stepson on the verge of leaving him for good.

## Francis Dolarhyde

Francis Dolarhyde, aka the Tooth Fairy or, as he prefers to be known, the Red Dragon, is a pitiless serial killer with the physique of a linebacker, making him a terrifying enemy to confront. However, he is also a man we get to know well, and even sympathize with to some extent. As strange as this may sound, Francis Dolarhyde is a romantic. If Michael Lander is motivated by hate, Dolarhyde is motivated by love, or an excess of love distorted into possessiveness skewed sideways into murder. In a novel about family bonds, Dolarhyde may arguably be the novel's main character. The title of the book itself refers to Dolarhyde. His actions clearly redirect the lives of everyone else in the story. Certainly, we know a lot more about his past than, say, Graham's.

Dolarhyde was born in 1938 with a severely cleft palate, in Springfield, Missouri, to an impoverished woman named Marian Dolarhyde Trevane. Abandoned by her husband, Marian, in turn, abandons her deformed baby boy in the hospital. A surgeon does the best job he can to repair the infant's cleft palate. Dolarhyde is raised in an orphanage until the age of five, when his grandmother brings him home to live with her. His grandmother abuses him physically and psychologically, a state of affairs that only worsens when she develops dementia. He begins to kill small animals during this time. His mother and her husband take him in for a few months, but he is sent away at the age of nine for hanging his stepsister Victoria's cat. At the age of seventeen, he breaks into a neighbor's house and is then given the choice of enlisting in the Army or being charged. He joins the Army, where further repairs are made to his cleft palate.

While in the Army, he learns to develop aerial reconnaissance photos. He is stationed in Hong Kong. Upon his return to civilian life, he is employed at Gateway Labs as division chief. He spends his leisure time body-building. After being captivated by his viewing of a print of William Blake's painting of the Great Red Dragon, he travels to Hong Kong to have an enormous dragon tattooed on his back. He may or may not have killed in Hong Kong, just as he may or may not have killed a number of elderly women in St. Louis and Toledo earlier in life. Five months after his vacation, he kills his first family.

Harris spends a lot of time (and pages) on Dolarhyde, giving us the most detailed past history of anyone in the novel. Perhaps some of this history even explains why Dolarhyde becomes a killer, or at least suggests some possible reasons. Moments of trauma emphasized in the back story certainly correspond to unique features of Dolarhyde's identity as the Red Dragon. The false teeth he uses for his murders are his grandmother's. The wooden wheelchair he uses for Lounds's murder is his grandmother's. His hated childhood nickname of "cunt-face" may motivate him to attack the labias of his female victims. The stepbrother who slams Dolarhyde's face into a mirror until it breaks gives rise to Dolarhyde's need to use mirror shards to cut into the faces of his female victims. And so forth.

However, all of these traumas are incidental to the central theme of Dolarhyde's life—his extreme isolation. From the very beginning, Dolarhyde is left unattended in the newborn ward to see if he can survive without oxygen. On that first day of life, abandoned without a mother, he cries nonstop and no one comes to help him. Isolation from all human contact serves as a metaphor for Dolarhyde's entire wretched, lonely life. Even his name, Dolarhyde, suggests "dolor," or pain, grief, and sorrow. He knows isolation is his natural state. Incapable of forming relationships with other people, his isolation motivates him to kill families that he can finally become a part of.

He feels unwanted, largely because he is unwanted. The list of those who reject him is a litany of loss. He is the shunned result of a union between his mother, Marian, and a father who leaves town before Dolarhyde is born. Marian leaves the hospital without him. She does not tell her mother about the pregnancy or the birth, thus denying Dolarhyde any possible support from an extended family. Dolarhyde ends up in an orphanage, where the other children and potential parents shun him because of his facial deformity, further excluding him from the socialization process so critical to healthy social interactions. When Dolarhyde is taken from the orphanage by Grandmother, she cruelly uses him as a weapon of vengeance against her daughter, the very sight of him costing Marian's husband, Vogt, a political election. Bitter about the election and lack of money, Marian and Vogt's children beat their stepbrother by repeatedly slamming his head into a mirror. Queen Mother Bailey, the one maternal figure who does show love to him, leaves him after a fight with Grandmother. Time after time, the people Dolorhyde cares for leave him for one reason or another. He matures without ever having known an extended, loving relationship. Other people treat him, for the most part, with ugliness. He craves the beauty of love but has no idea how to experience it.

Dolarhyde's childhood relationship with his grand-mother is damaging in so many ways it's hard to know where to start cataloging the trail of destruction. It is bad enough she uses him as a weapon against her own daughter. It is certainly sad that she places him in a big rural house where his only contact is with the elderly indigent who have been taken in by his grandmother for extra money from the county. She demonstrates none of the warmth that he seeks from her. Many of her behaviors are abusive. Most dramatically, she threatens to castrate him with a pair of scissors held to his penis as punishment for wetting his bed as a five-year-old boy. She uses the threat again when she observes him "playing doctor" with a neighbor girl. The memory of this terrifying threat still haunts him as a forty-two-year-old man.

He learns to associate sexuality with violence early in his life, another dangerous nexus of thought and experience often found in the personal histories of serial killers, a detail no doubt gleaned by Harris in his visits to the FBI's Behavioral Science Unit (BSU). During the episode where Dolarhyde and the neighbor girl show each other their private parts behind the chicken house, the grand-mother's black female cook beheads a chicken that careens around the corner, flapping and spurting blood onto the girl. The threat of castration following this incident solidifies Dolarhyde's connection of sex with extreme violence. To make up for the shame he imagines he has inflicted upon his beloved grandmother, he decides that the best way to redeem himself is to sneak into her bedroom at night and stand guard over her sleeping form, armed with a hatchet to protect her from burglars. Compelled to strike her with the hatchet like a burglar might do, he instead goes out to the chicken house under the full moon to slaughter a chicken. The adult Dolarhyde's modus operandi (MO) is clearly rooted in this twisted childhood manifestation of love.

Love expressed as violence characterizes Dolarhyde's life, even down to his treatment of the animals that people hold dear. As the Red Dragon, he kills family pets as foreplay leading to the consummation of his love. He learned this behavior early in his life, demonstrated by his decimation of the pets in his neighborhood. Slaughtering animals is a dry run for the much larger task of killing humans—another detail Harris gleaned from his shadowing of the FBI profilers. As far as the people he kills, Dolarhyde selects families that fit his own idealized image of the kind of family life he has been denied. By killing the families, he becomes part of a family. He can do anything he wants with them—cavort naked through their house, rearrange their bodies as a silent audience, and rape the dead wife/mother. In Dolarhyde's mind, this is the only way he can experience the loving family life he covets.

Voyeurism is a theme in his life. He turns a childhood obsession with peeking into the windows of neighborhood females into a career in the military, developing medical and aerial surveillance films. Watching movies, of course, is a vicarious method of experiencing the lives of other people, since Dolarhyde has no real life of his own. After leaving the military, Dolarhyde, like Lander, parleys his training into a civilian job, which in turn is leveraged into a means of committing murder. For Dolarhyde, his ideal job is developing film at Gateway Labs, where he can peer into the lives of the countless hundreds who send home movies to him.

As an adult, before he begins to kill, Dolarhyde is consumed by past hurts and rage, all carefully hidden behind the polite face he presents to the world. He lives alone in his grandmother's vast house, lifting weights for diversion. The tipping point for Dolarhyde consists of two key epiphanies: the first being the recognition of aging skin on the back of his hands at the age of forty, and the second being his glimpse of the William Blake painting *The Great Red Dragon and the Woman Clothed with the Sun* in a *Time* magazine article about a London art exhibition. The sight of this painting sparks within him a hallucinatory fantasy life that liberates him from his lonely misery.

He expresses his fantasies through art, specifically, film-making. He splices footage from the Leeds home movie together with shots of himself standing with an erection in front of the Blake painting, approaching the camera to swallow its lens with his mouth, and dancing through the carnage in the Leeds bedroom. The film's last shot shows him having sex with the dead Mrs. Leeds. To almost any audience, this film would be a ghastly atrocity, but to Dolarhyde, it's both a source of physical pleasure and aesthetic frustration. Though he masturbates to the movie, he criticizes it for not showing the murders themselves and for his own limitation as an actor who gets way too lost in the frenzy of the part. Like any auteur directing and starring in his own work, next time he vows to do better.

Dolarhyde's intense fantasy life as a relief from the unbearable loneliness of his sad existence is consistent with the BSU's case studies of serial killers, many of whom reported such a rich inner life. Where Harris seems to take some artistic license with Dolarhyde is his beginning a career as a serial killer at the age of 42, since the pathology often manifests earlier in life, but it's not unprecedented. In any event, Dolarhyde's mid-life crisis does not present itself as something so mundane as buying a really fast car or dressing younger. Rather, he decides to kill people.

Once his fantasies fully take hold, Dolarhyde's mind is split into two entities: Francis and the Red Dragon. While immersed in the character of the Dragon, Dolarhyde is a fearsome, muscled monster. He forgets his self-consciousness, his timidity, and his loneliness. Like many a serial killer before him, he keeps a self-aggrandizing journal of his thoughts, clippings about his crimes, and grisly souvenirs taken from his victims, such as pieces of scalp and Freddy Lounds's lips. When parading before the terrified Lounds, Dolarhyde soars on dragon wings into flights of supercharged rhetoric that reveal his mega-lomania: "Before me you are a slug in the sun. You are privy to a great Becoming and you recognize nothing. You are an ant in the afterbirth. . . . Fear is not what you owe Me, Lounds. . . . *You owe Me awe* [italics in origi-nal]."[21] This fearsomely eloquent entity is a very different Dolarhyde than the one who tolerates Eileen's boyfriend mocking his "harelip" speech impediment at the party. The Dragon controls Francis, shows him what to do and how to outwit his pursuers at every step, empowers him to kill, goads him into lifting ever more weight in his attic weight room, and occasionally frightens him. The Dragon and Francis frequently enter into two-way dialogues, which are dominated by the Dragon reminding Francis what a loser he is and calling him "cunt face," his hated childhood nickname. The Dragon possesses aspects of his domineering grandmother's personality, which definitely places Dolarhyde in the genre tradition pioneered by the mother-obsessed Norman Bates in *Psycho*. Like Norman Bates borrowing his mother's clothes to commit murder in them, Dolarhyde dons his grandmother's false teeth to bite his victims. Dolarhyde apparently suffers from a type of multiple-personality disorder, a not uncommon malady for fictional serial killers, even if less common in real life.

In the other part of his psyche, Dolarhyde is a lost, bewildered, hurt, and lonely soul. Tragically, he begins to rediscover what is good in him only when it is far too late, during the midst of his Dragon murder spree. The catalyst is Reba McClane. When he realizes she is blind and therefore cannot see his face, he is immediately drawn to her. When he learns that she has experience in working with speech- and hearing-impaired children, the memory of his own childhood speech impediment further connects him to her.

As their relationship blossoms, he finds himself wanting to share with Reba something of what he is, so he takes her to the zoo so she can run her hands over a sedated tiger. The tiger represents for Dolarhyde his inner Dragon. Sexually excited by the sight of Reba with the tiger, Dolarhyde later is empowered enough to have sex with Reba. Emboldened by this encounter, Dolarhyde finds the strength to defy the Red Dragon when that murderous part of his mind tells him to kill Reba. He first considers the idea of suicide to save Reba from the Dragon, but rejects it because Reba has given him some modicum of pride. Instead he goes to the Brooklyn Museum to eat the Blake painting that put the idea of the Dragon in his head in the first place. Through absorbing the power of the painting, he gains enough power to conquer the Dragon and feel love for Reba. Love is what motivates Dolarhyde to kill, and love is almost what stops him from killing.

However, he cannot escape his past. When Will Graham and the FBI close in on him, Dolarhyde turns to the Red Dragon for help in evading the police dragnet. The final blow to his Francis identity occurs when he sees Reba kiss Ralph Mandy at her doorstep. Painfully unsophisticated in matters of mature relationships, he does not see the kiss for what it really is—Reba kissing Mandy goodbye after breaking up with him. In a moment remarkably similar to the description of Lander's human self dying following a traumatic relationship setback,

Dolarhyde loses the Francis part of his psyche forever. What is left behind is the Dragon, pretending to be Francis Dolarhyde. In the end, though he had tried to conquer the evil within him, Dolarhyde surrenders entirely to the Red Dragon.

## Hannibal Lecter

The world-famous "Hannibal the Cannibal" makes a modest first entrance as a supporting player. In a stroke of precognitive genius that ensured the success of his future writing career, Harris provided Graham with an incarcerated serial-killer nemesis for Graham to interview. Harris does not provide much backstory on Lecter in this novel, but it's probably safe to assume that any thoughts of Lecter's European heritage came much later to Harris. Primarily, this embryonic Lecter exists in *Red Dragon* to provide a suitably chilling atmosphere as well as to give Graham a previous profiling success. Lecter establishes Graham's professional bona fides as a successful tracker of preternaturally cunning serial killers practicing gruesome MOs.

So the scant facts as we know them about Lecter's history in *Red Dragon* are as follows. He is a small, well-groomed individual. He is born with maroon eyes, an outer marker of something quite unusual about his soul. No mention is made of Lecter's eleventh finger, which first appears in *Silence*. He exhibited sadism toward animals as a child, a trait consistently referenced in serial killer lore as an early warning sign.[22] In most other respects, however, Lecter appeared normal, staying out of trouble with the law and establishing a career. As an adult, Lecter first served as an emergency room physician in Baltimore. He treated a man suffering from an accidental arrow wound who would later become one of his murder victims. Lecter then became a psychiatrist in Baltimore. His aesthetic sense, much developed in later novels, is satisfied through his collection of antiques. Of course, during this rising professional career, he also collected victims.

According to Graham, Lecter had eleven known victims, two of whom didn't die. A passing reference to one of these surviving victims as being on a respirator in Baltimore later morphs into the character of Mason Verger in *Hannibal*. Four of the victims were killed in a period of ten days, approximately three years before the events of *Red Dragon*. The rapid succession of victims implies some kind of stress or crisis in Lecter's life at that time, but we may never know what that was unless Harris revisits Hannibal's pre-incarceration life in another prequel. Nor do we know who Lecter's victims were at this early point, other than some general details about the sixth victim (the one mutilated to resemble the *Wound Man*). The sixth victim is significant because his murder leads to Graham's epiphany about Lecter as murderer. Following Lecter's near-gutting of Graham, Lecter is arrested and eventually imprisoned in the Chesapeake State Hospital (later changed to "Baltimore State Hospital" in *Silence*) for the Criminally Insane, sometime in 1975. A year later, he nearly kills a nurse by ripping out one of her eyes and her tongue. Since then, he has lived quietly in his cell away from all the tabloid attention to his crimes. He keeps up with his professional correspondence and torments his jailer, Dr. Chilton. After the Tooth Fairy murders begin, Graham renews his acquaintanceship with Lecter.

Lecter is nowhere near as transcendentally evil in this incarnation as he will be in the other novels, but many of his signature characteristics are present. First, he resists easy categorization. He does not look like a sociopath, and he is only called one because no one is quite sure what to call him. Lecter's electroencephalograms show some abnormal patterns, but no one can decipher their significance. His resistance to being analyzed or comprehended is often remarked upon by others. Graham, for example, tells Detective Springfield that Lecter is not crazy, but commits atrocities because he enjoys them. Because Lecter is beyond our understanding, he is forever alone, a mythic exile who inspires fear and a certain shuddery fascination, like watching a deadly animal merely an arm's length away behind some rather flimsy bars or a short retaining wall.

Also on display is Lecter's chilling mix of brutality and intellectual refinement. He is both a man of medicine and a serial killer, two raging contradictions in one body. By the time we meet Lecter, lying in repose on his asylum cot, we have been primed to expect a monster in behavior if not appearance, the man who earned the tabloid nickname of "Cannibal" and eviscerated Graham with a linoleum knife. Graham captures the paradox of Lecter in one memorable passage, calling him a monster, "one of those pitiful things that are born in hospitals from time to time. . . . Lecter is the same way in his head, but he looks normal and no one could tell."[23] But we first see him surrounded by books, with *Le Grand Dictionnaire de Cuisine* open on his chest. Certainly, the "big dictionary of cooking" is a pun in this context, but it also reinforces the idea that Lecter is a gourmand, albeit a cannibalistic one.

Lecter is an intellectual, with refined cultural tastes to match. His use of language is educated and even civil, in spite of the hideous things he sometimes says. We know he was an antique collector in his "civilian" life. He's an accomplished, published writer. With ease, he can understand Dolarhyde's book-coded communication and reply to it in the same code. When he cleverly manipulates Dr. Bloom's graduate assistant over the telephone to reveal Graham's address, he shows how truly skilled he is at charming people. Because of his superior gifts, Lecter finds it easy to feel contempt toward others, typically mocking them at every opportunity. He adopts the air of the smug, arrogant professor who just knows he knows better than anyone else. Because of his intellectual persona, it is sometimes easy to forget what he is, as the asylum nurse now missing her eye and tongue found out to her sorrow. But the knowledge of what he has done always comes back to us, even if in this first outing we don't see him kill or eat anyone. Captivity has done nothing to change his murderous nature, as demonstrated when he sends Dolarhyde like a guided missile toward Graham's home address. We feel by the end that Graham had it right when he called Lecter a monster who looks like a man.

Lecter possesses extraordinarily enhanced senses, another characteristic we shall see developed in the other novels. All of his senses are hypersensitive, but the most attuned is his sense of smell. When Graham enters his cell, Lecter smells his aftershave through the nylon net separating the two men, just as Lecter later smells Clarice Starling's skin cream. If Dolarhyde's strongest sensory input is sight, then Lecter's is the sense of smell, which has the strongest power to evoke the past.

Lecter endures the boredom of captivity by living in his head, where time has no meaning, and savoring sensory input. Through his memories and his senses, he occupies both the present moment and the past. Though Lecter's memory palace is not mentioned, it's sketchily present here. He becomes a transcendental being to an extent that Dolarhyde can only aspire to be. Lecter's ability to transcend the limitations of most human beings is profound enough for him to withstand the coercive power of the sodium amytal injected into him in a vain effort to make him reveal the location of a buried Princeton student. His self-control is formidable.

His murders are part of his freedom from human constraint, putting him (at least in Lecter's mind) on par with God's power. He implies his equivalence to God in his "consolation" letter to Graham following Lounds's murder: "[Murder] must feel good to God—He does it all the time, and are we not made in His image?"[24] Lecter's mocking question leads us toward an uncomfortable reckoning with the duality of human nature: its potential for acts of grace hand-in-hand with its capacity for murder. Lecter is a man who, for all of his civilized refinement, embodies the primal instinct to kill and in a way stands as a metaphor for all of us in supposedly more enlightened times. Lecter's last written words to Graham capture the feeling of this modern dilemma: "We live in a primitive time— don't we, Will—neither savage nor wise."[25]

## Freddy Lounds

There is little mistaking what Harris thinks of Lounds as a character, right down to the reporter's unattractive appearance. Lounds is described as small and ugly, with buck teeth and rat eyes. Then there are Lounds's more unsavory traits—materialism, attention-seeking, and unethical tactics. One cannot help but wonder if Harris is exorcising some bad memories of his own journalistic career by creating this pathetic, obnoxious reporter and then subjecting him to excruciating torture at the hands of Dolarhyde. Harris has no use for the tabloid press Lounds represents, if *Red Dragon* is any indication. Lounds pays dearly for the excesses of an entire profession by the time Dolarhyde leaves him as a flaming ruin outside the *National Tattler* office.

Lounds did not begin his career as a reporter for the *Tattler*. Instead, he worked in what Harris calls "the straight press" for ten years. During that time, Lounds sharpened his skills as a journalist. In fact, he was a good one, possessing smarts, guts, patience, and energy. He was also a good organizer and writer, but he could not achieve the degree of success he sought in mainstream journalism. He realized his employers would use him and take the information they obtained through him, but never reward him. Then one day in 1969, Lounds had an epiphany while watching an older alcoholic reporter, who was no longer capable of doing anything except taking dictation over the telephone, ask a female editor for a

Kotex to use on his bleeding behind. Seeing his future embodied in this pathetic man, Lounds resigned from the newspaper and found a higher-paying job with the *Tattler*. At the *Tattler*, he receives the outward affirmations of worth he craves—a parking space with his name on it and a salary of $72,000 a year. Because he takes this career path, he is considered a pariah by the "straight" press reporters who used to be his colleagues.

Above all, Lounds likes to be noticed, which is why he could not stay in what he believed to be the professional oblivion of respectable journalism. He makes his living writing bogus cancer-cure stories, which the *Tattler*'s market research proves to move issues off the stands into the hands of those desperate for any cure. He also chases sensational serial-killer stories, another proven crowd-pleaser. He is no longer motivated by something so naïve as professional integrity, but pure greed and vanity. These desires drive him to lengths many consider obnoxious at best when covering a story. He does not care that people detest him, so long as he gets the story and photographs he needs to advance his career and salary.

Lounds's pushiness is one of his distinguishing characteristics. Following Graham's near-fatal slashing, Lounds came into Graham's hospital room while Graham was asleep and photographed his temporary colostomy for the *Tattler*. During the Tooth Fairy case, Lounds has to be removed by the police from the Lombard Funeral Home, where he is trying to take pictures of the bodies of the Leeds family. He later impersonates the killer during a telephone call to Graham in order to verify that the FBI is using the *Tattler* personal ads to contact the killer, which initially subjects Lounds to the threat of arrest by an enraged Graham but directly leads to Lounds working with Graham on a bogus story to entice the Tooth Fairy into a trap. Lounds's grand plan in all this is to rush a paperback into print almost as soon as the Tooth Fairy is captured, so he can accumulate the wealth and attention that has thus far

eluded him on the scale he believes he is entitled to. Whatever else can be said about Lounds, he embodies the quality of persistence unencumbered by shame.

In spite of his materialism and obnoxiousness, Lounds
is not completely one-dimensional. We begin to see him
in a slightly more sympathetic light through his relationship with Wendy, who owns a topless bar named
"Wendy City" in Chicago because Lounds co-signed the
loan with her. Wendy is a curvaceous blonde whose
physical attributes are an obvious part of her attraction
for Lounds, but not the only part. She also strokes his ego
by calling him by a pet nickname of "Roscoe," praising
him for his smarts, and lulling him to sleep. She understand Lounds is a self-promoter with many personality
defects and very little luck. It's true their relationship has
a mercenary side to it, but she is obviously fond of the
sad little man. When Lounds is horribly burned and
dying after the assault by Dolarhyde, Wendy sits with
him at his bedside. In his last moments of life, she
promises him everything will be okay again.

Lounds shows some admirable qualities under duress.
During his torture by Dolarhyde, Lounds demonstrates a
certain amount of fortitude in a hopeless situation. Since
Lounds's mind is always racing and scheming, he thinks
quickly of ways he can negotiate with the Dragon, even if
his strategies ultimately fail. After being burned, Lounds
retains enough presence of mind to gasp out a license
plate number he glimpsed during his abduction and to
accuse Graham of setting him up. The overall effect of
Lounds's brutal treatment by the Dragon is to moderate
our judgment on Lounds. Not matter how obnoxious he
is or how badly he treated Graham, Lounds doesn't
deserve what happens to him. Wendy says as much to
Graham at Lounds's graveside. Perhaps the final verdict
on Lounds is delivered by Captain Osborne of Chicago
Homicide: "Lounds was a ballsy little guy, you have to
give him that."[26]

## Jack Crawford

Graham's mentor and former boss in the FBI is Jack
Crawford. If Graham stands apart from the FBI, Crawford
is squarely in the middle of it. Crawford is a career agent
who supervised Graham on the two occasions Graham
left the FBI Academy to return to the field to investigate
serial murder cases. We know little about Crawford's
home life in this novel, except that he is married to a
woman named Phyllis. Instead, we know him as defined
by his profession. A tough but fair teacher, Crawford is
the kind of man who calls trainees on assumptions by
yelling at them, "Assumptions make an ASS of U and ME
both." He once had a drinking problem but now substitutes hard work for the narcotic of booze. Through long
experience, he has a superb command of the administrative world in which he lives. He knows who to call, what
equipment he has at his disposal, and how to navigate
the Byzantine labyrinths of bureaucracy and institutional
process. But more than any of that, what Crawford
knows how to do is motivate (or manipulate, if you will)
people to do what he wants and how to pick the best
people to do what he wants. It's the difference between
management and leadership. Crawford is a leader.

He demonstrates his leadership in many ways both
large and small. But critical to his success is picking the
right people to work cases. He does this with an honest
recognition of his own limitations. He knows he does not
have the intuitive genius necessary for the kind of profiling required in the Tooth Fairy case, so he turns to
Graham. He also knows the personal touch works best in
convincing people to do something they don't necessarily
want to do, so he travels down to Marathon to make a
face-to-face plea to Graham to return from retirement.

Of course, Crawford's skill in selecting good people
has a hard edge to it. He does not exhibit mercy. Since
the mission is key to him, he is manipulative in his

handling of Graham and others to get the results he wants. He gauges carefully the precise moment at which to strike, knowing just what appeal will sway Graham to carry out his wishes. Crawford does not hesitate to place Graham in possible danger by using him as bait in a trap for the Tooth Fairy. When he fears that Graham is burning himself out by obsessively going over the victims' possessions, he makes the calculated decision that it is worth the risk to allow Graham's intuition to emerge. However, Crawford is as a rule not dishonest or disingenuous in his manipulation. Whatever he tells people is usually straightforward. Whatever else may be said about him, he's open about his agenda.

Another aspect of Crawford's leadership gift is his ability to unify people behind the goal of catching a killer. The world of law enforcement is notoriously territorial, with different jurisdictions routinely competing with one another for the glory of solving cases, hoarding valuable information from supposed allies, blaming one another for procedural mistakes and missed evidence, and generally huffing and blustering. Crawford rightly views this macho posturing over turf as a serious threat to the success of a murder investigation, so he finds ways to appeal to a higher good for the sake of unity. For instance, when Crawford faces a passively hostile contingent of Atlanta detectives shortly after the Leeds murders, he reassures them he only cares about catching the killer, not who does the catching. His speech settles the audience enough so that they listen to Graham. In the end, Crawford's genuine commitment to catching killers is what makes him such an effective leader.

## Reba McClane

Reba McClane works at Baeder Chemical, next-door to Gateway. She is about thirty years old, with short red-blonde hair. After three months of employment there, she meets Dolarhyde in a professional capacity. She quickly develops a romantic interest in him because of his directness and refusal to patronize her because of her blindness.

Before Baeder, she worked at the Reiker Institute in Denver for ten years, training the newly blind how to reintegrate into the sighted world. However, she found the Institute environment far too removed from the outside world. She thought the Institute's mission was inherently contradictory, in that the trainers were preparing the blind to live in a world that the trainers did not actually venture into. So, she planned to become a speech therapist for speech- and hearing-impaired children. Fate decided otherwise. When she sees an advertisement at Reiker for Baeder, she applies for a job and gets it. She is under no illusions as to why. She cynically tells Dolarhyde she was selected because as a blind woman, she fit in two different categories to satisfy the diversity requirements of a defense contract.

This observation is characteristic of Reba's direct approach, a quality that she also appreciates in Dolarhyde. She likes that he does not play the usual games men play in order to get women to go to bed with them. Her words to him are straightforward, even blunt. For example, she directly raises the issue of his slight speech impediment, complimenting him for his ability to speak well. When Dolarhyde asks her what the other women at work say about his appearance, she responds honestly that they are intrigued by his aloofness and his bodybuilder's physique. Her directness manifests in ways other than her words. Reba is the sexual aggressor with the inexperienced Dolarhyde, apparently performing fellatio on him on the couch in Dolarhyde's parlor before they move to his grandmother's bed to have intercourse. Both in speech and action, she knows what she feels and wants.

The experience of being blind has grown in her a certain set of skills, such as the ability to navigate through physical space based on touch. It has also given her specific attitudes about relationships. She has been involved with a few people who were attracted to her because they believed she would become dependent upon them. Consequently, she is cautious, even skeptical, about people's motives and actions. She has heard all the common myths the sighted world holds about blind people—the blind hear better than the sighted, or the blind are purified in spirit by their condition—and knows the myths to be patronizing misconceptions. Regarding men, she is heterosexual and enjoys sex, but she knows most of them do not want the perceived burden of caring for a blind woman. She sees this reluctance clearly in Ralph Mandy, the man she is dating casually at the time she begins her relationship with Dolarhyde. Mandy whines to her often that he is incapable of love, which aggravates her because the last thing she wants is to own him. Reba responds to Dolarhyde quickly because she recognizes a certain shared kinship in their respective distances from other people.

She refuses to let her blindness prevent her from achieving her goals or make her the object of other people's pity. She won't feel sorry for herself as a blind woman, and when she does feel anger, she channels it into constructive energy. Like Molly Graham, Reba knows the value of every moment. Her time is too precious to squander on self-pity, learned helplessness, or the worry of others. She gets very angry with Dandridge, for example, when he persists in offering her a ride home from work. His sympathy is an affront to her sense of independence. Dolarhyde, by contrast, appeals to her because she finds him just as independent.

For all of her clear-headedness, however, Reba has made a tragic error in believing Dolarhyde is a kindred spirit. She mistakes his moments of distance from her as signs of shyness, when instead he is restraining himself from biting off her fingers or killing her as an offering to the Red Dragon. She has no idea of the kind of inner struggle Dolarhyde goes through, torn as he is between his identities as both a man and murdering dragon. However, she is introduced dramatically to his Dragon personality when he chloroforms her and abducts her as a reaction to seeing her goodbye kiss with Ralph Mandy. Her literal blindness is a metaphor for how she never sees Dolarhyde as he really is, even at the end. She believes while held prisoner in his house that she is listening to him argue aloud with his Dragon personality as to whether to kill her. In reality, the whole scenario is a ploy to fool Reba into thinking Dolarhyde has killed himself. The traumatic experience leaves Reba questioning herself, her perceptions, and her judgment. Graham's attempt to cheer her up aside, the novel leaves us uncertain as to whether Reba will re-engage with a treacherous world or retreat back into the blind cloister from which she came.

## Molly Graham

Molly Graham is the wife of Will Graham and the mother of an eleven-year-old boy, Willy, from another marriage. Graham is Molly's second husband. Her first husband, a farm-league baseball player, died of cancer on the verge of making it to the big leagues. She moved to the Florida Keys to open up a shop. She met Graham while he was working as a diesel mechanic in Marathon in the Florida Keys following his retirement from the FBI. She lives a content life with her son and Graham in Sugarloaf Key as the novel opens.

As the story's other primary female character, Molly Graham carries a lot of symbolic weight. Like Mrs. Leeds and Mrs. Jacobi, she represents the qualities of being a good wife and mother in this book about threatened families. Unlike those two women, she not only survives a vicious attack by Dolarhyde but kills him, thus saving her family. As this outcome makes clear, she is clearheaded and fiercely protective of those she loves. Aware of the danger in advance, unlike the unfortunate Mrs. Leeds and Mrs. Jacobi, she is fully prepared to kill when the time comes. Graham has trained her out on the firing range so she can protect herself. As it turns out, of all the mother characters, Molly is the only survivor, the only one who saves her child. She does for Willy what Marian never did for Francis.

We see her protectiveness from the beginning. She resents Crawford's intrusion into their home, knowing he is bringing nothing but trouble for the Grahams. The sight of his forearms repulses her; he looks like an ape to her. She demands for him as a friend to leave Graham alone, then makes him promise to keep Graham away from the action. She fears Graham's fragile mental equilibrium will be threatened by returning to his former life and that he may have to come face-to-face with his third serial killer.

As it turns out, the third time is no charm. The case nearly kills Graham, and it does kill his marriage. From her point of view, Molly was right to fear Crawford's violation of their family space. In a way, his action brings the Tooth Fairy right to their front door—which Dolarhyde gets no further than because Molly shoots him dead. At the hospital later, with Graham recovering from emergency surgery, Molly lashes out at Crawford one more time, asking him caustically if he wants to give Graham a face transplant. She practically runs from the hospital, leaving Crawford behind as a symbol of the outside world that shattered her marriage.

Before everything goes so wrong, one of her functions as stalwart family guardian is to provide the stability of a loving relationship for Graham. In many ways, it's a clichéd role—the wife staying at home with the kid while the husband is out saving the world. At night, Graham calls Molly when he's feeling lonely and/or horny out on the road. She makes it clear she misses him in her home and in her bed. She promises him she is there for him and that she knows he is doing the right thing, even though it is costing him. The story is full of examples of her love for him, including her ill-fated reconciliation with him after the tragically premature celebration of the end of the Tooth Fairy case.

However, Molly's love is not unconditional. It's predicated on his providing stability for her and her son so that they do not have to experience another tragic loss. When it becomes clear that Graham's involvement in the case has compromised her son's safety, she begins a gradual process of distancing the two of them from him, first emotionally and then physically. When she greets Graham at National Airport in Washington after their home address has been revealed in the *Tattler*, her fingers are cold on his cheek, symbolizing her retreat from him. Her mistrust of Graham and apprehension about what he may be bringing down on her and her son's heads is captured in her nightmare about "heavy crazy footsteps coming in a house of changing rooms."[27] When talking on the phone to him, she is vigilant for the tell-tale signs that he has been drinking. When she hears him slur, she calls him on it at once. She makes all of the arrangements necessary to move to Oregon to stay with her first husband's parents, without Graham's help or knowledge. She hands her shop over to a friend and gives Graham's dogs to the animal shelter. Once in Oregon, she gets a part-time job. All of these are steps in her gradual journey of breaking away from Graham, a man she still loves but no longer believes to be reliable.

Her protectiveness stems in part from her acute awareness of the preciousness of our time on earth and the elusive nature of happiness. The untimely death of her first husband taught her that "time is luck." So she now insists on quarterly medical checkups for Graham and Willy and examines herself regularly for lumps. From her vigilance, Graham learns how to relish each day. As the relationship with Graham deteriorates, she tells him how hard it is to get something and then keep it in this life. Ever on guard against threats to happiness, she shuts Graham out in self-defense when it becomes clear he is endangering her, however noble his cause. In a dangerous world, her wariness allows her and her son to survive.

## STYLE

Words such as *understated*, *lean*, and *spare* are often used to describe Harris's writing style. In his second novel, the prose is still fairly minimalist, but it is interspersed with many more poetic phrases, images, and rich metaphors and similes than before. The sensory appeal is strong in lines such as these describing the carnage left behind by the killer in the Leedses's bedroom, where "bloodstains shouted . . . from the walls, from the mattress and the floor. The very air had screams smeared on it."[28] The imagistic quality of the writing is notably more pronounced than it was in *Black Sunday*.

We've seen how Harris handles intense action sequences before, running his sentences together breathlessly as if everything were happening at once. A good example of this occurs in the climactic confrontation between Molly and Dolarhyde: "She forgot the stance and she forgot the front sight but she got a good two-handed grip on the pistol and as the door exploded inward she blew a rat hole through his thigh . . . she ran to him and shot him twice in the face as he sprawled against the wall, scalp down to his chin and his hair on fire."[29]

In quite another context, the same technique is used to run together the words and thoughts of Reba and Dolarhyde during their first sexual encounter: "*Do you feel me now yes . . . Your heart is loud yes . . . And now it's quick and light and quicker and light and . . .* [italics in original]."[30] In passages such as these, Harris attempts to capture the pacing and rhythm of what he is describing, all the better to engage his audience.

The present tense frequently disrupts the past-tense narrative, another favorite technique of Harris's. It creates a type of mythic present, where past events take on the immediacy of the moment. For example, when Graham reconstructs the movements of the Leedses's killer in his mind, he "sees" it happen in the present tense: *"His hand in the tight glove snakes in through the hole [in the glass], finds the lock. The door opens silently. He is inside. In the light of the vent hood he can see his body in this strange kitchen* [italics in original]."[31] The present tense becomes associated with the killing mindset—a consciousness estranged from civil society, a psyche both alien and disturbingly recognizable. It's all by way of warming us up for Lecter's entrance, a man described in the present tense: "Dr. Lecter's eyes are maroon and they reflect the light redly in tiny points. . . . He is a small, lithe man. Very neat."[32] By his spilling over from the past into the present, it's as though Lecter, thought of by Dolarhyde as a dark Renaissance prince, exists independently of the particular events of the plot. He is a mythic presence. Even the words and the conventions of popular story-telling cannot fully contain Lecter.

## ALLUSIONS

An allusion may be defined as a reference to something that exists outside of the story. Harris comes into his own in *Red Dragon* as a "master of allusion." He researches his subjects exhaustively, loading his narratives with esoteric facts, specialized processes, and cultural references and hints to an incredible degree. While this ability is on competent display in *Black Sunday*, Harris becomes a mature writer fully in mastery of his craft in *Red Dragon*. We've examined earlier how Harris learned a great deal about serial killers from his visits to Quantico. The novel is packed with many forensic details not often found in crime thrillers, an even more remarkable feat when one considers that Harris is not a policeman. However, his background as a crime reporter and his continued associations with law enforcement figures serve him well in this capacity.

One of *Red Dragon*'s most memorable and chilling scenes, Graham's nocturnal inspection of the blood-soaked interior of the Leeds house, is packed with fascinating insider information that makes the scene authentic. We learn about comparison of blood-spatter patterns against standardized comparison plates to determine victim movements; the use of a red fingerprint powder appropriately called Dragon's Blood (which makes an appearance again in *Hannibal*) on the bathroom mirrors; the increased level of free histamines and serotonin in Mrs. Leeds's gunshot wound, indicating that she lived for several minutes after being shot; and hair and oil samples on a light switch revealing the order in which victims died.

As the story unfolds, we learn more. The corneas and finger- and toenails of victims can be dusted for fingerprints. The Smithsonian Museum can make a plaster cast of teeth from bite marks on the female victims. The FBI can test a severed branch to reveal the type of cutting edge used upon it, and it can subject a note written on toilet tissue to a battery of tests for hair, fiber, and fingerprints. Harris meticulously describes these processes to enhance the story's realism. Though fascinating in their own right, the forensic details are not merely background context. When filtered through the matrix of Graham's formidable combination of knowledge of criminal investigation procedure and vivid imagination, the crime scenes speak to him clearly enough to enable him to make the intuitive leaps that ultimately lead to the final identification of Francis Dolarhyde as the Tooth Fairy. The research Harris absorbed allows him to make this outcome plausible.

Harris demonstrates he has done his homework in many areas besides law enforcement. For instance, he encapsulates his study of psychology in two characters. One is Dr. Alan Bloom, who speaks knowledgeably of paranoid schizophrenia, suicidal ideation, delusional thinking, and the origins of sadism in the fusion of aggression and sexuality at a young age. Bloom, in contrast to the hardened Jack Crawford, is a bookish academic who expresses some degree of compassion for the Tooth Fairy on the basis of the killer's nightmarish childhood. The other character is Lecter, a psychiatrist. Lecter at one point refers to Winfred Overholser's text *The Psychiatrist and the Law* (1953), a title that also serves as a helpful way of thinking about the alliance between law enforcement and psychology/psychiatry represented by criminal profiling.

Extremely arcane knowledge from diverse scientific fields is almost casually dropped in throughout. Graham, for instance, has written the standard monograph on determining the time of death through insect activity, thus putting the fictional character into the real-life company of forensic entomologists Mant and Nuorteva in Tedeschi and Eckert's *Forensic Medicine* (1977) reference volume. Graham's intellectual foil, Lecter, publishes scholarly articles on surgical addiction in the real-life *Journal of Clinical Psychiatry*. Law-enforcement characters speak in shorthand professional jargon of insect invasion waves, families who cover for "biters" in the family by saying animals inflicted the injuries, aniline dyes in colored inks being transparent to infrared, eidetic (or photographic) memory, and so on. The "Abbe Flap procedure," a surgical method pioneered by Robert Abbe for the repair of cleft palates, is mentioned. Also referenced is the illustration *Wound Man*, found in medieval surgical texts, depicting the many varieties of battle injuries on one human figure. These references fit organically into the flow of the story. They do not seem forced or irrelevant. They do add to the story's realistic texture.

Allusions or references to the arts and humanities are numerous in this book, far more than in *Black Sunday*. Having mastered the basics of pacing and plot in his previous novel, Harris strives for an intellectual as well as visceral thriller. The book's epigraphs set the appropriate tone. One is from Alphonse Bertillon, two from William Blake, and one from the Biblical book Ecclesiastes. The quote from Bertillon, the father of anthropometry (an early scientific method of identifying criminals through physical measurements), is a brilliantly paradoxical circular argument cutting to the heart of Graham's troubled relationship with his gift for imagining the fantasy life of killers: "One can only see what one observes, and one observes only things which are already in the mind." The next two epigraphs, taken from the English Romantic poet William Blake's linked poems "The Divine Image" and "A Divine Image" in *Songs of Innocence* (1789) and *Songs of Experience* (1794), respectively contrast the "innocent" qualities of mercy, pity, love, and peace against the "experienced" qualities of cruelty, jealousy, terror, and secrecy. At the end of Graham's confrontation with Dolarhyde and his own capacity for evil, the reader encounters the quote from Ecclesiastes: "And I gave my heart to know wisdom, and to know madness and folly: I perceived that this also is vexation of the spirit." The line sums up the tragic fall of Will Graham, surely a vexed spirit. With his empathetic knowledge of the extremes of human emotion, Graham may have gained some level of insight and wisdom from his experience, but the pain of the loss of his innocence will be a source of spiritual suffering for him.

Several allusions are drawn from music and art history. Dolarhyde listens to Handel's *Water Music* (1717) in his van, an orchestration composed by George Frideric Handel for King George I. Interestingly, King George I had to deal with a Jacobite Rebellion during his reign, and the name of one of the families slain by Dolarhyde is Jacobi. Paintings also appear at prominent spots in the book. A version of Gilbert Stuart's famous Landsdowne portrait of George Washington greets Dolarhyde during his visit to the Brooklyn Museum, a frightening moment for Dolarhyde because Washington's hooded eyes and bad teeth in the portrait remind him of his grandmother.

The allusions to William Blake's art are particularly important to the novel. The title of the book is taken from a series of "Great Red Dragon" watercolors painted by William Blake between 1805 and 1810 to illustrate the Biblical book Revelation. Dolarhyde chances upon a photograph of the painting *The Great Red Dragon and the Woman Clothed with the Sun* and becomes obsessed with it as a depiction of his own fantasies of transcendence through sexual power.[33] Dolarhyde hangs a large print of the painting in his bedroom and features it in his home-made "snuff" movies of the killings of the Leeds and Jacobi families. Another print of the painting is on the wall beside the mirror in his attic weight-lifting room. He quotes the phrase, "And There Came a Great Red Dragon Also," from the book of Revelation in his ledger of clippings and more grisly mementoes of his murders. By structuring this pathetic but terrifying killer's modus operandi around Blake's painting and the Dragon of Apocalypse in the book of Revelation, Harris provides an artistic and literary depth, all too lacking from his many imitators in the serial-killer genre, to the narrative.

The Web site *Dissecting Hannibal* makes a fairly convincing case that several textual clues point to Mark Twain as one of Harris's primary literary influences, albeit unacknowledged. For instance, Graham's youthful thievery of a watermelon corresponds to a similar incident in Mark Twain's speech *Theoretical and Practical Morals* (1899). Using this and other examples, Twain concludes that committing such sins ultimately vaccinates one against them, which is echoed in Graham's reflections on Bloody Pond at Shiloh. This same location is mentioned in Twain's nonfiction travelogue, *Innocents Abroad* (1869). Dolarhyde lives in Missouri, which is another possible reference to Twain's home state. Twain was born in Florida, Missouri, which possibly explains the author's choice of Florida as the site

William Blake, *The Great Red Dragon and the Woman Clothed with the Sun*. Brooklyn Museum 15.368, Gift of William Augustus White. Copyright 2009 by Brooklyn Museum, New York.

of Graham's retreat from police work. Hannibal, Missouri, was the fictional home of Tom Sawyer and Huckleberry Finn, and of course we all know what Lecter's first name is.

Another unacknowledged but likely influence is Edgar Allen Poe, whose character C. Auguste Dupin is the first fictional detective. Dupin is centrally featured in Poe's "The Murders in the Rue Morgue" (1841), "The Mystery of Marie Roget" (1842), and "The Purloined Letter" (1844). Dupin's method is known as ratiocination, or the act of identifying with a criminal's point-of-view in order to know everything the criminal knows. In this way, Dupin through an act of imagination and logic can solve the crimes he investigates. Clearly, Graham employs ratiocination to investigate crime scene evidence.

Other literary allusions abound. The book on Hannibal "the Cannibal" Lecter's shelf in his cell, *Le Grand Dictionnaire de Cuisine* (1873) by Alexandre Dumas, is certainly a pun in the context of Lecter's crimes. However, Dumas is also the author of *The Count of Monte Cristo* (1844), a novel about, among other things, the unjust imprisonment of Edmond Dantes. Lecter probably finds much to sympathize with in the plight of that novel's main character. Even the name of the bar Graham finds Niles Jacobi in, the Hateful Snake, is probably taken from a line in Edmund Spenser's epic poem *The Faerie Queene*, Book I, Canto III (1590). In the allegorical structure of Spenser's poem, "the hateful snake" represents the hidden hatreds and malice within the human breast, certainly a fitting reference for a novel about an outwardly normal serial killer.

Finally, several of the allusions are drawn from the world of popular culture, including musicals, cartoons, and fads. For instance, Graham mentions Ezio Pinza when he says he won't be able to pick out the Tooth Fairy from across a crowded room. Pinza was the famed opera singer who appeared in the stage musical *South Pacific* (1949) by Richard Rodgers and Oscar Hammerstein. His rendition of "Some Enchanted Evening" was a national sensation. One of the lines from the song says, "You may see a stranger across a crowded room and somehow you know," an appropriate description of Graham's intuitive process. Sometimes the allusion works to give us a vivid sensory image of a character. One example is Wendy's comparison of Lounds to Morocco Mole, a Hanna-Barbera cartoon character modeled after actor Peter Lorre from the mid-1960s television show *Secret Squirrel*. Another of the allusions evokes the specter of one of the real-life serial killers Harris no doubt studied in researching the book. A T-shirt printed in Chicago after the murder of Lounds says, "The Tooth Fairy is a One-Night Stand," a reference to a popular saying in Aspen, Colorado, in the widespread furor following the escape of suspected serial killer Ted Bundy from the courthouse where he was facing trial. These many allusions signify Harris's intent to combine the so-called "high" and "low" arts to produce a densely layered work of popular fiction.

## SYMBOLS

The symbolic structure of the novel bears some similarity to *Black Sunday*, particularly in the prevalence of scar imagery. Scars, as they did in the previous novel and will continue to do in all the subsequent novels, symbolize the residual effect of past trauma. Both Graham and Dolarhyde are scarred by their pasts. In the first few pages, we find out that Graham has a nasty scar extending from his left hipbone to just under his right rib cage. The scar represents the psychic damage Graham has sustained as a result of his encounters with two serial killers. Both times he ended up in the hospital, once for the damage to his mind and the second time for the damage to his mind and body. The dead flesh's inability to tan symbolizes the permanence of Graham's mental instability.

Dolarhyde wears his scars too. The physical one is the scar on his upper lip, left by the corrective surgery years before. In a sense, he was born scarred, with a cleft palate that made him resemble a leaf-nosed bat more than a baby. As an adult, his physical scar is minimal, but the past trauma it represents is colossal. Ostracized and abused as a child, he grows into a man who is unable to connect with others in any meaningful way. Harris compares Dolarhyde's inability to communicate to a scar's inability to blush. Scars can neither tan nor blush; they will never change. Neither, it seems, can Graham or Dolarhyde.

Animal imagery pervades the story to a greater extent than it did in *Black Sunday*. Harris creates a veritable bestiary, in which every creature takes on allegorical significance within the Green Machine of nature. For example, he links insects to scenes of either captivity or aggression.[34] One of the imprisoned insects is the beetle Dolarhyde as a child kept in a pill bottle, representing his own trapped state of being. In another instance, Reba hears crickets while held captive in Dolarhyde's van. The insects associated with aggression are more numerous, as we might expect in a serial killer book. The moths batting against the Grahams' screen door are harbingers of the death and devastation to come, a symbol Harris returns to in much more detail in his next novel. Graham believes Mrs. Leeds was the killer's target, "as surely as a singing cricket attracts death from the red-eyed fly."[35] The fly is an ominous symbol in the book; in another example, Lecter's scrutiny of Graham feels to Graham like a fly inside of his head. Bees with the potential to sting swarm in the rotting orchard surrounding Dolarhyde's property, symbolizing his internal state. In another kind of symbolism altogether, Graham sees a caterpillar in the Jacobi yard. The caterpillar represents the power of metamorphosis, linked to Dolarhyde's quest to transform himself.

The larger birds, reptiles, and mammals take on their own meanings. The shrike, a bird also known as the "butcher bird" for its predatory habits, is the nickname of Garrett Jacob Hobbs. The snake, another predator, is linked to Graham when the *Tattler* quotes an unnamed source who calls Graham a king snake hiding underneath the house. The bar he enters during his investigation is called the Hateful Snake, suggesting Graham harbors his own anger within his breast. Graham is himself a kind of predator, killing other hunters; however, he is vulnerable to them as well, as the dying chicken snake near the pond at Shiloh symbolizes.

Dolarhyde is associated with the bat, possum, and rabbit as a child. His appearance at birth resembled a bat, but more often he was cruelly called a "harelip," linking him to the rabbit. Queen Mother Bailey called him a little possum. The rabbit and the possum are both prey animals, symbolizing the child Dolarhyde's victimization by others. As an adult, now transformed from prey to predator, he associates himself with the tiger in the critical scene where he shares a glimpse of his true inner self with Reba in a way she can survive. Animals play an important part in his twisted psyche. In fact, he kills family pets, a ritualized behavior established in his adolescence when he began killing farm and neighborhood animals. The only families he will kill are those who own pets.

Certain other animals are linked to Graham. Besides the snake, another of Graham's "totem" animals is the dog, an appropriate association for his status as a human bloodhound in Jack Crawford's pack. Dogs are a constant theme in Graham's life. As a boy, Graham was chased by dogs when he stole the watermelon, indicating in his innocence he is not yet the hunter, but the hunted. But as he grew, he developed an affinity for dogs. Just like Harris at his lonely house in the field, Graham takes in a motley collection of stray dogs. The barking of a dog signals some key moments in the story. For example, Graham hears a beagle barking somewhere near the Jacobi backyard, where he discovers a vital clue. The Scotty barking at Mrs. Leeds in the Leeds home movie is another signal that the film is a vital piece of evidence. Waugh relates the persistent canine imagery in the book to Cerberus, the mythic hound that stands "in front of the labyrinth and the night-journey into the underworld."[36] The juxtaposition of dogs with the crime scenes signifies Graham's imminent entrance into a dark and perilous place, the labyrinth of the psychopathic mind, to discover the answers he seeks.

## THEMES

Several themes are prominent in the novel. All of these themes support the book's basic contention that man is always potentially a killer. What makes us human is the act of channeling that murderous aggression into more constructive pursuits, such as hunting killers. But the beast (or Dragon, if you will) is the enemy within us, always ready to undermine our own civilized urges.

First, this is a story about the threat to the family posed by threats both internal and external, among them child abuse, crime rates, and work pressures. The book begins with the murder of an upper-middle-class family, making it clear from the start what the domestic security stakes of this serial killer investigation are. The manhunt must stop cold a fundamental threat to one of America's most cherished cultural myths—the traditional family achieving the American dream of happy home, many children, a family pet, and enough income to classify them as consumers with disposable wealth. Dolarhyde's crimes are earthshaking not only because of their extreme violence and perversion, but the kinds of victims he selects. With chilling madman's logic, Dolarhyde progresses from slaughtering the family pet on through the elimination of the family's husband and children to the gruesome insult of the last act of raping the wife's corpse in front of the dead family. It's a violation so fundamental, it reaches mythic proportions. Society recognizes the threat immediately, as illustrated by the media's instant widespread focus on the crimes and law enforcement's response of diverting massive state and federal resources and personnel to the investigation.

The murder of the entire family serves as a metaphor for the dangers facing traditional American families. Besides the threat of violence committed by strangers, the most insidious threats come at us from loved ones within the home—child abuse, divorce, alcoholism, and devotion to work over family. Look at the *real* villains in *Red Dragon*. Child abuse, whether passive neglect or active torture, is the catalyst for the chain of events leading to the murders of two families. Dolarhyde himself is a victim of childhood abuse inflicted upon him by a mother who abandoned him and a grandmother who tormented him because of her own sexual neuroses. His peers ridiculed, mocked, and beat him. The incessant abuse leaves him irreparably damaged to the point where the only meaningful family relationship he can safely have is with dead people.

Graham's family both complements and differs from the Leeds and Jacobi families. Unlike those affluent families, Graham's lower-middle-class family is a rather patchwork assembly, bulging with unspoken resentments and mounting tensions even before the stress of the Red Dragon investigation. Graham's eleven-year-old stepson, Willy, idealizes his dead father, a Florida State League baseball player who met Molly in grade school and took his family traveling with him. Dead for five years, his ghost haunts the Graham family. When emotionally vulnerable, both Molly and Willy watch baseball. Graham cannot compete with such idyllic memories or occupy as central a place in his stepson's feelings. As a result, Graham feels resentment toward Willy during times of stress, particularly when the family's fragile peace is shattered by the various revelations in the pages of the *Tattler*.

Like Dolarhyde, Graham germinates a mixture of envy of and anger toward happy families. Witnessing and thinking about the aftermath of Dolarhyde's murders brings out Graham's latent hostility. For instance, when Graham first inspects the Leedses' numerous belongings, he compares them against his own meager belongings:

fishing equipment, a used Volkswagen, and some Montrachet wine. The source of the animosity lies in Graham's childhood. His family was poor. His father worked on boats in different places across the country, taking Graham with him. So Graham was always being uprooted and placed in new schools. His resentment toward the affluent Leeds and Jacobi families is based on a certain degree of class envy. His long-held grudges erode his family relationships. As I have written elsewhere, "Harris suggests that family life, no matter how apparently stable or based on love and mutual respect, is inherently fragile and probably pathological for those concerned."[37] The inevitable dissolution of the Graham family reinforces the point. While both movie adaptations of the novel have finally restored the Grahams to some degree of stability, in Harris's original, the Grahams are doomed to fail. In this book, the family is the site of great stress, danger, and finally tragedy.

Second, the book presents the act of seeing as pseudo-murderous, with definite gender implications. The sense of sight, particularly the visual technology that expands it, is shown to be lethally invasive. The most obvious embodiment of this theme is the voyeuristic Dolarhyde selecting murder victims on the basis of their home movies. The act is not complete without filming it first and watching it later in his own parlor. He masturbates to a film montage of scenes from the Leedses' home movies and images of himself standing with his Blake print, raping Mrs. Leeds, and taking the camera lens into his mouth. The montage cements the connection between murder, sexual perversion, and film technology. Like any aspiring filmmaker, he thinks about how he can improve his art, such as maintaining more control of his on-screen performance and using infrared film to avoid the harsh glare of regular lighting. Dolarhyde's actions represent an almost Hitchcockian linkage between murder, visual technology, filmmaking, and voyeurism.

Lounds's actions further highlight the invasive nature of photography. He photographs Graham standing in the doorway of the Chesapeake State Hospital, a shot later cropped by the *Tattler* so that the words "Criminally Insane" show in the picture with Graham. This photograph, taken and published without Graham's permission, yields terrible consequences. It brings Graham's face and name to Dolarhyde and directly puts Graham and his family at risk. To return the favor, Graham poses in a *Tattler* photographic session with Lounds, fatally placing Lounds in Dolarhyde's sights. Besides an early instance of Harris's trend of meting out poetic justice to certain "rude" characters, Lounds's fate shows the punishment for irresponsible use of "surveillance" technology, in this case the tabloid media. Graham resists being "seen" in this way, so Lounds pays the price for violating his wishes.

It's worth noting that the book's practitioners of surveillance technology are men, one of whom is a serial killer. Dolarhyde represents the extreme end of a continuum of visual appropriation of other people, especially women, by men. It's no accident he believes his murderous alter ego originates in the act of technological seeing represented by photography. He thinks the Dragon is reborn in countless images in art books and magazines. Though he never clearly articulates it, he clearly considers murder and photography to share a kinship. Therefore, he resists being seen. The red, insect-like goggles he wears at Gateway shield his eyes from the scrutiny of others, providing him with a mask through which he can observe without being observed.[38]

Mrs. Leeds and Mrs. Jacobi are the book's foremost victims of photographic reductionism, existing within the story as sexualized images in film only. Both Dolarhyde and Graham obsessively watch their images over and over, admittedly for far different purposes. Reba McClane complicates the formula. In a way, she too is complicit in the visual voyeurism business by working at Baeder.

However, her blindness poses a clear plot counterpoint to and rebuke of Dolarhyde's hyper-acute, murderous visual sense. Her inability to see puts her in danger of being gawked at and "accidentally" felt up by lecherous males and patronized by men like Dandridge. Her blindness is a metaphor for not seeing Dolarhyde's true nature at first. She does survive, however, indicating that her blindness gives her an edge in a world of dangerous, sighted men.[39]

Aside from gender, intriguing (and problematic) questions of race arise in studying Harris's fiction. Thus far in Harris's career, the African American characters have all been secondary characters, in subordinate positions to the white characters. Queen Mother Bailey, the cook for the Dolarhyde family and one of the few positive influences on young Francis, is one example. Though slavery had ended almost a century before, her position in the narrative is at first glance indistinguishable from that of a house slave. This portrayal opens up Harris's fiction to charges of racism. Giving the book the benefit of the doubt, however, it can be argued that the retention of African Americans as household servants was a common enough phenomenon among some Southern families in the postwar years. Having such a servant also characterizes Grandmother Dolarhyde as a faded Southern belle clinging to the past in the best Blanche DuBois/Amanda Wingfield/Emily Grierson literary tradition. Harris's working within the Southern Gothic literary movement may explain his presentation of the way in which social mores of the antebellum South persist stubbornly into the present, haunting men and women still with the specter of racism.

Another theme is the binary or divided nature of humanity, forever aspiring to decency but mired in clotted pools of blood resulting from its willfully unleashed brutality. Just as the safety of the home is called into question, so too is the sanctity of one's own psyche. The individual mind may fracture or split because of threats within and without. As Graham knows, psychic defense mechanisms are too porous to restrain the primal instincts inside and keep bad influences outside. The mirrors Dolarhyde shatters represent not only his resistance to being reflected but his own fractured mind. His psyche is too badly damaged by trauma for him to ever be whole, though he aspires to be whole as part of his delusion. When he connects with Reba, her attraction for the civilized face he presents to the world creates a crisis that splits him into two distinctly different personas—the weak Francis and the strong Dragon. Through these two characters, we see that the life of the mind is as fraught with danger as a battlefield like Shiloh.

In *Milton: A Poem* (ca. 1804), William Blake emphasizes the power of the imagination to shape our lives in this line: "The Imagination is not a State; it is the Human Existence in itself." *Red Dragon* makes the case that imagination, as the defining characteristic of humanity, is a dangerous gift. If imagination creates reality, the released imagination may take a turn to the murderous, causing a meltdown of the mind. A real danger is posed by the mind's capacity to imagine alternative viewpoints, thus becoming changed by the contact for the worse. It's the Gothic answer to the Romantic notion of the individual's connection to nature and others through imaginative projection. Graham cannot stop his thoughts no matter how disturbing they may be to him, reminiscent of the adolescent Lander's inability to control his internal dialogues. This ability may make Graham an unusually effective criminal profiler, but his success costs him his family life—all because of an enhanced imaginative capability.

Graham fears his own susceptibility to madness and violence, a valid enough concern given his rage toward Lounds and his unconscious complicity in getting the man killed. Sometimes this fear leads him to overreact defensively to innocent remarks, such as Molly's joke that he had a criminal mind as a boy stealing a watermelon. When in proximity to genuine madness, he becomes hyper-aware of its infiltration of his mind. For instance, he leaves Lecter's presence when it becomes too much for him, but he feels as if Lecter's spell leaves the hospital with him. His friend, Dr. Bloom, comments that fear is the price of Graham's imagination. Graham's downfall is a cautionary note to all of us to show a little restraint in the things we imagine.

Dolarhyde also pays a price for his imagination. Through his fantasy life, he creates an imaginary persona, the Red Dragon, to give him a sense of power. At first, he revels in his newfound liberation to act on his long-repressed urges. However, his creation spins out of control when his affection for Reba complicates his life. The Dragon becomes a separate entity, speaking to him for the first time. It heaps abuse on him in language borrowed from his past tormentors, calling him "cunt face" and threatening him with castration if he chooses Reba over Becoming. Rejecting suicide as a way to prevent handing Reba over to the Dragon, he instead consumes the original Blake watercolor to become even more powerful than the Dragon. His mind fractures under the tension between his civilized self and his primal self. When he does want to stop killing, he finds it's not so easy to call it off once his primal self has been unleashed. His case illustrates Harris's theme of the danger of a mind at war with its own murderous urges.

Another danger to the integrity of self is child abuse. We've already seen how Dolarhyde is motivated by a deep reservoir of anguish originating in his childhood and his perception of himself as a deformed freak. His anguish turns him into an angry adult, to say the least. At first he directs his anger inward, absorbing countless insults from people without reacting. Under the empowering influence of his new-found fantasy life, however, he begins to redirect his anger outward at life's everyday small irritations. His repressed anger has a much more dire consequence, of course, because it motivates him to take out perceived injustices on his victims as a means of self-empowerment. Criminologists and psychologists alike warn us about the long-term effects of child abuse and how its victims often grow up into victimizers. Following their lead, and in no small way shaping one of the primary themes in the serial killer genre, Harris presents us with a worst-case scenario of the role of child abuse in criminal violence and psychopathology.

A fourth key theme is the human desire to transcend the material and achieve immortality through grand actions. Dolarhyde seeks to facilitate his own rebirth from the material world to the divine realm. Certainly, transformation in and of itself is not necessarily a destructive act, but in Harris's Gothic world, the romantic idea of achieving individual godhood transmogrifies into a debased mystic impulse to seek renewal in the sacrifice of others. Dolarhyde, for example, imagines that there is a transfer of energy from his victims to him, which in turn fuels his Becoming. The more life force he absorbs, the sooner he transforms. Graham gets it. He knows that Dolarhyde wants to meet Lecter in order to kill him and absorb his energy to become even more powerful.

Dolarhyde's quest to transform himself through murder is expressed symbolically in his interest in astronomy. The stars and the planets exist in the same ethereal realm he aspires to. Therefore, he murders by the light of the full moon each month. He likes to watch his home movies in a darkened room with a revolving light filter casting star-like pinpoints of light down onto him. He does not want to miss the Perseid meteor shower, which reminds him of one of his favorite passages in the book of Revelation: "And his tail drew the third part of the stars of heaven, and did cast them down to the earth." To Lounds, he compares himself to the guest star of 1054.[40] Reba is more correct than she knows when she thinks of him as a black hole and her own success in reaching him as equivalent to a radio astronomer receiving a return signal. He experiences sexual intercourse with Reba as an act of earthly transcendence out among the stars. This particular act of transcendence, which does not depend upon the one-sided energy exchange of murder but on a mutual exchange, is the only time in his life he feels everything is all right. Most of the time, however, his concept of transformation is entirely self-centered, directed at becoming the Red Dragon so he will no longer have to suffer at the hands of others.

Dolarhyde's metaphysical goal is paralleled by his earthly physical transformations, specifically the surgical repairs to his cleft palate. They leave him with a dimple in his upper lip, a scar he magnifies out of all proportion to its actual prominence. He shuns looking directly into mirrors because he still believes himself to be deformed. By way of overcompensating for his insecurities, he transforms his body into a massively muscled killing machine through obsessive weight-lifting. He travels to Asia to have a fearsome dragon tattooed onto his back. All of these changes are ritualistic preparations for his transcendence. They are part of the obsessive continuum that leads to the ritualistic murders. In the mystic logic of the book, the physical rituals culminating in blood sacrifice are an integral part of the process.

The book implicitly condemns religious ritual. Lecter, in his mocking way, cuts to the heart of the book's message about the futility of efforts at mystical communion and material transcendence for self-betterment in his letter to Graham. In it, Lecter argues that murder must feel good to God, because He does it all the time. Lecter mockingly suggests that since we are made in God's image, we too should feel good about committing murder, and concludes by pointing out that God just collapsed a church roof on thirty-four worshippers in Texas. Lecter's sarcasm conveys a deep skepticism in the existence of God, let alone that He is good. With less mockery, Graham reaches the same conclusion when he reflects on the indifferent beauty of nature, or the Green Machine in which there is no God.[41] The only grace afforded us is that which we make, in defiance of our basic reptile brains. The agnosticism, or outright atheism, of Graham and Lecter offset Dolarhyde's murderous transcendentalism.

Dolarhyde's sad, bloody attempt to become something more than what he is sets up a successful template for Harris to follow. *Red Dragon* changed Harris's career in a direction he has not yet turned away from. With this book, the Harrisverse begins to take on a coherent form. Harris continues to work through the implications of the many themes of *Red Dragon* in his next novel, *The Silence of the Lambs*. As we shall see, *Silence* became a genuine cultural phenomenon.

# 4

# "Can You Stand to Say I'm Evil?": *The Silence of the Lambs*

If *Red Dragon* is about the violation of the sanctity of our homes and families, then *The Silence of the Lambs* (1988) is about the violation of the integrity of our skins. All kinds of violations of protective outer coverings occur in this novel, some literal and some metaphoric, almost all directed against females by males. On the literal level, the serial killer Buffalo Bill removes the skins of his female victims, a gruesome violation of bodily integrity. Figuratively, Hannibal Lecter peels away the layers of protective defenses erected by FBI trainee Clarice Starling against the cruel memories of her childhood. If Harris's previous novel disturbs us with its images of home invasions, then this one strikes at an even more elemental level—the invasion of our innermost physical and psychic privacy.

In this book, skin is a symbol of the various covers we construct to protect us from the scrutiny of others. Buffalo Bill, who covets the skin of his victims with his cold gimlet eyes, uses female skins to construct a female identity for himself. In doing so, he robs his victims of far more than their lives. First, he destroys their dignity through abduction, captivity, and murder. He then literally opens them up by stripping portions of their skins from them. If Buffalo Bill's gaze is that of the destroyer, then Starling's empathetic gaze is that of the restorer who can give back some sense of dignity to these skinned women. She metaphorically gives the dead their skins back and literally prevents Buffalo Bill's latest captive from losing hers.

Before succeeding in her quest to save Catherine Martin, however, Starling as a "sister under the skin" must suffer the loss of some of her own protective covering through forced psychotherapy with psychiatrist Hannibal Lecter. Only when she has confessed a source of childhood pain to Lecter can she move forward to save the young woman held in Buffalo Bill's oubliette. Through the painful baring of her soul, Starling finds at least some temporary peace from the haunting childhood memory of the screaming, slaughtered lambs. Her symbolic "skinning" gives her what she needs to save a young woman from a literal skinning.

Lecter is clearly a costar this time around, rather than the bit player he is in *Red Dragon*. Will Graham meets with Lecter exactly once in *Red Dragon*. In *Silence*, Lecter and Starling meet face-to-face on five separate occasions. He asks her if she can "stand to say I'm evil," forcing her to examine her pat assumptions about the nature of evil and ultimately confront her own past. Their encounters constitute some of the most emotionally powerful parts of the story. Whereas Graham was a hated enemy, Lecter bonds with Starling and even decides to help her personally and professionally. However, Lecter remains dangerous. He orchestrates events from his asylum cell to an even greater extent than he did in *Red Dragon*. Armed with his privileged knowledge of the identity of Buffalo Bill, he manipulates the law enforcement apparatus at every level for strategic advantage. For the first time, we see him in his full unleashed brutality during a bloody escape from the Memphis courthouse. In *Silence*, Harris has created in the character of Lecter a truly memorable and chilling villain—a superstar serial killer.

For all of Lecter's evil glamour, however, *Silence* is Starling's story. In Starling, Harris achieves an enviable feat for a male writer by creating a female character appealing to both men and women. Her tale is a dark coming-of-age story, in which a plucky heroine of modest circumstances finds herself in a very dangerous environment of sexist and/or homicidal men, navigates a potentially fatal labyrinth with the help of two male mentors (one of them a killer), and succeeds in her quest to save a captive female from a hideous monster. Unlike Will Graham, whose troubled relationship to his own investigative gifts ends in tragedy, Starling's quest is rewarded with a happier ending. *Silence* provides a sad epilogue to Graham's story, informing the reader that Graham is a drunk in Florida with a face not pretty to look at. Starling fares much better, at least in this novel (*Hannibal* is another story). Perhaps a critical difference between Graham and Starling is that while the older Graham tends to identify with the killer in order to unmask his identity and increasingly isolates himself from his family and society to do it, the younger Starling relates more to the plight of the victims and moves toward a reintegration into society—for now.

## CRITICAL RECEPTION

Early reviewers of *Silence* were generally enthusiastic about the book. Typical is Douglas E. Winter, who first begins by calling Harris "the best suspense novelist working today," even if he waits for maddeningly long intervals before publishing novels. Winter calls the book "a virtual textbook on the craft of suspense, a masterwork of sheer momentum that rockets seamlessly toward its climax." Noting the difference in tone between *Red Dragon* and *Silence*, Winter says *Silence* "offers an optimistic, outward-bound escape from the maelstrom of a world gone mad."[1] Christopher Lehmann-Haupt writes, "Mr. Harris's chilling story lowers the reader's blood temperature by a few degrees."[2] William Leith praises Harris for his "excellent sense of how to match the most lurid and twisted activities with very down-to-earth practical details" and concludes, "You find yourself feeling sick with the horror of it all, not because there's so much blood or perversion, but because you believe it could happen."[3] John Lanchester speaks to the power of Lecter as a character: "Lecter is straightforwardly a monster, bearing no relation to any murderer who ever lived, but achieving an archetypal quality through his brilliance and inexplicability, his mythic quality as instantly apparent as, say, Sherlock Holmes's."[4] Offering a less effusive review, John Katzenbach calls the novel "fast paced, intriguing and exciting" but ultimately inferior to *Red Dragon*.[5]

The academic criticism following a few years later tends to grant Harris more kudos than demerits. None is more forthcoming than David Sexton, who states uncategorically, "It is impossible to read [*Silence*] and not recognise it as a masterpiece of its form."[6] Daniel O'Brien more circumspectly calls Crawford's deployment of Starling against Lecter implausible and Harris's prose overwritten, but gives Harris high marks for penning "a classic fairy tale of escape and rescue."[7]

Scholars approach the novel from varying theoretical perspectives. Some are interested in finding a genre home for *Silence*. Joe Sanders, taking note of the novel's winning the 1989 Bram Stoker Award and being nominated for the World Fantasy Award, investigates the question of how Harris's non-supernatural fiction uses "'real-world' elements to produce effects similar to supernatural horror fiction."[8] Tony Magistrale uncovers Gothic elements in the novel's treatment of "identity transitions and transmogrifications."[9] Peter Messent makes the case *Silence* is more within the Gothic Horror tradition than the crime genre, given the amount of taboo transgression that occurs within (cannibalism, for instance).[10] Alternatively, S. T. Joshi, in attempting to classify the novel in either the suspense or horror genre, finally places it in the former on the basis that Harris seems more interested in the processes of detection than presentation of the horrible.[11]

Other writers single out specific themes for discussion. Linda Mizejewski hones in on the partnership between Starling and Lecter to explain the undeniably popular appeal of "this tale about a beautiful FBI agent and a flesh-eating mass murderer."[12] She argues that the two are really a couple, in keeping with a tradition in the crime fiction genre that the investigator and the criminal share an attraction toward one another.[13] Similarly, Harriett Hawkins enthusiastically makes the case that Starling and Lecter's reciprocal relationship helps liberate Starling from both painful childhood memories and bitter class resentment against privileged individuals like Senator Ruth Martin, thus representing "an important crossing of the bridge between pre-feminist and post-feminist portrayals of ambitious women in popular art."[14]

Bruce Robbins, while writing primarily about the film adaptation, notes that the novel's positioning of a criminal as mentor to the female Starling striving for success in a patriarchal institution is fitting, given that she too is a type of outlaw.[15] John Goodrich identifies Lecter as a teacher who puts Starling through an increasingly grueling series of tests, each one of which she passes, in order to prove her worth as a pupil.[16] Breaking the norm somewhat in focusing on Jame Gumb, Edith Borchardt singles out Gumb as an artist (in his case, a tailor) whose psychopathology causes him to murder.[17] Robert H. Waugh describes Lecter as a mythic character ever in the process of molting and transformation, much like the butterfly that plays such an important role in the novel.[18] Finally, Robert Ziegler points out that the novel's ambiguous ending, in which Starling's blessed silence is only a temporary victory and a vicious serial killer is on the loose, denies any global interpretation of the text and ends with the unsettling observation that reading itself is an act of cannibalism in which a text is broken up and devoured by critics.[19]

All of these arguments testify to the complexity readers have discovered in the novel. Its slippery ability to evade final classification (Is it suspense? Detective thriller? Crime fiction? Horror? Gothic? Neo-Gothic?) and its multiplicity of themes mark it as a superior work of fiction in any genre. For many, it is Harris's masterpiece.

## PLOT DEVELOPMENT

*Silence*, like the two novels before it, has essentially a three-act structure. Act 1, consisting of Chapters 1–14, establishes the relationship between Starling and Lecter as the FBI hunts for a serial killer, "Buffalo Bill." Act 2, Chapters 15–38, begins with the abduction of Catherine Martin by Buffalo Bill and concludes with the escape of Lecter from police custody in Memphis. Act 3, Chapters 39–61, brings the hunt for Buffalo Bill to its successful resolution and Starling to the verge of graduating from school to become an FBI agent.

The plot itself is, as Daniel O'Brien accurately diagnoses, "a reworking of *Red Dragon*. . . . This time, a female trainee FBI agent is taken out of school to hunt a serial killer, though her initial brush with Lecter is supposedly on an unrelated matter."[20] *Silence* replicates the formula established by *Red Dragon*, to the point where one could almost consider the former a "remake" of the latter, as opposed to a sequel or a continuation. The greatest difference between the two storylines is that *Silence* is told from the point of view of a young woman at the beginning of her career, as opposed to an older, bitter male at the end of his. The switch in protagonists allows for a much different dynamic, and more interaction, with Lecter.

Act 1 begins with Clarice Starling, a trainee at the FBI Academy in Quantico, called in from the firing range to meet with Section Chief Crawford in his office. Crawford asks her to question Hannibal Lecter, still incarcerated at the Baltimore State Hospital for the Criminally Insane. While there, Lecter gives Starling a clue that leads her to a storage facility, where she finds a severed human head. She returns to question Lecter, who explains how the head ended up in the storage unit. He next offers to trade information about Buffalo Bill's identity in exchange for a transfer to a federal institution. Crawford then enlists Starling to go with him to examine the body of a Buffalo Bill murder victim in West Virginia. Examination reveals a moth cocoon stuffed in the dead woman's throat, just like the one in the throat of the severed head.

Act 2 begins with the abduction of Catherine Martin, the daughter of a powerful female senator, by Buffalo Bill. Since Buffalo Bill keeps his victims alive for several days before killing them, a massive federal response is launched to find Catherine in time. Starling returns to the asylum for more interviews with Lecter. He parcels out clues to Starling only if she shares painful personal memories about the death of her father when she was a child. Slowly, Starling gathers information about Buffalo Bill's identity. However, the process is interrupted on the verge of success when the obnoxious hospital director, Dr. Chilton, transfers Lecter to a holding cell in Memphis, Tennessee, to reveal what Lecter knows to Senator Martin. Lecter provides a false clue to the senator to misdirect the investigation. During a final meeting with Starling, she reveals to him that her childhood memory of screaming lambs during the spring slaughter now drives her to rescue Catherine to make the screaming stop. In return, he gives her the final clue she needs to find Buffalo Bill. After she leaves, he escapes in bloody fashion from the courthouse where he is being held and becomes a fugitive.

During the third act, while Catherine struggles to find a way out of the basement where she is being held captive by Buffalo Bill, Starling chases down Lecter's leads in Belvedere, Ohio, the hometown of the first victim. While searching the victim's bedroom, Starling realizes Buffalo Bill is using the skins of his victims to make a suit. The trail leads her to the house of Jame Gumb. While talking to him, she sees a death's-head moth in the room and realizes Gumb is Buffalo Bill. A deadly cat-and-mouse game ensues between Starling and Gumb in the darkened basement. Ultimately, Starling shoots Gumb and rescues Catherine.

The novel's denouement is brief. In a letter sent to Starling, Lecter asks her if the lambs have stopped screaming. He also warns her that she will have to earn the "blessed silence" again and again, as human cruelty never ends. He concludes his letter by saying he has no plans to kill her.

## CHARACTERS

### Clarice Starling

Clarice M. Starling is a twenty-five-year-old trainee in the FBI Academy at Quantico, Virginia. She grew up in rural West Virginia in less-than-modest circumstances. When she was eight years old, her father, a small-town marshal, was fatally shot by two drugstore burglars. Her mother worked as a motel cleaning woman in an effort to make ends meet. Clarice helped her bring towels, soap, and other cleaning supplies into the motel rooms. However, their financial situation became so desperate that when Clarice was ten, her mother sent her away to live with her mother's cousin and husband at a sheep and horse ranch near Bozeman, Montana. There, Clarice developed an attachment for one of the horses, which she named "Hannah." She began to worry that Hannah, gaining weight and losing her sight, was destined for the slaughterhouse. One night, after the screaming of the spring lambs being slaughtered out in the barn woke her up, Clarice took Hannah from the ranch. The refugees ended up at a livery stable in Bozeman, trying to convince the owners to let Hannah live out her days giving rides to children. Angered by the local stir over Clarice's actions, her foster parents sent her (and Hannah) away to a Lutheran orphanage.

From there, Clarice's life was a succession of boarding schools. Her good grades and scholarships earned her entry into the University of Virginia, where she double majored in psychology and criminology. She obtained her counselor's license and worked two years in a mental health center while going to college. When Jack Crawford taught criminology seminars at the university, she signed up for the class. Inspired by his teaching, she decided to apply to the FBI Academy. Once there, she wrote him a note, but he never replied. At the time the novel begins, she has been at the Academy for three months.

The vast majority of the novel is told from Starling's point of view, so we get to know her as a character quite well. Hers is basically a coming-of-age or rite-of-passage story. She is certainly the most positive of Harris's characters to date, though she exhibits some character traits (anger, for one) that make the events of *Hannibal* not completely unexpected. What makes her so appealing for fans, both male and female, is her mix of intelligence, courage, independence, compassion, integrity, and toughness.

Starling is a successful college graduate on the brink of a career with the FBI, a remarkable feat considering the obstacles placed in her path early in life. Her high intelligence has earned her the grades that gave her the scholarships that allowed her to escape rural poverty. An excellent student, she is often given special attention and opportunities by her instructors and mentors, such as Hannibal Lecter, Jack Crawford, and John Brigham, the gunnery instructor.[21] Almost literally alone in the world, armored only with the memory of a beloved father and a courageous mother, she uses her intelligence for advancement, which the perceptive Lecter picks up on immediately in their first meeting.

More than professional success, however, she seeks the approval of her parents, especially her father, even though both are dead. During a moment of reflection in the otherwise headlong pace of the Buffalo Bill investigation, Starling wonders if her parents would be ashamed of her, and comes to the conclusion that no, they would not. Crawford acknowledges this need within her when he says to her after Buffalo Bill's death that her father sees her. Through the opportunities that her intelligence has brought her, she honors her parents.

Independence is another of Starling's most obvious qualities, going hand in hand with her courage. She relies on her own strength and abilities because she knows she is pretty much alone in the world (like many of Harris's characters). Through the harsh circumstances of her birth and early childhood, she is abandoned by family. We learn that she has brothers, but we never know their names or what happened to them. At many critical junctures in the story, Starling goes it alone, without backup. She enters the asylum dungeon alone to confront the dangerous madman that ultimately got the best of Will Graham, she goes into the storage unit alone to discover the head in the jar, she chases down other important leads alone, and she enters Buffalo Bill's underground labyrinth alone. She does all this without hesitation and in spite of her fear, simply because, as Lecter might say, it is in her nature to do so.

Compassion is also part of her nature. Unlike Will Graham, who finds it easier to empathize with killers than victims, Starling more easily identifies with the plight of the murdered. Reviewing photographs of the flayed victims fished out of rivers, for example, she finds it hard to look at them because of their loss of dignity. After examining the body of Kimberly Emberg, the West Virginia victim, Starling feels the case become very real and personal to her on the behalf of this poor anonymous woman who at one time had put glitter polish on her nails to make her feel more pretty. The memory stays with her. She tells Ardelia Mapp she can't stop thinking about Kimberly. Starling's attachment to Kimberly is almost filial.

The bond to the skinless woman solidifies Starling's commitment to law enforcement in a way that all of her schoolwork had not truly prepared her for. What she learns about the cruelty of human nature as a result of seeing the violated corpse creates a knowledge in her that will "lie against her skin forever . . . she had to form a callus or it would wear her through."[22] She acknowledges the downside to her empathy—that it is possible to care too much when presented with atrocity, that to be undone by its brutality is to render her ineffective in stopping it. She recognizes this when she slightly misquotes from T. S. Eliot's poem "Ash Wednesday": "Teach us to care and not to care, teach us to be still."[23]

Starling's compassion extends to the other victims, but particularly the first victim, Fredrica Bimmel, and the captive Catherine Martin. When Starling learns Catherine lost her father at a young age, she feels close to her. Similarly, while searching Fredrica's room, Starling comes to know and like Fredrica through the left-behind evidence of Fredrica's efforts to pretty herself up. This quiet moment of identification with a dead woman immediately precedes Starling's epiphany that Buffalo Bill knows how to sew and killed Fredrica for her lovely skin. Starling's empathetic gift, similar to Graham's in some ways but different in that it favors victims rather than killers, creates the breakthrough in this particular manhunt.

She also feels a bond with another, far larger class of victim—the lower socioeconomic classes in America. At the sight of the West Virginia deputies outside the funeral parlor, Starling knows instantly that these men used to carry their lunch to school in paper sacks that were used over and over. Crawford, far removed from any true understanding of Starling's background, sees the depth of her bond with the West Virginians when she asks the male deputies to leave the room to let Starling take care of the female murder victim. He sees her as the descendent of the strong country women who function as the healers and caretakers of their folk. Her empathy with the downtrodden classes gives her insight that Crawford and his middle-class male agents literally cannot see.

Complementing her compassion is her toughness, making her all the more effective as a fledgling detective. Besides her physical courage, Starling stands up to authority whenever she is pushed, a tendency that will bring her to grief in *Hannibal* but nevertheless speaks to her strong sense of self. She does not suffer fools gladly. Dr. Chilton in particular aggravates her, with his petty officiousness and his sexual harassment of her. At first, her resistance to him is courteous. She politely but pointedly suggests he not accompany her to Lecter's cell if Lecter views him as his nemesis. Later, she pushes back against him hard when he accuses her of not sharing information with him. She next confronts Senator Martin and Paul Krendler from the Department of Justice at Catherine's apartment. When Krendler insults Crawford's judgment, Starling pointedly asks him if he knows anyone else who has caught three serial killers. This exchange initiates Krendler's long enmity to Starling. It doesn't help any that she defies his direct order to return to school in Quantico, instead going to Memphis to see Lecter.

In her multiple dealings with Lecter, she exhibits great strength as well. In their first meeting, for example, she stands up under his withering verbal assault upon her rural background, and then counters by asking him if he's strong enough to turn his perception upon himself. She even accuses him of being afraid to do so. Though respectful of the danger he poses, she unflinchingly deceives him with a fake offer, to elicit information from him about Buffalo Bill. Her strength originates in part from her hardscrabble background and the legacy of her parents. For example, the memory of her mother washing blood from her father's hat in the kitchen sink provides her with a symbol of courage, which she draws upon in times of stress. She thinks of her lost family as a source of grace in her life.

Like any Harris protagonist, however, Starling has her tragic flaw. She is angry. Lecter, her psychotic psychotherapist, pinpoints this trait spot-on when he asks her how she manages her rage. Crawford observes it in her as well, after Chilton derails her interviews with Lecter. When Starling is mad, she loses it. She rants to herself about forcing Chilton to look at Catherine Martin's dead body as payback for his meddling. This kind of rage stems from her lower-class rural background and her history of loss. Her working-class father dies when she is young, and her impoverished mother gives her away to relatives when she can't afford her anymore. Forming deep attachments to animals as familial surrogates, she builds up a deeper reservoir of resentment against a heartless world that slaughters lambs and aging horses. Then she moves from foster family to foster family, preventing her from forming lasting bonds. The schools she attends provide the only stability in her life.

Her background leaves her with a lasting bitterness against the privileged, an ironic development since fate puts her in the position of rescuing the pampered daughter of a United States senator from a slaughter not unlike that of the lambs in Starling's childhood memories. Like Will Graham, she acknowledges her class resentment to herself. When Senator Martin calls her a thief, she reacts not only to the insult but to her own buried anger against such privileged women. In spite of being equal to the senator in terms of looks and drive and intelligence, Starling still remains angry because of the injustice of her childhood.

To the extent she feels any sense of lasting family identity, it's a fairly abstract emotion for her and more than a little negative. She thinks her family's luck has been bad for hundreds of years. She visualizes her ancestors as pissed off and lost. Her belief in her flawed genetic heritage contributes to her latent anger over the needless death of her father. It's only a step further to extrapolate that Starling's fear of her own destiny as a loser drives her to excel in order to avoid her father's fate. Whenever she falls short in her own judgment, she angrily blames herself and then redirects the anger outward in search of targets.

Through all of her emotional highs and lows, Starling rescues Catherine and finds momentary peace. At the end of the novel, she sleeps in the silence of the lambs. However, as Lecter observes in his letter to her, she judges herself so harshly that she will need to earn that silence many more times. Lecter tells her she is driven by her need to redress injustice—the never-ending plight of humanity. Of course, Lecter is intimately familiar with the uglier manifestations of humanity. Starling is just now beginning to face them head-on. Her journey into experience begins with her sight of Kimberly lying skinned on the slab, a journey destined to take her into some very troubled waters indeed.

## Hannibal Lecter

So what else can we add to the emerging character portrait of Hannibal Lecter based on this novel? It's already been established that he's highly intelligent, educated, refined in taste and manner, paradoxically brutal, and ingeniously manipulative. This time, he assumes a vital role in the education of Clarice Starling into the ways of the world. Though serving as a consultant to Graham in the previous novel, he was never truly interested in helping Graham. Starling is a different story. Perhaps surprising even himself, he eventually gains enough respect for Starling that he gives her just enough information to allow her to succeed.

Harris provides us with a few more details about Lecter's psychiatric practice and the murders that landed him in the asylum. For many years, Lecter performed psychiatric evaluations for courts in Virginia, Maryland, and other East Coast states. Ironically, he evaluated many cases of criminal insanity. He also maintained a thriving practice during that time. One of his regular patients was Benjamin Raspail, principal flutist for the Baltimore Philharmonic Orchestra and Lecter's ninth known victim. At some point during the course of Raspail's therapy, Raspail introduced Lecter to his former lover, Jame Gumb, and confessed to Lecter how Gumb had killed and flayed a lover. During a therapy session, Lecter killed Raspail. On the following evening, indulging his macabre sense of humor, Lecter served Raspail's thymus and pancreas as part of a dinner to the president and the conductor of the Baltimore Philharmonic.

Graham calls Lecter a monster in *Red Dragon*, largely because the workings of Lecter's mind are incomprehensible to outside observers. Harris continues to present Lecter as monstrous, endowing him with nearly supernatural abilities and malice. In a description of Lecter's enjoyment of his spacious hotel room following his escape, Harris links him to Satan through biblical allusion to Job 1:7 in the King James Bible: "He enjoyed going to and fro in his suite and walking up and down in it."[24] Lecter's metaphysical evil is outwardly marked by exceptional physical attributes, truly setting him apart from other humans. In addition to his maroon eyes, he was born with six fingers on his left hand, a condition known as polydactylism.[25] In other particulars of his appearance, he is small and sleek, leading Starling to think of him in a startling image as a *"cemetery mink"* living *"in a ribcage in the dry leaves of a heart* [italics in original]."[26] He has dark hair swept back from his forehead in a widow's peak, contrasting sharply with pale features bleached from his years of living away from sunlight, like a creature turning albino in the depths of a cavern. To Starling, Lecter's unnatural eyes seem to gather all the shadows in his cell, and behind those eyes is nothing but darkness. His movements are always graceful, his body lithe.

Additionally, his internal life is extraordinarily rich. He possesses a phenomenally keen sense of smell, able to discern the minute scent traces of Evyan skin cream and L'Air du Temps perfume left behind on Starling's ID card. Quite capable of entertaining himself for years deep within his formidable mind, he suffers no real ill effect from his long imprisonment. These attributes set Lecter apart from the rest of humanity.

We also see Lecter in murderous action this time around. Through the sheer power of his words to inflict harm, he convinces his fellow asylum ward Multiple Miggs to swallow his own tongue and choke to death. In a flashback, we first see him kill his patient Benjamin Raspail with a knife to the heart. Then, in an elaborate escape sequence later in the book, we see him claw, bite, and beat two police officers to death with the aid of a riot baton. Nor is he squeamish in the slightest, as demonstrated when he removes Officer Pembry's face to wear over his own as a way of taking on Pembry's identity to escape. His fiendish intelligence combined with ruthless brutality takes him from the hell of Chilton's asylum to a luxurious room in the Marcus Hotel under an assumed identity, sipping a glass of Batard-Montrachet and readying to fly to Rio.

He takes great pleasure in manipulating others. Since he knows almost from the beginning who Buffalo Bill's identity is, his enjoyment in helping Starling derives not from puzzle-solving but in how long he can play games with her, the FBI, Chilton, and indeed the rest of society. Crawford has him pegged, saying he looks only for the fun. Fun for Lecter involves the pain of others. He is never troubled by remorse or humanitarian considerations, pursuing only his own intellectual and sensual gratification. In the previous investigation, he had dedicated himself to the destruction of Will Graham; this time around, he is intrigued enough by Starling to help her, as long as he can have fun. He enjoys misleading others even while keeping Starling on track. His "big reveal" of Buffalo Bill's "real" name of Billy Rubin to Senator Martin is a medical joke, bilirubin being a pigment found in human bile and feces.

Lecter's insistence on social courtesy is more pronounced here. Genuinely upset by Multiple Miggs's ugly act of throwing semen at Starling, Lecter tells her that discourtesy is unspeakably ugly to him. However, like much about him, his courtesy masks inner violence. His words are frequently cruel, even if exquisitely phrased. He sips pain from the tears of others as if through a straw. Certainly, he does not hesitate to torment Dr. Chilton, Senator Martin, or Crawford, all of whom he views as pawns for his pleasure. So whatever his protests about discourtesy, Lecter uses his words as the only weapons remaining to him in captivity. Even his so-called civilized gestures, like sending a mocking sympathy note (cribbing verse from John Donne to boot) to Crawford about the imminent death of his wife, are sharp-edged and meant to harm, like the stiletto that pierced Raspail's heart.

Mockery is a key weapon in Lecter's verbal arsenal. He mocks individuals and social institutions alike. Christianity in particular is one of Lecter's favorite targets of ridicule. As he did in *Red Dragon*, he continues to collect news accounts of church collapses recreationally. He finds fascination in the iconography of crucifixion, even attempting to patent a crucifixion watch of his own design (using Starling's face in place of Christ's). Another of his sketches shows Golgotha after Christ's body has been removed from the cross. These drawings are motivated not by reverence, but contempt. Lecter directs another broadside against the FBI's division of criminal offenders into organized and disorganized, saying that a "real bottom feeder" thought of that classification. He expands his contempt to include both the FBI and the academic discipline of psychology, calling psychology "puerile" and "that practiced in Behavioral Science . . . on a level with phrenology."[27] Even when not speaking, he exudes a scornful air. Only once in Starling's experience, when they exchange a simple touch of fingers, does Lecter not appear to ridicule her earnest quest to save Catherine. More than anything else, this one moment of genuine respect from Lecter toward Starling hints at the kind of sincere emotional connection and underlying sexual attraction later developed to an extreme in *Hannibal*.

He undeniably feels something for Starling, and it happens pretty quickly. Even the obtuse Chilton sees Lecter's feelings for Starling. At the end of Starling and Lecter's first meeting, Lecter offers her a Valentine's gift (the location of Raspail's car), which will lead to her professional advancement. The "valentine" implies an attraction to her. He then talks Miggs into killing himself after Miggs offended Starling, so Lecter exhibits his own unique brand of chivalry to her. Lecter later asks her if she thinks Crawford fantasizes about having sex with her, a question Starling refuses to entertain but nevertheless is suggestive of Lecter's own sexual interest in her. In their third meeting, he sketches Starling as if she were sleeping, another suggestive moment. When he begins to elicit personal background information from her, they enter a level of intimacy almost sexual in its intensity. When he finally hears all of Starling's most painful childhood memory, he is as satiated, as grateful to her, as if they had shared physical intimacies. When their bodies finally do touch (one quick brush of fingers through the bars of a cage), the touch seems to electrify him. The monster can feel human emotions after all, and clearly he feels something for Starling.

For all of Lecter's monstrosity, the relationship with Starling humanizes him, leading the way for us to view him in a positive light as Starling's helper. It's the beginning of Harris's rehabilitation of his creation into the "hero" role. When we see Lecter help the hebephrenic religious zealot Sammie communicate again, it's also the first time we get a sense of how tragically Lecter has squandered his own gifts as a therapist through committing himself to a life of murder. We believe him when he reveals to Starling his true motive in helping the FBI. Knowing he will never be let out while he's alive, he asks for a room with a view where he can see trees or water. Nor is their relationship one-sided. It really is quid pro quo. However obliquely, he does give Buffalo Bill's identity to her in enough time to save Catherine. She succeeds because of her relationship with Lecter, a fact not lost upon the *Tattler*, which calls her the Bride of Frankenstein. As promised, Lecter gives good value for his inside knowledge, even though she had attempted to scam him while he remained honest with her. It may have been difficult for some first readers of the novel to think of Lecter as a sympathetic figure. But nevertheless, through the relationship with Starling, Harris turns him into exactly that.

## Jack Crawford

The Jack Crawford of *Silence* is a more fully drawn character than the one we saw in *Red Dragon*. We learn that he loves his wife Bella very much, considering her his life's companion. He was in the Army and is a Korean War veteran. Through his foreign experiences, he has learned to speak French fluently. As a young man, he was apparently quite full of life and happiness. Now, crippled by melancholy and stress, he is burdened figure.

Consider the following. His beloved wife is dying. He is responsible for a major criminal investigation. He has lost his brilliant profiler, Will Graham, who is now a drunk in Florida. Crawford's professional reputation is still sound, but in keeping with the rather funereal tone of *Silence*, he is now isolated in his underground office at

Quantico. Out of desperation, as the death toll mounts, he turns to Clarice Starling—who while bright, is definitely untested—to interview Lecter for any scrap of information helpful to the investigation. Through this move, Crawford demonstrates once again that he has an eye for talent. As a mentor to the young trainee, he is sometimes gruff or unreadable, but he serves as a loyal surrogate father for Starling.

His leadership capacity has already been firmly established. We've seen how he leads men. Now we see how he inspires a strong young woman to follow him, to the point where Starling would kill for him. While learning from Crawford, part of Starling's mind is always analyzing and reflecting upon his leadership strategies. She wonders when Crawford knew he would use her in the Buffalo Bill case and how long he'd waited for her to get hungry enough for success. She sees what he is doing to manipulate her and it still works on her. However, their relationship did not begin warmly. He must overcome a rough start with her. For example, he ignores her presence at Quantico for her first three months of schooling, even though she'd been in his seminar in college. When he decides he can use her in some capacity, he dispatches her as his emissary to Lecter without sharing with her what he knows. Then he reacts so coldly to her over the phone following her first interview with Lecter that she curses him. In the end, she appreciates his willingness to teach her and give her a chance to prove herself professionally. She no longer worries about his courtesy, or lack thereof.

His trust in Starling is critical to his success as a teacher. He gives her tough tasks so she can hone her skills, while correcting her when she goes astray or misses something. He relishes catching her in assumptions so he can say his signature line about assuming "making an ass" out of them both. But for all of his stern pedagogy, he fiercely defends her to others. When she has her stand-off with the television crew at the storage unit, he immediately shows public trust in her by bringing her with him to West Virginia to examine the latest floater. Being a stand-up guy counts for a lot as a leader; Crawford as strong leader definitely takes a stand for Starling throughout.

Like Lecter, Crawford is an oracle for Starling. Crawford knows about human nature and leadership from his service in the Korean War, so he routinely transfers those hard lessons into his post-war FBI career. Sometimes Crawford's advice to Starling takes on a Zen-like quality, as when he tells her how to be a successful criminal profiler: "Live right behind your eyes. Listen to yourself. Keep the crime separate from what's going on around you now. Don't try to impose any pattern or symmetry on this guy. Stay open and let him show you."[28] He often shares his leadership theories with her, such as honest disclosure to the people in one's command as the only strategy that works long-term. Often he advises her on the practicalities of navigating the treacherous politics and competing bureaucracies of law enforcement agencies. All of these insights, broken down into different categories depending upon the type of situation at hand, are hard-earned lessons from Crawford's own vast experience. He passes them on to her as an act of faith in her ability to learn.

He remains exceedingly cautious in his dealings with Starling so that he does not give her bad advice or steer her wrong in her hunger to prove herself. He is keenly aware of the responsibility he takes on by becoming Starling's teacher. Realizing how desperate a middle-aged man can be to sound wise to a trusting youngster, he speaks only about the things he knows about. Like Socrates, Crawford is smart enough to know that he is not smart enough to know it all. His sense of honor will not allow him to mislead Starling.

For all of his wisdom, however, Crawford is distracted, on the thin edge of defeat, haunted. As the story opens, Crawford seems like a ghost of his former self. He is too thin, he dresses too drably, and he has dark circles under his eyes. For all intents and purposes, in his underground bunker, he is a barely animated corpse. This is quite a contrast from the aggressive take-charge agent of *Red Dragon*. Something is wrong with him, Starling recognizes, but she's not quite sure what.

We find out before she does. He is the sole caretaker for his terminally ill wife, Bella, at home. The emotional turmoil of watching his wife die slowly while he remains healthy is taking a toll on him. Facing his life partner's mortality throws him into an existential crisis, leading him to question the existence of God and the possibility of hope in such a world. Harris captures this crisis in one poignant image of Crawford after Bella dies: "His empty hands hanging palms forward at his sides, he stood at the window looking to the empty east. He did not look for dawn; east was the only way the window faced."[29] "East" is traditionally associated with the dawning of hope and medieval conceptions of Paradise as toward the east. However, for Crawford the east is empty. His wife's terminal illness leaves him with little hope or faith. Certainly, he wants to believe in God, as his goodbye blessing to Bella makes clear. Finally, Harris offers some resolution for Crawford. Crawford's life with Bella has given him something to live for besides his career in the FBI. He hopes she is comfortable somewhere else now, her suffering ended. His character arc takes him from grinding despair to the very beginning of some acceptance of his loss.

## Catherine Martin

The privileged daughter of a powerful senator, Catherine Martin is the next intended victim of Jame Gumb. She is essential to the story, since her captivity initiates the same kind of "ticking clock" plot device used in *Red Dragon*. Starling has a week to find her, just as Graham has a set amount of time before the Tooth Fairy strikes again. Certainly, Starling's determination and investigative skill brings her to the rescue in the nick of time, but for all of that, she would have still been too late if Catherine had not used her own resourcefulness to delay Gumb's plan long enough for Starling to show up at his front door. Catherine plays a major part in her own salvation. In a way, Starling and Catherine are united in sisterhood against a world of men who want to harm them.

Catherine initially does not seem to show much promise for being especially brave or resourceful. While bright, she is best described as a "slacker" or "underachiever." Before her abduction, she is a spoiled child of wealth and privilege. She grew up with a housekeeper named Bea Love taking care of routine domestic chores. Her father died when she was young. She did not do well in school. She is now a student at Southwestern, working as a practice teacher. With her cat, she lives in an apartment more lavishly decorated than most student dwellings. Definitely a party girl in some aspects, driven by zesty hedonism, Catherine enjoys her sex and her drugs. She smokes hashish, eats blotter acid, and takes Polaroid pictures of herself engaged in sexual intercourse with her boyfriend. Altogether, she is an unremarkable young woman until her ordeal puts her to the test. She has to leave behind her slacker-dom, fast.

Knowing she cannot climb or plead her way out of Buffalo Bill's oubliette, she has to rely on her wits to think of a way to escape. Providentially, her youthful experience with sailing a small boat during heavy weather aids her now in calming her mind. She knows that if she can get up out of the pit she is big and strong enough to fight the man holding her captive. She is also willing to use her body as an enticement to bring him close enough to snap his neck with her legs. To get close enough to fight, however, she has to think of a way out of the pit. She must use whatever limited resources are available to her.

The only items in the pit with her are a futon to sleep on and whatever scraps of food Buffalo Bill throws down to her. Her only link to the world above the pit is the bucket and rope lowered to her. Therefore, she devises a plan to lure the dog Precious to the rim of the pit with a chicken bone tied to the rope and bucket. Then, when Precious is pulling at the bone, she yanks the bucket back into the pit, dragging Precious with it. Using the dog as a hostage, she holds Gumb at bay until Starling arrives. The helpless woman held prisoner in the pit of death proves not to be so helpless after all. In a situation very close to hopeless, Catherine devises a stratagem for survival that no one else previously in her position thought of or was able to carry out. She does well enough when put to the test to earn her survival.

## Dr. Frederick Chilton

First introduced in *Red Dragon* as a minor bureaucratic annoyance to both Lecter and Graham, Dr. Frederick Chilton is now a full-blown obstacle to Starling's quest to save Catherine. His vainglory and sexism place him within the same loutish category Freddy Lounds occupied in the previous novel—they even share the same first name. Chilton's thirst for publicity and tendency to grandstand nearly derail Starling at several junctures. His ineptitude is a major contributor to the chain of events leading to Lecter's escape. Little more than a glorified jailer with delusions of professional eminence, Chilton embodies another aspect of Harris's generally dim view of psychiatry as a science. He further represents the worst kind of patriarchal condescension toward professional women.

As head of the Baltimore State Hospital for the Criminally Insane, he is fifty-eight years old when he meets Starling. He is a bachelor living alone and probably always has been. In appearance, he has a mottled-pink complexion (from drinking?) and red-brown hair. The first impression he makes on Starling is anything but positive. Almost immediately he makes a sexist remark about the FBI going to the girls, a remark probably intended as a charming witticism. He compounds the insult by making a clumsy pass at her, offering to show her around Baltimore and then asking for a phone number at which he can reach her. Starling fends off his clumsy verbal advances, which immediately turns Chilton against her. This scene introduces a patriarchal threat of a different kind than a murdering madman—a hostile, rejected professional male with the power to harm a woman's career. Chilton is emblematic of the kind of men, like Paul Krendler, who do, in fact, ruin Starling's career in the next novel.

Once rebuffed, Chilton's enmity toward Starling progresses exponentially. He deliberately offends her by telling her Crawford is clever to send a young woman to Lecter to "turn him on," then follows that up by delighting in showing her the photo of the female nurse brutalized by Lecter several years before. He uses what limited power he has to make Starling uncomfortable and then takes mean pleasure in watching the result. It's a way of demeaning her while simultaneously making himself feel better for having been rejected by her.

The duel of wills now engaged between them, Starling and Chilton spar the next time they meet. Chilton attempts to intimidate her with every weapon at his disposal. He throws around references to his connections and authority. He tries his best to make Starling feel professionally inadequate by asking her if she's been published in professional journals and if she feels she knows what she's doing. He insists on her recording Lecter's conversations, even though he is surreptitiously recording them on his own. Finally, he protests her coming into his hospital and refusing to share information. For all of his bluster, though, he folds quickly when his slip of the tongue about having only one ticket to *Holiday on Ice* lets Starling see into his lonely bachelor's life. Clearly, Chilton is a weak tyrant, wilted by Starling's visible contempt toward him.

His petty tyranny extends to his hospital charges, in particular Lecter. For many years, Chilton has exercised his power to punish Lecter by taking away his books and toilet seat, holding his mail, turning up the volume on a religious television channel outside Lecter's cell, and so forth. Lecter returns these annoyances by ridiculing Chilton in letters published in the professional psychiatric journals, a highly public insult guaranteed to hit Chilton where he lives and inflame his deepest insecurities. Lecter also criticizes Chilton's lack of medical credentials at every turn. This specific bit of mockery plays a critical part in one plot twist. Chilton completely misses the significance of the name "Billy Rubin," the supposed real name of Buffalo Bill given to the authorities by Lecter. The name is derived from bilirubin, a pigment found in bile and human feces, but also conveniently the exact color of Chilton's hair. Chilton makes a public ass of himself by talking about the "search for Billy Rubin" on the evening news shows. Bile is further appropriately associated with Chilton because he harbors great anger as a result of his humiliations. Proven intellectually inferior to Lecter in every way, Chilton aches for revenge.

He thinks he finally has the upper hand when his taping of the sessions between Starling and Lecter alerts him to the bogus offer from the FBI to transfer Lecter if he helps Senator Martin. Chilton takes great satisfaction in telling Lecter that he has been scammed by Starling. Not content with this, Chilton threatens him with incarceration in state institutions. He claims Crawford and Starling are having an affair, a direct attempt to provoke Lecter's jealousy. Finally, he offers Lecter a deal with Senator Martin on the condition Lecter speak only to him and publish nothing. While claiming to protect Lecter, Chilton's real agenda is to garner some favorable publicity. It doesn't take long for Senator Martin to realize she has cast in her lot with a dangerously unreliable publicity hound. This realization frightens her terribly.

Lecter's refusal to grant Chilton access through interviews has long frustrated his goal of recognition within the medical community. Without a medical degree, Chilton seems to be suffering from a massive insecurity complex. He's in way over his head as director of a hospital for the criminally insane. Now he thinks he will gain recognition by inserting himself into the Buffalo Bill case. Instead, the deal Chilton brokers with the senator is a catastrophe, ending in many deaths and Lecter's escape. Like Lounds before him, Chilton's need to be noticed woefully backfires on him. The novel ends with Chilton, disgraced and terrified, hiding in federal protective custody. It seems only a matter of time before Lecter drops in on him to have, as Anthony Hopkins's Lecter says in the film version, "an old friend for dinner."

## Jame Gumb

Harris's third serial killer, Jame Gumb, is a flat character, almost a plot device to create the necessary situation to bring Starling and Lecter together. Arguably, Gumb is one of Harris's missteps; since Gumb is such a loathsome, unsympathetic monster, we have no real interest in him except as a cardboard villain. Unlike the pitiful yet frightening Dolarhyde, Gumb is merely contemptible, barely known to us except in superficial, even clichéd, broad strokes. His murderous transgendered aspirations sometimes seem like clumsily ironic extensions of the novel's feminist focus on Starling as a female in a man's world of murder and law enforcement. However, Gumb remains an example of childhood emotional deprivation as a contributing factor to the kind of rage that makes murder within the heart of the adult.

Gumb's history before the events depicted in the novel is a litany of horrors, all of which are important in understanding how he evolves into a killer.[30] From the moment of his birth, he never really has a chance to develop a strong sense of identity, as symbolized by the accidental omission of the "s" from his first name on his birth certificate. Gumb's insistence on being called "Jame," even though it's a mistake, indicates his desperate overcompensation when his identity is threatened. His mother, a failed beauty contestant and actress in California, descended into alcoholism. The state took Gumb away from her and placed him in a series of foster homes. At the age of ten, his maternal grandparents took him into their care, but he killed them two years later. He was committed to a psychiatric hospital until he reached eighteen, when the state shut down the hospital and released him. Though Harris implies that an unhappy childhood is not sufficient explanation for Gumb's sociopathology, it seems undeniable that the ugly details of Gumb's early history create the profound identity crisis that leads him to kill.

While in the hospital, Gumb received vocational education in tailoring, a skill he later put to a use definitely not intended by the state. Following his release, he obtained marginal employment throughout the years. Murdering the occasional homeless person as an expression of his rage, he hit rock bottom when his lover Benjamin Raspail rejected him and he lost his job at a curio shop. However, his life changed when he chanced upon a butterfly emerging from a cocoon. He believed that he, too, could transform into beauty. He killed, flayed, and beheaded Raspail's lover Klaus, then shoved a cocoon down his throat (an act that leads to his future doom at Starling's hands). To continue his transformation, he applied for sexual reassignment at Johns Hopkins but was rejected during the screening process for a history of violence. Frustrated in his attempt to literally transform his body, he turned to a more imaginative approach, which involved dressing in skins taken from young women he killed across the country. When he kidnaps Catherine Martin, however, his killing time begins to run out.

Gumb is a risky character for Harris to write, since Gumb exhibits behaviors that easily fit into gay stereotypes and thus may offend some readers. Our first glimpse of Gumb at home shows him to be singing along to a musical (*Ain't Misbehavin'*) in falsetto. He fusses over his champagne-colored poodle, Precious. He preens in front of a mirror, at one point tucking his genitals between his legs to appear female. When he becomes excited as the time of Catherine's death draws near, he wants "to fly about the room like Danny Kaye."[31] Harris does attempt to inoculate himself here and there against the charge of homophobia. The director of Johns Hopkins insists to Crawford that transsexuals are not violent. More importantly, Lecter tells Starling that Gumb is not really a transsexual, but believes he is. Gumb acts in a way he perceives as feminine, except it's really a grotesque caricature.

His eagerly anticipated transformation blinds him to the humanity of the women he kills. He thinks of Catherine and the others as "material," kept alive only long enough for starvation to loosen their skins so he can harvest them more easily. He treats them as a means to an end rather than as human beings. Of course, as Harris knows, the research on serial killers shows they typically dehumanize their victims, the better to torture, abuse, mutilate, and/or kill. Certainly, Gumb does have his sadistic side. In the past, he has hunted women through his darkened basement, aided by his night-vision goggles. His current interest in his victims, however, is almost entirely postmortem. Other than keeping them imprisoned for a period of time for practical reasons, he kills them cleanly with a single gunshot to minimize the damage to their skins. While they are alive, he wants no meaningful interaction with them. When he finally is forced to communicate with Catherine after she takes Precious hostage, he despises it. He doesn't want them talking—he wants them dead so he can skin them.

Gumb's goal is to make a woman suit out of those harvested skins in order to effect an imaginative transformation into the beauty he desires. He wants to "preen" and be admired for his tailoring efforts by those with the taste to appreciate them. His longing to achieve feminine beauty originates in the same kind of Freudian mother-fixation that afflicts Norman Bates and, in real life, Ed Gein.[32] For inspiration, he frequently watches a homemade videotape of footage from the 1948 quarterfinals of the Miss Sacramento contest, where his mother competed (but failed to win). Following that footage is a scene from a vintage 1950s "naughty" film depicting naked, or nearly so, women cavorting in a pool and going down a water slide. Gumb falsely believes one of those women is his mother. The juxtaposition of his mother's swimsuit competition and the B-grade skin flick emphasizes Gumb's incestuous desire, which redirects itself into his longing to become as beautiful and desirable as his "Mommy." To underscore this point, Gumb when talking to Precious the poodle often refers to himself as "Mommy" and how beautiful he will be when his project is completed with Catherine's death. The prospect of wearing his completed vest fills him with excitement, primarily because he believes he will then be so beautiful someone will finally find him attractive. Even at the moment of his death, terminally frustrated just at the point of realizing his fantasy of transcendent beauty, he gasps in his ghastly voice to Starling, the beautiful woman who kills him: "How . . . does . . . it feel . . . to be . . . so beautiful?"[33] These last words are a fitting, self-bestowed epitaph for Gumb. All of his life he has coveted beauty that he will never himself achieve.

## STYLE

If *Red Dragon* is a departure from the journalistic style of *Black Sunday*, *Silence* sees Harris achieve mastery of the form. He combines the spare, taut style of his first novel with the poetic lines and multiple allusions of his second. Sensory details are carefully selected to say a lot about a character in a few words. Consider, for example, this vivid speculation from Starling's point of view, as she remembers the roar of an airplane and the sound of voices calling to one another during a Marine airborne nighttime drop above the deserted Hogan's Alley: "And she wondered how it felt to wait for the jump light at the aircraft door, how it felt to plunge into the bellowing dark."[34] This noisy plunge aptly describes Starling's state of mind as she is invited by Crawford into an active serial killer manhunt.

Lecter, living in his own vivid world of tastes and sounds and smells but inaccessible to outside comprehension, owns some of the more striking image-driven moments in the story. In one of the few scenes placing us inside Lecter's consciousness, we experience the world as he processes sensory input in his cage in Memphis. He hears the music of Bach's *Goldberg Variations* as "discrete notes glittering off the steel around him." A paper napkin sliding off his lap to the floor takes a long time to fall—its every descending motion described. Moving his tongue around his mouth searching for the ballpoint tube he has secreted there is described as "a long and interesting trip for his tongue, like a good walk in the Alps."[35] The richness of Lecter's sensory world is so complex, he inhabits a sort of abstracted, waking-dream state in which other people move very slowly.

Other characters in the story cannot enter Lecter's mind or even speculate what might be in there, so they only have visual images of him. Note this description of Lecter in his cell: "The only colors . . . were his hair and eyes and his red mouth, in a face so long out of the sun it leeched into the surrounding whiteness."[36] Another description of Lecter in the prefabricated cell in Memphis sounds similar: "These white bars ribbed the walls. Dr. Lecter had a sleek dark head."[37] These passages vividly convey Lecter's pale and remote otherworldliness, accentuating his exile status. It's worthwhile to compare the description of Lecter's antiseptic white cell to the gloomy underground dungeon assigned to him in the Jonathan Demme film. As opposed to Demme's dark vision, Harris creates a space for Lecter in which the whiteness of the environment stands in for the cold nullity or void Lecter inhabits in his long winter of the heart.

Analogies, similes, and metaphors are also important to Harris. Most of this figurative language has to do with the unhappiness of being human. Given the wintry coldness of the world Harris paints for us, it's not surprising that pain is the most common human experience—the pain of death, the loss of faith and identity and values, the prevalence of childhood physical and emotional trauma, and so forth. Starling's meditation on moths and Buffalo Bill as predators that live on tears compares them both in terms of the pain they metaphorically feed upon. Desolation is the prevailing mood in the description of the maximum security ward in the Baltimore hospital as a place where the tormented inmates "sense beginning day as oysters in a barrel open to their lost tide."[38] Like the oysters far removed from the bay, these pitifully lost souls, far from the rhythms of everyday life and cut off even from the life-giving sun, cry out their anguish to an uncaring, even cruel universe. Wrenching comparisons such as these make the novel an elegy for the human condition.

Harris deliberately fuses his sentences together ungrammatically to create a fast-paced, anxious effect suitable for the scene's tone. It's easy to imagine Harris composing words in a rush to capture simultaneous or rapid consecutive actions, such as Starling's shooting of Gumb in the basement: "He cocked the Python as he brought it up snick snick and the figure blurred, bloomed bloomed green in his vision and his gun bucked in his hand and the floor hit him hard in the back and his light was on and he saw the ceiling."[39] The series of clauses joined by "and" rhythmically carry the action forward in a rush, speeding up the scene overall.

The "mythic present" verb tense we have seen in the first two novels appears in the first sentence of this book, describing the Behavioral Science section in the basement of the Academy building at Quantico. Though the events of the story are relayed in the traditional past tense, the FBI stands apart from the narrative flow, an enduring subterranean stronghold against darkness. The mythic present verb tense is used again when Crawford first mentions Lecter to Starling: "A brief silence follows the name, always, in any civilized gathering."[40] Lecter's first physical description is present tense, emphasizing his transcendence of time and space. Even his cell is described in the present tense, establishing this particular space as a realm apart from the normal ebb and flow of human existence. He exists both within the story time frame and the timeless other-world of legend.

## ALLUSIONS

Verisimilitude is another hallmark of the Harris style. Whatever he writes about is researched so thoroughly that its details are real enough to convince us to suspend disbelief. Even more than in *Red Dragon*, we see many details of police work that reveal Harris's insider knowledge and speak to the privileged "guest" status he enjoys with law-enforcement agencies. Obviously he has been to Quantico, interviewed agents such as John Douglas and Robert K. Ressler, toured the BSU section, and seen Hogan's Alley. He knows police weapons and how to shoot them. He describes how to trace the registration of a car with only a vehicle serial number and the make. He recognizes the jurisdictional rivalries that plague murder investigations and the budgetary fear that the Gramm-Rudman law strikes into the hearts of governmental institutions. He's familiar with a palatal reflector, a Litton police fax, and the Latent Descriptor index. He knows the jargon—"floater" for a body recovered from the water. Showing the details of Starling's education is a natural way for Harris to educate his readers about law enforcement and the criminological and psychological theories underpinning its profiling efforts.

Besides the macho world of police work, many details from the world of sewing, fashion, cooking, and other such traditionally "female" knowledge make their way into the text, as seems appropriate for the narrative focus on a young woman and a killer who wants to shed his male identity in favor of a female one. Gumb applies a hair remover named Friction des Baines. Starling wears Evyan skin cream and L'Air du Temps perfume, which, in combination with the role fragrances play in *Hannibal*, attests to a certain authorial knowledge of cosmetics.

Harris often recasts relatively innocuous details into a new and sinister light. Harris as a gourmand knows what sweetbreads are, so naturally these are the organs removed from Raspail's body to serve to the president and the conductor of the Baltimore Philharmonic. Gumb's character allows Harris the opportunity to turn knowledge of leather works into a macabre recipe for turning the hides of young women into a vest. The recipe in its particulars: Gumb has learned from experience that it takes sudden weight loss to make a human skin, weighing 16 to 18 percent of body weight, easier to remove. The skin of young adults is tightest of all. Collagen bundles within the skin do not allow human skin to be stretched in all directions.[41] Gumb soaks his skins in Native American vegetable extracts and uses beef brains to tan them. He uses underarm and waist darts and a center dart to create a seamless bodice for his "woman suit." As these examples demonstrate, Harris has a gift for putting everyday or even trivial factual information to horrifying use.

Diverse scientific fields are represented as well, all related in one way or another to the thematic progression.

To give one example, entomology, a specialty of Will Graham's in the previous novel, plays a more expanded role here. At the Insect Zoo at the Smithsonian Museum, entomologists Noble Pilcher and Albert Roden play chess with a rhinoceros beetle on the board and preside over a vast collection of 30 million insects and spiders. The entomologists drop jargon freely, such as "mandibles," "paired galae of maxilla," "cremaster," "Lepidoptera," and "mesal margin." We find out there are several varieties of moths that consume only the tears of large land mammals. Since Buffalo Bill uses the death's-head moth, *Acherontia styx*, as his personal emblem, we learn a great deal about them as well. An eerie image of a human skull adorns their backs. They are from Malaysia and steal honey from beehives. An exotic, even alien species, they perfectly fit within a book populated by exiles and outsiders of all types.

The book presents a great deal of information about sexual reassignment or transsexualism, though this resulted in controversy about the novel's perceived homophobia. Dr. Lecter helpfully identifies for us the three centers for transsexual surgery: Johns Hopkins, the University of Minnesota, and Columbus Medical Center. We learn that these centers use various batteries of tests for testing male applicants for the surgery: the Wechsler Adult Intelligence Scale, House-Tree-Person, Rorschach, and Thematic Apperception, among others. On the House-Tree-Person test, we find out exactly how true male transsexuals will draw males, females, houses, and trees. Lecter explains that applicants are rejected because of criminal records, severe childhood disturbances associated with violence, and inappropriate testing responses. Gumb uses his own process to transform himself physically. He takes the hormones Premarin and diethylstilbestrol to enlarge his breasts and thin his hair. As always with a Harris novel, these mini-tutorials on generally unfamiliar subjects, in this case the how's and where's of transsexual surgery, place the audience in the position of a student eagerly

learning from a fascinating but possibly demented professor with an interest in, shall we say, esoteric knowledge.
Harris's research makes this author/reader pedagogical
dynamic possible.

Having settled upon a formula for combining popular
and "high" art into fiction in *Red Dragon*, Harris refines
his approach in *Silence*. Epigraphs once again introduce
the story, taking us into the Harrisverse and priming us
for how to understand it. A passage from 1 Corinthians
(King James translation) is the first epigraph: "If after the
manner of men I have fought with beasts at Ephesus,
what advantageth it me, if the dead rise not?" What isn't
included is the next line, the more commonly known: "Let
us eat and drink for tomorrow we die." This extract from
Paul's epistle to the Corinthians has long been the subject
of analysis to decipher its exact meaning. Nevertheless,
the general premise seems to be that for many people
without religious faith (specifically Christian), life is a
struggle analogous to a battle with wild beasts, resurrection from death is uncertain, and immediate physical
gratification is the only comfort in the face of death. Since
the idea is expressed as a rhetorical or hypothetical question, however, the implication is that the contrary human
condition is also possible. Essentially, both opposing possibilities are united in one statement, a common happening
in metaphysical literature. We've seen this before in
Blake's concept of the marriage of heaven and hell, obviously an important influence on Harris. The choice of the
second epigraph strengthens this metaphysical interpretation. The passage is taken from John Donne's poem "Devotions": "Need I look upon death's head in a ring, that have
one in my face?" Specifically, the poem is from *Devotions
upon Emergent Occasions* (1624), Devotion XVI. Donne
(1572–1631) is best known as a metaphysical poet, famous
for his sermons. From these two epigraphs, it is clear that
Harris is writing no mere potboiler (with apologies to
Mischa Lecter). He promises metaphysical ideas to follow.

Harris cites many poets throughout the book. John Donne makes another appearance, this time unattributed, in Lecter's mocking "condolence" note to Crawford on the fatal illness of his wife. The lines are from "A Fever": "O wrangling schools, that search what fire/Shall burn this world, had none the wit/Unto this knowledge to aspire/That this her fever might be it?" The poem is a plea for a beloved woman not to die from her sickness, which fits Crawford's situation exactly.

e.e. Cummings's meditative poem "Buffalo Bill" probably provides Jame Gumb with his *nom de plume*, though in the story the name is said to originate in Kansas City Homicide. A line from the poem is found in Buffalo Bill's case file: *"how do you like your blueeyed boy Mister Death."* The poem refers to the death of the famous Wild West showman, "Buffalo" Bill Cody. Cody was renowned for his marksmanship, which the poem references in his rapid-fire shooting of clay pigeons. He also re-enacted his scalping of a Sioux chief in his show on a few occasions. Similarly, Harris's Buffalo Bill kills women ("pigeons") one after the other and skins his victims.

When forcing herself to be calm in spite of the need for haste, Starling slightly misquotes a line from T. S. Eliot's poem "Ash Wednesday" (1930), as we've already seen. The actual line ends with "teach us to sit still." It's a plea to the Virgin Mary for spiritual serenity amidst life's travails. The poem is Eliot's "Christian conversion" poem, written after he converted to Anglicism, describing the tension in accepting religion after a life lived without faith. By citing this meditative poem, Harris asks us to reckon with the struggle to reconcile opposite extremes of the same question—in this case, faith and secularism.

In addition to poets, the story directly and indirectly alludes to many novelists, short story writers, and/or philosophers. Each of these writers contributes to the intellectual richness of the book. In some ways, the unacknowledged authors are the most influential, going to the story's very essence. Waugh argues that English novelist John Fowles (1926–2005) provides a fictional template for Gumb in the character of Frederick Clegg in *The Collector* (1963).[42] In Fowles's novel, the sexually obsessed Clegg kidnaps a young woman, Miranda Grey, and holds her prisoner in his basement until she dies. He must then "collect" another woman as if she were a beautiful butterfly. The parallel to Gumb's modus operandi, if not underlying motive, is striking.

Sexton contends that Sir Arthur Conan Doyle (1859–1930), and Bram Stoker (1847–1912) are important to Harris's treatment of detection and, in particular, Dr. Lecter as a character. Sexton succinctly claims there is "one straight line of descent for Hannibal Lecter: Professor Moriarty and Sherlock Holmes combining their talents."[43] Like Holmes, Lecter deduces much about a person based upon few clues. Both Holmes and Lecter share extraordinarily heightened senses, such as smell. Lecter also greatly resembles Moriarty. In the story "The Adventure of the Final Problem" (1893), Professor Moriarty is a criminal mastermind, the "Napoleon of crime" whose formidable intellect matches Holmes's. Professor Moriarty is a clear precedent for Dr. Lecter, the nemesis of the best minds in the FBI. Sexton also delineates the similarities between Lecter and Bram Stoker's character of Dracula, appearing in the novel of the same name in 1897. The parallels between the vampire and the cannibal are obvious—the red eyes, the nocturnal life, the feeding off others, the pale face and red lips, the white teeth used for tearing, and the super strength.[44]

Several writers are directly alluded to. One of the most thematically significant is Lewis Carroll (1832–1898), author of the classic children's books *Alice's Adventures in Wonderland* (1865) and *Through the Looking Glass, and What Alice Found There* (1871). Starling thinks of Carroll when Crawford's tone reminds her of the caterpillar that dispenses advice to Alice. The allusion works in a couple of ways. Starling resembles Carroll's youthful heroine, in that both Alice and Starling leave their everyday reality ("down the rabbit hole") to enter a strange world transformed, with only their wits and courage to guide them.[45] The caterpillar itself is a symbol of transformation, since it will one day become a butterfly. Gumb gravitates toward the chrysalis of the death's-head moth as a token of his own desired transformation into beauty. The allusion to Carroll reinforces the transformation theme.

Another writer, the English novelist Jane Austen (1775–1817), is referenced when we see the orderly Barney reading Austen's novel *Sense and Sensibility* (1811). Lecter, the consummate reader, has been encouraging Barney to expand his intellectual horizons, which no doubt explains Barney's choice of reading material. The novel is Austen's first, about the personal growth of two sisters, Elinor and Marianne Dashwood. Starling also develops as a person through the course of her adventures, thus making the allusion to Austen's heroines a fitting one.

Harris alludes to a famous writer of philosophy. During a session with Starling, Lecter mocks Crawford for a speech he gave to the National Police Academy, during which Crawford quoted from the Roman writer/philosopher and emperor, Marcus Aurelius (121 C.E.–180 C.E.). Lecter explains the relevance of the stoic philosopher's ideas to the case: "The Emperor counsels simplicity. First principles. Of each particular thing, ask: What is it in itself, in its own constitution? What is its causal nature?"[46] Marcus Aurelius's principle of simplicity leads Starling to the conclusion (with a little helpful coaching from Lecter) that the killer is serving his need to transform into something beautiful. Keeping it simple, as it were, leads Starling right to Buffalo Bill's front door.

Harris alludes to several significant works of art and architecture. In his cell, Lecter keeps his sketch of the Palazzo Vecchio and the Duomo, seen from the Belevedere in Florence, Italy. The Palazzo Vecchio is the town hall of

Florence, the site of Inspector Pazzi's hanging and disembowelment in *Hannibal*. "The Duomo" is a short-hand reference to the cathedral church, or Basilica di Santa Maria del Fiore, begun in 1296 and completed in 1436. The church is capped by the dome designed by Filippo Brunelleschi (1377–1446). The Belvedere is the short name of a fort built between 1590 and 1595 by Ferdinando I de' Medici, a member of one of Florence's most powerful families. In one drawing and two sentences, Lecter captures a great deal of Florentine history and art. Incidentally, this reference also sets the direction of the whole future of the Lecter franchise.

Lecter refers Starling to paintings of the crucifixion by the Italian painter Duccio di Buoninsegna (ca. 1255–1318). Duccio is known to have painted at least three different crucifixion scenes on two triptychs and one altarpiece. According to Lecter, the details of the crucifixion in Duccio's work are accurate (a debatable claim, incidentally). In these paintings, nails have been driven through Christ's palms. The figure's feet rest upon a block of wood. In the painting housed in the Opera del Duomo Museum in Siena, Italy, Christ is flanked by the two thieves mentioned in the Gospel of John, whereas in the two paintings respectively housed in the Royal Collections of Hampton Court in England and the Boston Museum of Fine Arts, Christ is the sole crucified figure. In Lecter's drawing, Christ is missing from the center cross, while the two thieves hang on either side with their legs broken. Lecter, whose mockery of Christianity is a matter of record, says his drawing shows what the thief who had been promised Paradise really got—a horrible death.

Lecter also vouches for the veracity of the gory details of another painting, *The Flaying of Marsayas* (ca. 1570–1576). Tiziano Vecelli, or Titian (ca. 1485–1576), is the painter. In Greek mythology, Marsayas is a satyr who challenges Apollo to a music contest, loses, and pays a fearsome price. His fate is depicted in Titian's disturbing

Duccio di Buoninsegna, *Triptych: the Crucifixion; the Redeemer with Angels; Saint Nicholas; Saint Gregory*. Museum of Fine Arts, Boston, Grant Walker and Charles Potter Kling Funds. Copyright 2009 by Museum of Fine Arts, Boston.

painting. He hangs upside down while being skinned. Pan brings a bucket of water while dogs wait to lap up the blood and eat any fallen scraps. Lecter references the painting as evidence of his point that flaying victims are inverted so that they remain conscious.

Another painting Lecter appreciates is Theodore Gericault's (1791–1824) painting *The Raft of the Medusa* (ca. 1818), because Gericault studied numerous corpses in morgues and hospitals to get a sense of the proper skin textures. The painting depicts a haggard collection of survivors amid the dead and dying, on a raft cast adrift following the infamous wreck of the French naval frigate the *Meduse* in 1816. Cannibalism was one of the horrors the castaways suffered—probably another reason Lecter likes the painting.

As these paintings demonstrate, Harris delights in alluding to classical artistic representations of heinous deeds.

Another of Lecter's artistic interests is classical music. In his Memphis cell, for example, he listens to an aria named the *Goldberg Variations* (1741), composed by Johann Sebastian Bach (1685–1750), as performed by the famous pianist Glenn Gould (1932–1982) in 1955. This particular composition is renowned for its complex musical structure; Lecter's fine ear can hear every distinct note. Bach as played by Gould is obviously a favorite of Lecter's, since he listens to Bach's *Two and Three Part Inventions* (ca. 1723) while staying in the Marcus Hotel. Music is another dimension of the value Lecter places on art, a trait hinted at in *Red Dragon* but expanded upon here. The range of Lecter's tastes grows in each of his incarnations.

For Harris, popular arts stand side-by-side with the "high" arts represented by Bach, Duccio, John Donne, and others. References to Madonna, Walt Disney, *People* magazine, and professional wrestling crop up frequently. These details help to establish the narrative in the cultural fads of a particular time and place, but they also tend to advance the themes. For instance, Lecter slams both the banality of Christianity and popular culture by attempting to patent his design of a crucifixion watch modeled after a Mickey Mouse watch. Analysis of the more obscure allusions yields more interesting connections. When Starling visits Lecter for the second time, someone down the hall from his cell is whistling the Scottish tune "Over the Sea to Skye." As the Web site *Dissecting Hannibal* explains, the song is about the escape of Bonnie Prince Charlie (1720–1788) to the Isle of Skye, aided by a woman named Flora MacDonald. He was an exiled Jacobite who sought the English, Scottish, and Irish thrones. We've seen the Jacobite connection before, in *Red Dragon*.[47] Here, Harris may be playfully alluding to his previous novel, but the song also foreshadows Lecter's escape, made possible by his relationship with Starling.

The funeral home assistant, Lamar, talks about the professional wrestlers Duke Keomuka and Satellite Monroe,
both of whom played villains in their careers, as the
favorites of a couple of local ne'er-do-wells. The latter
wrestler is most likely an allusion to Sputnik Monroe
(1928–2006), who achieved fame in Memphis, Tennessee,
during the segregation era of the 1960s for his demand
that black patrons be allowed to sit anywhere they
wanted during his exhibitions. One of the themes of
*Silence* is the integration of women (represented by
Starling) into the FBI, so this allusion fits, as well as adds
some richness, to the rural West Virginia environment
Lamar inhabits. Through examples such as these throughout the book, Harris consistently closes the distance in
the traditional division between elite and popular culture
as a singular mark of his fiction.

## SYMBOLS

The symbolic structure of Harris's novels, as we have
heretofore seen, depends a great deal upon the associations attached to animals and insects in story context.
*Silence* both repeats and expands upon the meanings
attached to, say, moths and birds. Scar symbolism, on the
other hand, is not as prevalent as it has been in the first
two novels. The relatively minor textual emphasis on the
lingering effects of childhood abuse may explain this shift
in the underlying symbolic construction.

The ways in which moths are represented invest the
story with much of its meaning. The word *moth* already
carries some sinister connotations, probably for the
destruction that some moth species wreak upon clothing,
trees, crops, and so forth. The term *moth-eaten* derives
from such habits. The simile "like a moth to the flame,"
based on observation of the apparently suicidal tendency
of moths to fly too close to lights or fire, is often used to
describe the actions of people irresistibly drawn toward

certain self-destructive behaviors. Buffalo Bill, who embraces the moth as personal totem, is as doomed as the moth flitting ever closer to the desired consummation of light and heat.

Yet in doom he finds transformation. In the finest tradition of English professors, Lecter helpfully explicates to Starling that for Buffalo Bill the moth symbolizes the process of change. For many cultures, as Lecter certainly knows, the transformation of the humble pupa into the magnificent butterfly represents hope for a new life, rebirth, and the soul's freedom from the body. The moth, however, is a more ambiguous symbol. It represents the process of change, but given that the moth in this book is the death's-head, it symbolizes evil and death as well. Gumb's moth fetish captures the paradox in his character. He yearns for transformation into someone beautiful, but uses murder to facilitate that change. Inspired by the sight of the death's-head image, Gumb feels lighter, as if he were already leaving behind the indignities of being trapped in a hated body. Transcendence is both liberation and death, an association strengthened throughout the book by not only Gumb but other characters. Crawford is losing weight as he braces himself for widowhood. Lecter sheds his mask and straightjacket, dons Officer Pembry's face, and undergoes plastic surgery to change appearance. Starling herself, inexorably drawn into police work by the memory of a slain father, undergoes a professional transformation that brings her into close contact with death. Like caterpillars morphing into moths, all of the major characters change, but they circle the presence of death constantly.

Much like the moth, spiders are associated with death in the book. In the cosmology implied by Harris's symbolic structure, selected "low" creatures (the night-flying moth, mice, spiders) are denizens of the dark places, the underworld. Despite the museum guard's admonition to Starling not to lump spiders in with the insects, Harris uses them all to represent the underbelly of civilization. The otherworldly interior of the storage unit, where Klaus's head rots from the cap down in its bottle of alcohol, is one such place. In this forbidden zone, orb weavers bind their tiny victims and leave them to shrivel. Starling begins to worry about deadly brown recluse spiders as she explores the macabre landscape within the storage unit. Primed by this eerie first encounter with the world of Buffalo Bill, Starling thinks of him as a trapdoor spider. Like the subterranean spider, Gumb pounces upon his prey, immobilizes them, and drags them back to preserve their bodies (or at least part of them) in his vast underground abattoir. Through these scenes, Harris capitalizes on the widely recognized symbol of a spider's lair as a den of evil.

Much of the meaning associated with birds and larger mammals in *Red Dragon* (and to some extent in *Black Sunday*) is carried over. Canine imagery, for example, appears again briefly in association with Graham, described as one of Crawford's keenest pack hounds. This reference reinforces the association between bloodhounds and the act of detection/profiling, which Starling is now learning how to do. Waugh makes the interesting observation that the real hound is Lecter himself, "who attacks like a dog killing a rat"[48] and exhibits a sense of smell keener than anyone else's. As guardian of the secrets of the serial killer's mind, he is like the three-headed hound Cerberus, preventing access to the underworld. While Graham had some success in penetrating this barrier, Starling as a woman goes further than Graham ever could because Lecter grants her access. She quiets the baying of the hound.

Birds again serve a symbolic function. Starling's last name, for one, links her to birds. It's an almost daringly Hitchcockian flourish to name her after a bird, since after all, "bird" is British slang for female. Alfred Hitchcock's complex and arguably misogynistic deployment of bird imagery in *Psycho* (1960) and (naturally) *The Birds* (1963) is echoed here. Starling, with its *-ling* ending, is a diminutive word, suggesting she is tiny or puny, outgunned in a paternalistic world and potentially the prey of the female-slaying killer she seeks. However, she is always scrappy and resilient, qualities symbolically associated with the starling.

Many other birds have significant meaning in the story, specifically, owls, pigeons, and crows. In many cultures, the owl traditionally symbolizes intelligence, wisdom, and power. Appropriately, Starling's mentor Crawford is described as having an owl-like face. The comparison captures the paradox of Crawford's wise but predatory nature. In some Eastern cultures, the owl is an avatar of the guardian of the secrets of the underworld, which may explain why Klaus's head in the bottle is described as owlish in appearance. Klaus is a mute senti-nel at the gates of Buffalo Bill's realm.

Pigeons frequently appear in the story, usually as a symbol of female vulnerability to males. After a nasty face-off with the masculinized Senator Martin and Paul Krendler, Starling watches a pigeon foraging for food in a parking lot, wind ruffling its feathers. Starling's own feathers have just been ruffled, so she identifies with the pigeon's lonely quest. More ominously, Frederica Bimmel's father, Gustav, keeps hundreds of pigeons, of various sizes and colors, in coops in his backyard. The unsettling evidence of his activity reaches far down the river from his house, with feathers riding on the surface of the water. This image of the feathers on the "skin" of the river sets the tone for Starling's investigation of Frederica's lonely life and death. The imprisonment of the birds at Frederica's house foreshadows her fate as a captive in Gumb's house. Several pages later, it becomes clear why Gustav keeps so many pigeons. Starling sees a PVC pipe from his shed gurgle bloody water out into the river, fol-lowed by Gustav appearing with blood on his trousers and slaughtered pigeons in a plastic bag. She turns away from this sight, probably because it reminds her of the slaughter of helpless animals she witnessed on the Montana ranch. The bloody scene specifically genders the merciless slaughterer as male and, in light of Starling's identification with birds in general, the caged pigeons as female.

Not all birds are symbolic female victims of male killers. In one case, the bird is an active aggressor. The crow is a personal symbol of enmity for Starling. She forms this association in her childhood because of a crow that persistently steals shiny objects from the housekeeping cart belonging to her mother, a motel cleaning woman. Because she was told by her mother in one of these motel rooms that she was being sent to Montana, Starling now often dreams of the antagonistic crow and thinks of it again when Chilton's interference seemingly dooms Catherine. The crow symbolizes to her all of the obstacles she has endured because of the loss of her father and the impoverishment of her youth.

Other than birds, the most heavily symbolic animal in the book is the lamb. The book's title immediately makes that clear. The lamb is traditionally associated both with Christ's role as protector of humanity (the good shepherd) and victim of it (the crucified martyr). For the poet William Blake, a writer we know to be important to Harris, the lamb is a symbol of innocence and purity in Christianity, as represented in his poem "The Lamb" from *Songs of Innocence* (1789). The lamb's personal significance to Starling, however, does not become apparent to us until she reveals to Lecter how she was woken up one night by the sound of spring lambs being slaughtered out in the barn. Knowing she could do nothing for the lambs, she tried to run away (unsuccessfully, as it turned out) with Hannah.[49] Lecter accurately diagnoses her need now to catch Buffalo Bill and save Catherine as motivated by her memory of her earlier failure to save the lambs. Rather poetically, he asks her if she thinks she "could make the lambs stop screaming."[50] At this moment, with the clues falling into place in another of the "eureka" moments that characterize Harris's fiction, the enigmatic meaning of the book's title becomes clear. It foretells the happy outcome of Starling's rescue mission—the lambs will be silent. The last line of the book tells us that Starling "sleeps deeply, sweetly, in the silence of the lambs."[51]

## THEMES

*Silence* revisits some primary themes of *Red Dragon*, de-emphasizes others, and adds new ones. The danger to the normative heterosexual family is almost entirely absent this time around. In part, this occurs because *Silence* is written from the point of view of a young female protagonist without a family, so the most thematically appropriate kind of threat for this character to face is a killer of single women. Here, the traditional family unit is already lost beyond recovery, represented by Starling's abandonment by her parents at an early age. Starling grows up basically alone. Her family, to the extent that she forms a new one, consists of two surrogate fathers (three if we count the institutional affiliation with the FBI) and an African American sister. Starling has no serious romantic interest, excluding the pleasant distraction offered by Noble Pilcher as a reward for her rescue of Catherine. One of the novel's most important themes, then, is the difficulty the female outsider encounters in making her way through a patriarchal, white world and the strategies by which she overcomes these obstacles. Gender politics are front and center.

The antagonists who pose serious obstacles to Starling's quest are, with the exception of Senator Martin, white males. Two of them are doctors, representing the male-cloistered world of the medical/psychiatric profession. Dr. Chilton is a sexist both attracted to and threatened by Starling, first trying to get into her pants and then shutting her out when she rebuffs him. Though not her direct employer or colleague, Chilton's behavior constitutes a type of sexual harassment routinely faced by women. Dr. Lecter represents a different kind of challenge. He doesn't necessarily want to get into Starling's pants, although he certainly seems to enjoy asking her whether her foster father had sex with her or Crawford fantasizes sexually about her. What he wants most, it seems, is to get into her head. He refuses to give her valuable information until he, in effect, coerces her consent to rape her psychologically. While Lecter's forced "therapy" is at some level undeniably helpful to Starling's growth, it's worth noting the professional ethics violation he commits in forcing his "help" upon a reluctant patient. What he does to her is a melodramatically extreme version of workplace "quid pro quo" (to use Lecter's favored term) sexual harassment. Starling "consents" to Lecter's will, but only under the duress posed by the need to garner the necessary information to save Catherine.

Paul Krendler of the Justice Department poses a direct professional threat to Starling. He backs Senator Martin over Starling when they discover Starling looking for clues in Catherine's apartment. He then sends a request to the Office of Professional Responsibility that Starling be suspended from the Academy. Faced with a female who is not cowed by his authority, Krendler uses the power of his office to try to hurt her career. As we find out in *Hannibal*, he is successful in doing it. The "smart mouth" of the assertive female often brings down such patriarchal retaliation.

The paternalistic protection of well-meaning but misguided males represents another kind of threat. Protecting women from the more unpleasant side of living is a traditionally chivalric attitude, but it demeans them by implying that women are helpless to handle themselves. Crawford, as teacher/mentor to Starling, generally treats her with the proper respect as a colleague-in-training, but he does make one significant blunder at the West Virginia funeral parlor. To a get a sheriff who is resentful of federal interference away from an audience of deputies, Crawford says to him he'd rather not discuss certain elements of a sex crime in front of a woman. Starling must conceal her anger in front of a gawking male audience.[52] She later calls Crawford on his ploy since cops look at him to see how to act around her. To his credit, Crawford acknowledges his mistake to her. Nevertheless, the ease with which his men-only strategy worked on the rural sheriff illustrates the extent to which traditional paternalistic attitudes are ingrained.

The extreme misogyny of the male serial killer, embodied in Jame Gumb, poses the most direct threat to female survival. Starling, a woman attempting to succeed in a male-dominated profession, is the only thematically fit character to stop him. Gumb's desire to transform into feminine beauty adds another layer of complication to this literal war between the sexes. He never leaves biology or socially coded gender attributes behind. He may tuck his genitals from view, but he is never actually castrated. Although Gumb hates his own identity, he hates women even more. He clubs, imprisons, murders, and skins them without mercy or consideration for their humanity, an extreme manifestation of ordinary male fear, anger, and/or hatred turned sideways into violence directed against women. Ultimately, he is a caricature bearing little resemblance to actual women, or for that matter, male homosexuals, transvestites, or transsexuals. What he does represent is an extreme case of male fear/hatred of women. The mask he wears, or more literally the woman suit he constructs, cannot hide it.

Gumb's pathology is built upon one essential need. He covets the beauty of femaleness for himself to wipe out his perceived ugliness. To Starling, Lecter identifies the act of seeing as the means by which we identify those things (and people) we wish to covet. He does not exempt women from this implied moral accusation; however, the book's totality suggests pathological acts of seeing, that is, those designed to appropriate for destructive purposes, are a particularly male phenomenon. As in *Red*

*Dragon*, *Silence* features a serial killer obsessed with films and making lethal use of surveillance technology for stalking purposes. Gumb is primed for the kill by watching old film footage of his mother on stage during a beauty contest. Once he identifies a target, he lurks unseen in the dark, enjoying the superior technological advantage of night-vision goggles over his prey. In the Harrisverse, it is difficult to imagine a female "seeing" in such a murderous fashion. In fact, at the novel's climax, Starling is rendered blind (just like Reba McClane) while engaged in a deadly cat-and-mouse game with Gumb wearing his infrared goggles in the pitch-black basement. Repeatedly, Harris codes the male act of seeing as potentially murderous.[53]

Faced with the hostility of a male world, women adopt a number of protective strategies. One is to confront it head-on through integration. This is exactly what Starling does by entering the FBI Academy, a bastion of patriarchy. By wearing its uniform, she commits her own kind of cross-gender transgression against tradition. Senator Martin, in the men's club environment of the U.S. Senate, is even more transgressive in acquiring power. Lecter's bogus compliment to Senator Martin about loving her suit is not only a compliment but a mocking recognition of her accomplishment.

Starling does not shy away from confrontation with dangerous or powerful men. She defies Krendler's direct orders, stands up to Lecter, and chases Buffalo Bill to his lair. Her fierce drive to make the world right and silence her own inner demons takes her past these barriers. She realizes that as the only woman hunting a killer of women she brings insights to the case that her male colleagues do not possess. She knows the male investigators have overlooked many potential clues because they are not part of the female world she knows. Her knowledge of sewing, a traditional female craft, allows her to make the connection no other male investigator has made or is likely to make—Buffalo Bill has been seriously trained to sew. Starling forces her way into the all-male investigation and breaks the case, although ironically not without assistance from her two powerful male mentors, Crawford and Lecter.

Another strategy for women in a dangerous patriarchal environment is to create a sisterhood as a type of Maginot Line against all manner of sexism and misogyny. The model of how this works is found in the relationship between Starling and her roommate, Ardelia Mapp. Their dormitory room is both a peaceful oasis and a fortification for both of them after long, stressful days out among men. The two form both a support network and a working team for each other. Mapp is a helper on Starling's quest, chasing clues with her and comforting her when she cries. Mapp is a ferocious defender of Starling. When a male classmate makes a crude reference to Starling as Melvin Pelvis, Mapp verbally slams the young man to the extent that he leaves his breakfast uneaten on the table. Starling finds Mapp to be reliable in a way no man has ever been. The relationship between Mapp and Starling, while not sexual in nature, is nevertheless quite intimate. Their living and working together is a viable feminist alternative to the more traditional family unit Starling lost as a child and never regains. In fact, Starling and Mapp's sisterhood is probably the most positive family portrait to be found anywhere in Harris's fiction.

The sisterhood, theoretically, includes all women. Starling, usurping a traditionally male function, anoints herself protector of Catherine Martin and avenger of the murdered women. Standing over the body of Kimberly, the West Virginia murder victim, she commits to stopping this killer of women. She thinks of all past and potential victims of Buffalo Bill as sisters. Honoring this commitment to the endangered sisterhood brings her down into Buffalo Bill's basement, against her better professional judgment, to save Catherine.

Of course, not all female relationships in the book are mutually supportive. The one between Starling and Senator Martin becomes downright adversarial. The senator is furious when she learns Starling and Crawford have made a phony offer to Lecter in her name. Her anger increases when she finds Starling digging for clues in Catherine's apartment. Nevertheless, Starling tries to be sympathetic to her, knowing that she is facing the imminent death of a daughter. Starling appreciates Senator Martin's scrappiness. Overall, Harris achieves the task he sets for himself in creating strong, complex female characters.

Harris's few black characters continue to perform services for the white characters in settings far removed from the Southern Gothic world in which Dolarhyde exists in *Red Dragon*. In *Silence*, a black guard at the Smithsonian serves as Starling's guide to the entomology department. Starling idly compares him in her mind to a large statue of a South Seas chieftain, an association sounding almost neo-colonial. Ardelia Mapp, a black character more significant to the plot, supports Starling at home. When Starling needs a laugh or a cry, Mapp is there to serve her every mood. During one support session, Mapp looks older, perhaps even maternal, to Starling. We next see Mapp bringing her an Orange Crush, offering her tea, handing her a Coke and Jack Daniel's after the case is over, and generally doing other motherly kindnesses for her when she is tired. The black woman habitually serving the white woman of rural origins is a charged dynamic, to say the least, within the context of the nation's history of slavery.

Other aspects of Mapp's characterization verge on the offensively stereotypical. Her "street" talk is a rather common portrayal of African American women in popular culture. She says things like "You come talking that mushmouth, people say you eat up with the dumb-ass, girl,"[54] "I *been* knowing that,"[55] and "Girl, they'll sail you off the back steps like a dead Easter chick."[56] She applies the label "signifying" to Krendler, a term popularly associated with black culture. Its meanings are subtle and many, but boil down to "insulting." Additionally, Mapp is notably more sexualized than Starling. She shows more interest in men, for instance calling one classmate "hot" and eagerly telling Starling about seeing him in his python briefs through a window. She advises Starling to "go wild" with Pilcher, a thinly disguised directive for her to have sex with him. Mapp's earthiness, as represented by her vernacular and her sexual interest, is clearly a positive force in Starling's life. However, Starling represents the intellectual driver of the plot, whereas Mapp, an academically excellent student in her own right, does little to contribute in that direction. She's there mostly to make Starling comfortable and confirm the rightness of Starling's inductive conclusions. Harris is rightly praised for his skills in characterization, but the African American characters, to the extent there are any in the story at all, are definitely flatter than the primary white characters. Having tackled gender politics in *Silence* from the point of view of a young woman, and having done a laudable job by most critical assessments, Harris has yet to deal with race in any meaningful way.

Transformation, or the capacity to change toward some higher form, remains a central thematic concern for Harris. By this novel, he has developed a fully realized articulation of what might be called "Gothic transcendentalism." If American transcendentalism is a basically optimistic affirmation of the individual capacity to become godlike in terms of wholeness with nature, the Gothic variety of it examines the dangers of such an endeavor—the megalomania, the self-absorption, the cruelty, and frankly the futility of it. The novel takes the position that if higher ideals and forms are mere constructs of the mind, without some absolute basis in external reality, then individual attempts to achieve higher states or planes of existence are fundamentally flawed, self-delusional, and even doomed.

By now it's becoming clear, as Magistrale argues, that two of Harris's serial killers to date—Francis Dolarhyde and Jame Gumb—are pitiful failures of the transcendental imagination, however scary they might be. Only Lecter seems to have a more down-to-earth perspective, freed of any delusional belief there is a God to aspire to Become.[57] "Simplicity," Lecter coaches Starling—simplicity in all things, including keeping one's feet on the ground and head in the present moment. Gumb's imaginative project to become a woman by donning their skins fails because it is too magical, too based on a future idealized state, and too complex in its defiance of natural law.

We've already seen how the moth symbolism supports the theme of transformation. The caterpillar's progression into moth-dom is predetermined by genetics, rooted in natural causes and evolution. Gumb looks upon this sequence as a template for him to follow to change into a more beautiful being. Following nature's lead is not necessarily a destructive act. Nor is seeing the divine in natural processes, as American transcendentalist Ralph Waldo Emerson (1803–1882) did. Where Gumb gets it wrong is redirecting his inner hatred for women into his transcendental belief system. He takes the precedent of the caterpillar's transformation way too literally, thinking that if he changes his outer form to resemble the thing he wants to be, he will therefore *be that thing*. "Mommy's going to be so *beautiful*!" Gumb exclaims to Precious on the eve of harvesting Catherine's hide, about as optimistic a statement of anything as we are likely to find in Harris's fiction. Gumb really believes in what he is doing. The infusion of pathology into the process, while adding a poisonous dollop of magical thinking, deforms it into a grotesque parody of the transcendental drive.

The serial nature of Gumb's crimes, or those of Dolarhyde before him, suggest a certain frustration with achieved results, leading to the inevitable repetition of the act toward some future perfect realization of it. We discover Gumb has a long history of killing some men but mostly women, evolving through distinct phases. For instance, he goes through a period where he hunts young women through the dark of his basement warren, finally shooting them to end the game. Ultimately this proves unsatisfying, so he switches to his current project of skinning heavy women in order to become one. Had Starling not killed him, it is very likely Gumb would have remained full of hate at his core and found yet another way of killing women to provide some temporary relief from his past.

Another theme is the power of memory. Memory is a driving force behind both Gumb's and Starling's actions. Both characters acutely feel the memories of childhood abandonment in the present. Both spent various time in state institutions: Gumb in foster care and a psychiatric hospital, Starling in orphanages. Both lost beloved parents. Obviously they cope with painful memory in vastly different ways, but their memories remain influential in determining their actions for change now.

Starling's- life-long drive to become an FBI agent is rooted in memory. She wants to pay homage to her father while redeeming his pointless death at the same time. The memory of her mother's lonely struggle against poverty and widowhood also sustains her. She thinks of these empowering memories as "hand-me-down grace," wisdom inherited from the struggles of her ancestors. Lecter first articulates the importance of memory in the story when he tells Starling he has memory instead of a view. The narrative explores how memory plays a role in transformation. After all, if we do not remember where we came from, how do we know where to go next with any sense of purpose?

The power of memory is a common theme in Gothic and neo-Gothic literature, especially in the Southern Gothic. In the modern South, memory of the lost antebellum culture remains very close to the surface, so the Southern Gothic as a regional literature routinely visits the haunted past. Arguably *Silence* falls into this literary category. Though there are no truly supernatural elements, it's striking how haunted the narrative is. It circles repeatedly to what has come before. It's a sequel revisiting several characters and themes of *Red Dragon*. The memory of murdered women hangs over the story like a burial shroud. The plot revisits the places they lived and died, to reconstruct their lives. Starling and Gumb are driven by their haunted pasts. Crawford remembers happier times with his dying wife Bella. Only Lecter seems to have sprung from history without a history (and even that changes in the next novel). The power of the past to still harm us through memory is the key motivating force for change in *Silence*, whose very title is a plea for the quieting of the restless past.

As do all of Harris's books so far, this one asks us to consider the theme of what evil is and its role in making murder. The oracular character of Lecter is the primary means by which Harris explores this theme. During their first session, Lecter responds with what seems to be genuine indignation to Starling's suggestion that environment somehow played a role in his becoming a serial killer: "Nothing happened to me, Officer Starling. *I* happened. You can't reduce me to a set of influences. You've given up good and evil for behaviorism. . . . You've got everybody in moral dignity pants—nothing is ever anybody's fault. Look at me, Officer Starling. Can you stand to say I'm evil? Am I evil, Officer Starling?"[58]

Here Lecter argues against the power of the environment to shape human moral behavior. Put simply, one's surroundings do not explain or justify behavior. Some of these actions can be labeled "good" and others "evil." Like any teacher, he is forcing Starling to a reckoning with definitions. To understand the nature of evil, one has to define it.

Lecter scoffs at Starling's simplistic claim that destructiveness and evil are the same thing. Storms and fire and hail are evil if it's that's simple, he tells her. Then he asks her if church collapses are evil and, if so, who did them. If God exists, Lecter concludes, He loves destruction, and creates both the ugliness of typhoid and the loveliness of swans. In this exchange, Lecter gives voice to the kind of interrogation into the nature of God found in William Blake's poem "The Tyger" from *Songs of Experience* (1794). Blake concludes the existence of the "fearful symmetry" of predators like the tiger argues for a dualistic conception of God, perhaps one with two distinct "personalities" that could be respectively labeled "good" and "evil." There may even be two distinct creators, one being the "demiurge," an imperfect or even evil creator of the imperfect material world. Lecter doesn't cite Blake here, but he nevertheless raises the same theological question Blake does. Lecter's iconoclasm is obvious, but what is more ambiguous is whether he doesn't believe in God at all or whether he thinks God (or some aspect of God) is evil. Even his caustic remark to Starling about God dying in a mattress fire is more about hurting Starling for deceiving him than any firm statement about God's existence and role, if any, in the foundations of human morality.

One thing is for sure. Lecter cannot abide traditional Christianity. Through his crucifixion drawings and watches, he mocks its theology and what he sees as its obsession with the bloody sacrifice of Christ at every turn. Even the signature aspect of Lecter's murders—the cannibalism and the serving of human organs to unsuspecting dinner guests—is a parody of the Christian belief in transubstantiation at the moment of communion. Chilton, recognizing Lecter's animosity toward Christianity, routinely punishes him by turning up the volume on a television outside of Lecter's cell tuned to a religious channel. While the origin of Lecter's specific antipathy toward Christianity is never made clear, it's likely Lecter discounts it as a philosophical/theological framework because as practiced by most people, he believes its conclusions are too simplistic, too black and white.

The book does acknowledge the power of religious belief in one of its most traditional functions: offering solace. The scene where Bella dies at home with Crawford is poignant for the way Crawford attempts to embrace it in his time of grief. Crawford says a brief prayer over her, hoping his words are true but not knowing if Bella has any soul to find a home in the afterlife. As we have noted already, he then looks out a window to the empty east. Since east is the symbolic direction of the Christian promise of resurrection, it is obvious here Crawford's faith is based more on wishful thinking than devout belief. Whatever good or evil may be in Harris's fiction, these concepts cannot rely on any warrant of outside higher revealed truth. We make mercy and we make murder all on our own, to return to *Red Dragon*'s final words.

Beyond questioning the metaphysical basis for morality, Harris steadfastly refuses to offer any pat solution to the problem of human evil. What he does is return us, as surely as memory is the means by which we interrogate the past, to his overriding theory of dualism in human nature, first sketched out in *Black Sunday* and amplified in *Red Dragon*. Our civilized impulses exist side-by-side with our primal ones, with the contest going more often than not to the instinctual side. The bloody history of human civilization, with its painful progress forward and its frequent regressions to carnage, argues for the primacy of our reptilian-brain instincts. As human beings, we construct elaborate justifications for releasing our violent impulses and rationalizations for dealing with the consequences. Yet all is not lost, since our ability to make murders is offset by our ability to control them, if only we have the discipline to do so.

*Silence* is by far the most optimistic of Harris's books in its redemption of the central character through her ability to resist the moral contamination of being in close contact with murder. The Harrisverse has never looked so positive as it does in this book. However, the publication of *Hannibal* would offer a much bleaker assessment of our plight—and howls of outrage from those who had embraced Starling as an icon of female empowerment.

# 5

# "Pity Has No Place at My Table": *Hannibal*

Thomas Harris's fourth novel, *Hannibal* (1999), marks a radical departure from his earlier, rather formulaic crime-thriller novels. What does one make of a novel in which a cannibalistic serial killer is the romantic leading man, a strong-willed heroine dedicated to the protection of the helpless becomes a cannibal and the consort to a murderer, and a pitifully mutilated and crippled survivor of that killer's rampage is actually the villain plotting a nefarious revenge scheme involving man-eating swine? There is little of the rationalistic police-procedural tone and storyline of *Red Dragon* and *The Silence of the Lambs* present. If tension, a swift pace, and tautness of prose dominate Harris's first three novels, then this story lingers, meanders, and circles. The Baroque world of *Hannibal* is a surreal one, in which a liberated Lecter dodges a tangled, corrupt skein of authorities and vigilantes across half the world, all with unflappable aplomb, until he too, like Catherine Martin, must be rescued from a fate worse than death by Clarice Starling. He returns the favor by "curing" Starling of her father-fixation and memories of early childhood traumas. Starling in return heals Lecter's own traumatic childhood memory of his murdered and eaten sister, Mischa. The novel ends with Starling and Lecter, now lovers, on the lam in South America attending an opera.

Upon reflection, however, the plot twists and reversals of *Hannibal* are not quite so unexpected. Lecter has manifested a more-than-friendly interest in Starling since their first meeting, when he became agitated by the sight and scent of Starling marked with the semen flung at her by the inmate Multiple Miggs. Their relationship is built partly on paternal mentoring, partly on courtship. As for Starling joining her mind and body with a killer, one need only look at the law enforcement outsiders in Harris's previous novels to realize that Starling, like Graham and Kabakov, is vulnerable to corruption because of her marginalized status. She is a woman in what is traditionally a man's career. Her socioeconomic background as "poor white trash" from West Virginia stigmatizes her further. Her idealistic view of her mission destines her for eternal conflict with the political realities of her chosen profession. An honest woman among liars and craven opportunists, she finds it difficult to censor her comments when anger wells within her. But what characterizes her most, making her most susceptible to the attractions of a Hannibal Lecter, is her complex relationship to the revered memory of her father.

Starling's father was, to use Lecter's cruelly blunt label, a night watchman whom she has idealized as a result of his early removal from her life. To live up to his memory, Starling aspires to become an FBI agent. But as the climax of *Hannibal* makes clear, at least part of what fuels Starling's drive to succeed is her intense anger over her father's mistakes that got him killed by two addicts robbing a drugstore. As a psychiatrist trained to recognize outward signs of repressed emotions, Lecter has seen early in his relationship with Starling just how angry

she is. For example, during one of their dungeon meetings in *The Silence of the Lambs*, Lecter asks Starling how
she manages her anger. The answer is, by fiercely competing with and routinely defeating men on their own
terms in a rigidly patriarchal profession and, equally dangerously, smart-mouthing any of her professional superiors she finds offensive.

The payback for Starling's integrity and political tone-
deafness is a career that never truly takes off in spite of
its promising beginning. She is isolated, with only one
real friend. Her FBI mentor, Jack Crawford, is a middle-
aged man nearing retirement and the end of his professional influence. She is therefore ripe for the seduction
that Lecter has planned for her almost from the beginning. Though *Hannibal* is distressing to many of the
legions of Starling's fans, who see her as an icon of feminine strength doubly reinforced by actress Jodie Foster's
heroic portrayal of her in the film adaptation, Starling, as
Harris writes her, is a woman in desperate, neurotic need
of affirmation from older males, particularly those in a
mentoring capacity.

Starling's reservoir of anger, repressed as an unbearable truth in light of her reverence for her father, makes it
easy for her to participate in the cannibalistic feast upon
the brain matter of her enemy Krendler. "Pity has no
place at my table," Lecter tells her, and it's a lesson she
learns well. Though under the hallucinatory influence of
powerful drugs administered by Lecter, her complicity in
the murder of Krendler marks the point of no social
return for Starling. Then, through a complex remaking
process carefully instituted by Lecter, Starling continues
to uncover the source of her childhood traumas keeping
her from fully functioning as an adult. Finally, of her
own free will, she remakes herself as Lecter's elegant
companion in South American exile. The faint hope, for
those who wish to see Starling reclaim her former life, is
that Lecter built the sound of a certain musical note into

her reprogramming—a tone that will free her from his spell. The prospects for this awakening seem very dim, however, as the novel ends. Lecter's Pygmalion project has succeeded so well that Starling actually wields greater power than Lecter. So perhaps a better literary analogy is *Frankenstein* . . . could Lecter's own creation destroy him as her final act of healing? It is a novel that we may never see, but it is interesting to speculate where Lecter and Starling may go from here.

## CRITICAL RECEPTION

If *Red Dragon* and *The Silence of the Lambs* were met with generally high critical marks, *Hannibal* was greeted with a much more mixed reaction upon its publication. The negative reviews single out any number of flaws for examination in varying degrees of scornful tone. Lewis Grossberger settles for "snarky" in his review by addressing the fictional Lecter personally, while taking the book to task for its unbelievability:

> Though Mr. Harris' literary style unfortunately tends toward vulgar sensationalism dwelling, as he does, on the more lurid aspects of your career, Media Person feels confident that most readers will nevertheless emerge with a sympathetic attitude toward you. Indeed in this day and age, many will find your singular life downright inspiring.[1]

Jeff Giles criticizes Harris for the depiction of the book's villain: "The Verger character is a disaster, a failed effort to dream up somebody who'd make even Lecter look well adjusted."[2] Robert Plunket takes aim at the novel for its homophobia:

> In fact, never has a mainstream thriller been quite so fraught with stereotypically homosexual themes and motifs. Among the more prominent: opera, bodybuilding, pornography, fussy entertaining, drugs, cosmetic surgery, the daddy obsession, and—I swear to God—a lesbian couple contemplating artificial insemination.[3]

Terry Teachout calls the novel "embarrassingly pretentious" and faults it for daring to explain the root cause of Lecter's cannibalism: "What possessed Harris to tell us such a thing? With this wholly unexpected revelation, the dignified demon whose credo is Evil, be thou my good shrivels before our eyes into yet another sympathy-seeking victim, the sort of fellow whose pain Bill Clinton would hasten to feel."[4]

Teachout's lamentation of the demystifying of Lecter is a common complaint of the book's critics, most of whom, it seems, can barely stand to see Lecter as a mere human being of admittedly extraordinary abilities, as opposed to a pseudo-demonic entity of preternatural wiles. Robert Winder, observing that Lecter's earlier incarnations presented him as a mythic vampire-like figure in the tradition of Dracula, sadly notes:

> The more we learn about Lecter, the less resonant he becomes. In gaining his freedom, in shopping for expensive soap and driving a vintage Jaguar, he loses the magical potency with which he outwitted the world's best efforts to restrain him. Not since Samson lost his hair has a warrior been so crudely brought down to earth.[5]

Mark Dery argues that in addition to Lecter's childhood trauma, the book trivializes Lecter's evil in other ways: "The diminution of Lecter's moral stature is signaled by the reduction of his Mephistophelean superiority to a serial shopper's 'taste for rarified things': an 18th-century Flemish harpsichord from Sotheby's, an upscale picnic basket from Hammacher Schlemmer."[6] Christopher Lehmann-Haupt complains bitterly: "Lecter, the dark prince of chaos, giving away to wishful thinking, and wanting more order? Lecter being so dumb as to think if the universe contracted, time would reverse? Bring on the noisy lambs, then. They might as well be roaring."[7] Taking aim at Lecter's character from a different direction, David Edelstein excoriates the book as frightening in its glorification of vigilantism: "What [the book] shares with the perpetrators of Columbine and other massacres is the smug assurance that vigilantism is both noble and courageous, the province of the elite, and that the power to decide who lives or dies should be firmly rooted in the righteous individual."[8]

Some critics lament what has been done to Starling. Richard Alleva writes mournfully:

> Turning this plucky, caring, all-American heroine into Eurotrash may be the worst thing an author has done to a character in the history of popular fiction since Conan Doyle launched Sherlock Holmes over the Reichenbach Falls in the embrace of Professor Moriarty. But Doyle could resurrect Holmes. How can Harris redeem Starling?[9]

Slightly less disappointed but still regretful, Annie Gottlieb observes, "Clarice is here, but she's as disillusioned and cynical as Harris himself seems—as so many of us are in a time when every idea has proven hypocritical and every hero hollow."[10] Gottlieb's comment may penetrate to the core of what disturbs *Hannibal*'s legions of detractors—the book reeks to them of disillusionment and the failure of ideas.

However, for all of the critical lambasting, some balanced or even positive reviews do exist. Paul Gray, for one, calls Harris a virtuoso "orchestrator of suspense" and "at the top of his form," although he criticizes the novel for "a disquieting streak of sadism that Harris's two previous novels involving Lecter largely avoided."[11] Michelle West accepts the book for what it is, "a twisted, incestuous, and compelling read throughout [in] which the dark heart of Beauty and the Beast can be found, beating loudly."[12] Probably the most positive contemporary review was that of Harris's fellow novelist Stephen King. King, going much against the grain, deems the novel to be even better than *Red Dragon* or *The Silence of the Lambs*: "[*Hannibal*] is, in fact, one of the two most frightening popular novels of our time, the other being 'The Exorcist' by William Peter Blatty."[13]

The academic reception of the novel, a few years after its release, has been just as mixed, and sometimes equally as vituperative, as the spirited debate surrounding its release. S. T. Joshi blasts the novel, particularly its second half, for plummeting "into realms of dreadfulness not seen since the heyday of Harold Robbins and Irving Wallace."[14] Robert H. Waugh complains: "Several problems make the third novel . . . unsatisfying, albeit illuminating. Chief among them is Harris's betrayal of Lecter's unreadability when he offers a cheap psychoanalytic account of Lecter's childhood at the expense of his mythic power."[15] Daniel O'Brien strikes a more moderate tone but still brands the novel as "inferior to both *Red Dragon* and *The Silence of the Lambs*."[16]

For all of the condemnation of the novel as seriously flawed and even offensive, the sad result of a brilliant writer going rather inexplicably off the rails and inexcusably taking Clarice Starling and Hannibal Lecter with him, other academic appraisals find much more of merit. Benjamin Szumskyj, gamely engaged in rehabilitating the novel's reputation, celebrates Harris's artistic courage: "One would find it hard to locate another novel that was not only waited upon by millions, but delivered an ending that *no one* expected. . . . For those who wanted a predictable plot with a Hollywood*esque* resolution, direct yourself to the countless novels of mediocre authors who can provide you as such. Thomas Harris is no such author, nor are his written masterpieces."[17]

While acknowledging the imperfections of the book against its predecessors, David Sexton insists "it is, in its own way, like no other novel whatsoever, a masterpiece."[18] What Harris does masterfully, Sexton argues, is reclaim Lecter and Starling as his own characters from the public arena. Charles Gramlich makes the case that *Hannibal* works as the beginning of Harris's rehabilitation of Lecter into a mythic hero, and indeed the World War II backstory and romance with Starling are prerequisites to the cloaking of "Hannibal in the robes of the hero."[19]

Understandably, the evolution of the Lecter/Starling relationship is the focus of much of the academic analysis. Peter Messent finds the climactic dinner episode, which begins with Lecter and Starling dining upon Krendler's brains and ends with Lecter suckling at Starling's breast, a deliberate authorial recasting of Freudian psychology. Specifically, Lecter's presentation of Starling's father's corpse to her cures her of her Electra complex, and Starling's baring of her breast to Lecter cures him of his oedipal complex (which originated in his relinquishing his mother's breast to his younger sister Mischa). However, Messent concludes, it is an open question as to whether Starling is acting of her own volition or whether Lecter has, in essence, brainwashed her through hypnosis and drugs.[20] I have elsewhere written that the Lecter/Starling dalliance is entirely predictable, based on Harris's mining of Gothic themes for his fiction: "Those readers and critics who were horrified that Starling turned into a cannibal . . . are overlooking one of Harris's most obvious literary conceits—the intermingling of culture and primitivism central to the Gothic tradition."[21] O'Brien has the last word: "As a perverse sado-erotic fantasy, the Lecter-Starling coupling . . . wins points for imagination and attention to detail."[22]

## PLOT DEVELOPMENT

*Hannibal* has a much more complex, even convoluted structure than its predecessors. It is a Gothic cathedral of a book, in much the same way that Dante Alighieri's *Divine Comedy* (to which *Hannibal* makes numerous allusions) is. If the previous books have simple three-act dramatic structures, then this one has six distinct sections or movements, each dominated by different voices and moods. It's a big, sprawling book, moving between two continents and multiple narrative points of view. Harris's familiar police procedural framework is still present at times, particularly when the focus is on Starling. However, large sections of the book center on a plethora of other characters, including Lecter himself. Harris has ventured into multiple plot strands and points of view in his earlier work, but never to such an extent. The scenes set in Florence sit uneasily with the scenes in the United States, their linkage uncertain except through the plot contrivance of Verger's bounty on Lecter and a throwaway line in *Silence* referring to Lecter's fondness for the Duomo. Additionally, it is hard to find a precise locus of character identification within the plot; this aspect of the book alone may have frustrated many of Harris's readers, let alone the unexpected ending. Be all this as it may, Harris certainly does not content himself with replicating the thriller formula of his previous three novels. For better or for worse, he outdoes himself.

Starling makes her entrance in Part 1. Seven years after the events depicted in *Silence*, Starling's career is flatlining. Professional jealousy from many quarters and the enmity of Paul Krendler in the Justice Department, combined with Starling's tendency to backtalk to her superiors, have conspired to keep Starling assigned to routine stakeouts, surveillance duties, and drug raids. The book opens with one such drug raid, a multi-agency affair cobbled together for political reasons in an era of federal downsizing and budget reductions. Starling is accompanied on the raid by a number of officers and her long-time mentor John Brigham, one of her small but loyal support group (Jack Crawford and roommate Ardelia Mapp being the others). The raid is targeted against Evalda Drumgo, a major crystal methamphetamine dealer in the D.C. area, and her Crips bodyguards. When Starling kills Drumgo during the raid, the media goes wild. Her superiors use the negative publicity as an excuse to initiate termination proceedings against her. After years of silence, Lecter sends her a letter of support. Granted a professional reprieve by this turn of events, Starling travels to the family estate of Lecter's surviving victim, Mason Verger, to interview him. He lives there with his lesbian body-builder sister, Margot. The wealthy heir to a meatpacking dynasty and a man with a long history of pedophilia, he has been left paralyzed and hideously deformed (the result of cutting off his own face while under the influence of drugs given to him by Lecter). A giant moray eel endlessly circles in a tank by his bedside. He is obsessed with revenge, having publicly posted a million-dollar bounty for Lecter and established relationships with FBI and Justice Department officials behind the scenes to give him information. When the time comes, he intends to feed the doctor to specially bred man-eating boars in retaliation.

Part 2 of the novel shifts the scene to Florence, where Lecter has been living in anonymity for the better part of the seven years since his escape. This section of the novel is centered primarily upon a corrupt Italian detective, Pazzi. Pazzi is in professional disgrace because of his failure to convict a man he arrested for being a serial killer known as Il Mostro, who murdered lovers in Tuscany during the 1980s and 1990s. Pazzi discovers by chance that the interim curator of the Capponi Library, Dr. Fell, is really Dr. Lecter. Pazzi works with Verger's people to set up a trap for Lecter. However, Lecter easily sees the ambush coming. Instead, he turns the tables on Pazzi. He kills the detective by hanging him from the walls of the Palazzo Vecchio, an ironic end for a man whose remote ancestor was hanged from those same walls. Lecter eludes the remainder of Verger's men.

Part 3 parallels Starling's solo investigation to track down Lecter's current whereabouts with Lecter's return to the United States. Once back home, Lecter goes about re-creating a new identity and renting a new home. He often follows Starling, unknown to her. During his shopping, he attends a gun show, where an obnoxious deer hunter draws his notice. Lecter kills the man in the woods. Meanwhile, Verger and Krendler scheme to once again set Starling's termination in motion, in order to draw Lecter out to her aid.

Part 4 describes the process by which Starling is professionally executed at Verger's behest, with Krendler as the triggerman. After a short hearing, Starling is placed on administrative leave. Part 5 brings the various converging plot lines to their intersection. Verger's Italian manhunters stake out Starling, who in turn is being tailed by Lecter. The men capture Lecter and take him to the Verger estate, where he is held in preparation for being eaten by the pigs. After the FBI proves to be less than enthusiastic to investigate, Starling decides to take matters in her own hands. Just in time, she rescues Lecter from the pigs and Verger's henchmen but is rendered unconscious in the melee. Lecter carries her away from the estate. Margot, long bitter toward her brother for his sexual abuse of her in earlier years, seizes the opportunity to kill him by shoving the vicious eel down his throat.

Part 6 opens with Starling regaining consciousness. Lecter continually injects her with mind-altering drugs. The drug regimen continues for many days, a time during which Starling is listed as a missing person. At Lecter's urging, Starling confronts the unpleasant memories of her childhood once again, in more detail. Her therapy culminates in a dinner party, where the "guest" (really, the main course) is Paul Krendler. While Starling and Lecter consume sautéed portions of Krendler's brain, the lobotomized Krendler sings and makes crude remarks until Lecter kills him with a crossbow bolt. After dinner, Starling offers her bared breast to Lecter. The book ends with Starling and Lecter three years later, dancing on the terrace of their elegant home in Buenos Aires.

For many readers, this ending was maddening, loathsome, and downright unacceptable. The book's ending proved so controversial, in fact, that Jodie Foster and Jonathan Demme both said "no" to the film adaptation. The film that did result completely changed the ending to where Starling resists Lecter at the dinner party. He forces a kiss upon her but stops when he realizes Starling has handcuffed herself to him so he can't escape the police converging upon them. Forced to choose between maiming himself or Starling to escape, he cuts off part or all of his cuffed hand. The film ends with Lecter on the run again and Starling, apparently, restored to the FBI's good graces. Harris's original ending had been as cleanly excised from the story as if it never existed.

## CHARACTERS

### Hannibal Lecter

Lecter becomes at once more human and more mythic in this novel. He is more human because, true to Harris's other depictions of serial killers like Dolarhyde and Gumb, he has suffered terribly in his formative years, the memory of which distorts his adult thinking. He is more mythic, however, because his mental powers are more prodigious than ever. As an *eideteker*, he stores enormous reservoirs of learning in his memory palace. Yet this same memory palace contains memories of his traumatic childhood in wartime Eastern Europe. No mention is made of Lecter's nationality in the earlier novels, let alone any real details about his childhood except for Graham's reference to him torturing animals. Apparently, a mundane American background or a petty history of animal mutilation is no longer epic enough for Harris's design for the Lecter character. Instead, Lecter is descended from ancient and noble Italian families, including the Bevisangue, Machiavelli, and Visconti. His cousin is the great French painter Balthus. In this novel, the construction of Lecter's character resembles the intricacy of a medieval cathedral.

He was born to Lithuanian parents, who lived luxuriously on a vast forested estate. Hannibal and his younger sister Mischa were tended to by servants, their every need met. Then, World War II ended the Lecter family's idyllic rural existence. When Hannibal was six years old, artillery bombardments killed his parents. Hiwi deserters from the collapse of the Eastern Front in 1944 descended upon the Lecter hunting lodge. They kept local children prisoners in the barn, including Hannibal and Mischa. Whenever the deserters ran out of game from the surrounding forest, they killed and ate one of the children. One day, they came to take Mischa. Hannibal fought to keep her by his side, but they broke his arm and took her away to kill her with an axe. He never saw her again, except for some milk teeth in a stool pit. Ever since that terrible loss, Lecter wants nothing more in this world than to get his sister back somehow, someway.

We already know Lecter had a thriving psychiatric practice before his arrest. He handled many court referrals as well. We now learn that one of those referrals, a wealthy young man named Mason Verger, is one of the two surviving Lecter victims mentioned in *Red Dragon*. Verger, a pedophile court-ordered to do 500 hours of community service at the dog pound and seek treatment from Lecter, invited Lecter to his home. Lecter gave Verger a near-lethal dose of Angel Dust, acid, and methamphetamines. At Lecter's suggestion, a very high Verger cut off his face with a shard of mirror and fed the pieces of flesh to two dogs. Then Lecter broke Verger's neck with a noose Verger used for autoerotic asphyxiation—an act of poetic justice. Verger survived the attack—paralyzed, grotesquely disfigured, and crazed with the need for vengeance.

Lecter's arrest, trial, confinement to an asylum for eight years, and escape from police custody in Memphis are described in detail in the previous two books. Following plastic surgery in St. Louis, Lecter flew to Brazil, where his distinctively incriminating sixth finger was surgically removed. He may or may not have had something to do with the mysterious disappearance of Dr. Chilton while on vacation (although the "I'm having an old friend for dinner" ending of the film adaptation of *Silence* leaves little doubt what happened to Chilton). Eventually, he settles in Florence, Italy, a city he favors.[23] By killing the curator of the Palazzo Capponi, Lecter creates his own job opportunity. Now the interim curator of the library under the assumed name of Dr. Fell, he settles in for the life of an Italian gentleman of leisure, until news of Starling's plight in the United States comes to his attention.

Besides learning a great deal about Lecter's history, we also see more of his already established personality traits and some striking new ones. We already know of Lecter's distaste for rudeness, which is certainly expanded upon here. Barney, Lecter's orderly for many years, reveals to Starling that Lecter prefers to eat the rude. Donnie Barber, the deer poacher that Lecter kills and field dresses in the Virginia woods, certainly qualifies as rude when he curses at a gun show concessionaire within Lecter's field of vision. Barber's flagrant acts of poaching might also be considered a type of discourtesy. Lecter has no other reason to kill Barber than the man's rudeness. This murder solidifies Lecter's vigilante status.

Lecter's enhanced sensory powers are, if possible, even more sensitive now. Of these, smells are the most powerful for him. When he enters the Farmacia di Santa Maria Novella to buy soaps and bath oils for Starling, for example, he is overcome by the sensual aroma of the shop. He believes he can "smell with his hands, his arms and cheeks, that odor suffused him."[24] He can identify types of skin products and, by extension, those who use them by sniffing the lingering smells left behind in trace amounts on objects. He demonstrates this ability to Pazzi by sniffing a sheet of music Lecter had loaned to Signora Pazzi. Scent also plays a powerful part in Lecter's attraction to Starling. At their first meeting in the asylum dungeon, he took in her distinctive fragrances; when he returns from Florence to stalk her from afar in Virginia, he tracks her not only by sight but through scent. When he breaks into her Mustang at the state park where she is running, he sits in the driver's seat breathing in her scent in an intense, nearly sexual way. The smells excite him to the point where he leans forward to run his tongue over the steering wheel to taste the molecules she left behind—a literally autoerotic tableaux. Since scent is an easier sensory trigger for memory than any other, he also associates the bad memories of his childhood with bad smells. When immersed in the obnoxious and smelly throng of humanity crowding in eagerly to see the torture exhibition in Florence, for example, he presses a scented handkerchief to his face to filter out the stink. Because of this degree of olfactory sensitivity, who could prove more capable of driving away Lecter's bad memories than the delightfully scented Starling?

Taste, both sensory and aesthetic, remains important to Lecter. The aesthetics of the dining experience are as important to him as the flavor of the food. It's not enough for the food to taste good; he insists meals be treated as artistic creations in their own right. Of course, he needs the proper resources and tools to satisfy his sense of aesthetics. Starling recognizes that the best way to locate Lecter is to locate him through his purchases. While Krendler dismisses Lecter's interest in matters of taste as effete trivia, Starling shares enough of Lecter's intellect and aesthetic sensibility to know the life of the mind, the life of artistic fulfillment, and the life of owning fine things are what motivate him.

His art, if one may call it that, extends to his murders. This, more than anything else, gets at the lethal paradox of his character: both refined and savage. Starling calls this quality of his "whimsy." He finds whimsy in "presenting" the bodies of his victims in such a way as to make some larger metaphoric point. Remember the sixth victim, posed to match the *Wound Man* drawing? What is that if not art? The murders described in *Hannibal* are tableaux, artistic set-pieces designed to illustrate a theme. Lecter convinces Verger to feed his own face to the dogs as fitting punishment for starving them. Lecter next breaks Verger's neck with the same noose that Verger uses for masturbation games. Lecter eviscerates and hangs Pazzi as poetic justice for the man's avarice. To pay back Barber for slaying deer, Lecter kills the man with an arrow, then pulls the lungs out his back to leave them splayed in the so-called "Bloody Eagle" of Norse ritual tradition. He feeds Krendler's cerebral cortex to Starling as poetic justice for the abominable way Krendler has treated her over the years. These acts are not mindless aberrations, but acts of macabre whimsy designed to make a more serious point about each person's moral failings. Lecter is a profound moralist who makes a whimsical art of murder.

Lecter's whimsy masks an inner outrage against the kind of malicious God who could allow Mischa to die in such a hideous manner. Since that time, he has killed without worrying about God's disapproval, since he recognizes *how his own modest predations paled beside those of God, who is in irony matchless, and in wanton malice beyond measure* [italics in original]."[25] A man who collects stories of church collapses and mocks the iconography of crucifixion, he ridicules the spiritual solutions offered by Christianity. To others, this mockery makes him diabolical. Verger, whose born-again Christianity is portrayed as sinister in and of itself, thinks of Lecter loose as "going to and fro in the earth and walking up and down in it," a Biblical allusion to Satan used once before in *Silence*. Romula, the gypsy woman, takes one good look at Lecter and pronounces him to be the Devil. His influence upon the man-eating swine, devilish in both appearance and appetite, suggests something of the Biblical episode of the demon-possessed herd of swine later exorcised by Christ. Harris has a lot of narrative fun with the idea of Lecter as Satan, including a scene where Lecter retrieves a set of ID documents from the Devil's Armor at the village church of Santa Reparata. His mocking of Christianity, however, compensates for his inner anguish.

When people are not calling Lecter the Devil, they are calling him a monster. When Pazzi hypocritically prays to Heaven for the success of his avaricious scheme, he calls Lecter the "monster of monsters." Those of a more secular bent, freed of the constraints of traditional Christianity, also settle for calling him a monster. Behavioral scientists, for example, despair of measuring or quantifying him, calling him a monster rather than a man. Even the book's omniscient narrator frequently uses the term to refer to Lecter. The cumulative effect of these "devil" and "monster" references is to reinforce the idea that Lecter is more mythic than human. Something about him defies explanation.

Lecter has insisted before to Starling that his "evil" is essentially unknowable, that no one can or should explain him lest they end up like the census taker who unwisely attempted to quantify the monster. In *Red Dragon* and *Silence*, with no in-depth characterization or background information given to us, we may have believed Lecter. But now we are given a possible explanation for what makes Lecter so monstrous: the wartime atrocities of the Eastern Front. While the trauma may not explain him fully, it does humanize him. It renders him vulnerable. This Lecter suffers from night terrors. Lecter, who once asked Graham if he dreamt much, suffers from some pretty nasty dreams himself. In his waking hours, he is tormented by what a psychiatrist would call post-traumatic stress disorder. The sight of a deer in the Virginia forest triggers in him a flashback to the sight of the men who ate his sister pulling a wounded deer by the neck to the slaughter, a flashback so intense it makes him scream. His vulnerability bleeds over into many aspects of his life. We have not seen Lecter so impotent before. The inconceivable happens—the seemingly omniscient Lecter is taken by surprise and recaptured. He must even be rescued by Starling from the pigs. Though not every reader likes it, his vulnerability makes him a more sympathetic, understandable character.

Lecter is also humanized by his passionate feelings for Starling. His attraction to her has only grown stronger in her absence. When the news of her plight reaches him in Florence, he sends a letter of support to her immediately, rekindling the relationship. While Verger's psychiatrist-in-residence, Dr. Doemling, scoffs at the idea the relationship is anything more than mercenary on Lecter's part, Barney (who knows Lecter better than almost anyone else) disagrees with Doemling, saying that Lecter admires her courage. As events play out, Barney's viewpoint is proven most accurate. Lecter puts himself at great risk to come back to the United States to be near Starling again. His admiration, even love, for Starling becomes evident. What also becomes clear is how much the relationship with Starling is intertwined with Lecter's memory of his sister, Mischa.

His love for Mischa borders on the incestuous. Twisted by the manner of her tragic death to the point of becoming a cannibal himself, he desires nothing more than to undo what has been done to Mischa. His bond with Starling, a living woman and potential sexual partner, is key to his magical thinking. Even though Mischa is long dead, he thinks that reversing time in combination with the blood sacrifice of Starling will bring Mischa back to life in Starling's place. To bolster his wishful thinking, he reads the work of physicist Stephen Hawking, particularly his early theory that entropy may somehow reverse itself (a theory later disavowed by Hawking himself). These passages remarkably conflate Lecter's spiritual longings with the language of science.

This is an interesting development for an otherwise cynical intellectual who mocks simplistic belief in God by collecting press clippings of church collapses. Rather than Christianity, quantum physics and string theory offer the doctor a glimmer of hope to save Mischa, if only he could find a way to reverse time through the complex mathematical calculations he writes on butcher paper. He believes the merging of scientific principles—the paradoxical magic of the effect of extreme compression upon matter—and the ancient religious association of faith with the East will resurrect his sister in Starling's place. He believes Starling is the vessel through which Mischa can re-enter the present moment. Thus, he pursues Starling with the passion of the obsessed. His interest in helping Starling, although sincere enough, is predicated mostly on what she can do for him, in much the same way as Dahlia's interest in nursing Lander back to health following his pneumonia is not entirely selfless.

Starling in turn helps Lecter uncover his repressed feelings about Mischa. In what was undoubtedly the final straw for some of Harris's readers, Starling in a sudden clear moment of insight offers her breast to Lecter, and then asks, "Hannibal Lecter, did your mother feed you at her breast? . . . Did you ever feel that you had to relinquish the breast to Mischa? Did you ever feel you were required to give it up for her?"[26] He denies any such memories, but nevertheless responds to Starling's offer by kneeling to her breast and taking it into his mouth. She metaphorically becomes the generous, giving, and loving mother denied to him by the circumstances of his life. He becomes wholly integrated again, no longer dreaming of Mischa. Though still a monster, he is a rehabilitated one.

## Clarice Starling

As Lecter becomes more human, Clarice Starling becomes less human, more monstrous. This transformation commences in the first few pages, when she kills five people, including a mother carrying a baby, in a shootout. These killings, combined with Jame Gumb's shooting, land her in the *Guinness Book of World Records* as having killed more criminals than any other female law enforcement agent in U.S. history. She stars in the headlines of the ubiquitous *National Tattler* as the "FBI's Death Angel," the kind of sensationalistic over-marketing normally reserved for serial killers like Francis Dolarhyde, Jame Gumb, and Hannibal Lecter. The media, by blurring the line between Starling's shootings and the crimes of serial killers, effectively puts her in their same category. Being grouped in their company foreshadows her fate to become Lecter's willing opera date in Buenos Aires.

How could straight-arrow Starling, the embodiment of integrity and personal honor, ever possibly cross the line to this extent? The answer lies in a combination of factors, which include her deep reservoir of anger, her alienation from the male-dominated profession she has chosen, her history of poverty and abandonment, and her fixation upon a beloved but resented dead father. These factors render Starling all too receptive to Lecter's unique form of therapy. With his psychiatrist's insights, he breaks her down and rebuilds her in his image. The outcome of this treatment is shocking but not really so implausible as many of Starling's fans insist. Maybe this character is not Jodie Foster's Starling, but it is definitely Harris's.

For one thing, Starling aspires to the taste represented by Lecter. Lecter needles her about her taste even in their first meeting in *Silence* by mocking her good bag and cheap shoes. Seven years after that meeting, Starling hungers for some class and style in her life. Surrounded by men who resent her, faced with criminals engaged in sordid little crimes on a daily basis, is it any wonder Starling longs for some style? She is growing tired of the drab routine of her life. Primed to focus on style, she realizes that she shares with Lecter a hunger for fine things, such as turbocharged cars. Some of their stars are the same, as Lecter would say.

Another character trait is her anger, little noted by those who sing Starling's praises in *Silence*. Her rage originates from her poverty-stricken childhood and the untimely loss of her parents. She ventures out into the world, fails because of the professional jealousy of others and her own bad temper, and returns to the source of her anger to confront it once and for all (with a little assist from her demon therapist). Her anger leads her to pop off her "smart mouth" when provoked. Her temper flashes when she tells the men at her first FBI tribunal that their running from what happened at the fish market makes her sick. When unjustly accused or confronted by her superiors, especially Krendler, her rage literally seems to possess her, so that the very air shimmers with heat in her field of vision. When possessed like this, she is liable to do almost anything. When asked to surrender her weapons to the men who place her on administrative leave pending an investigation, for example, she briefly fantasizes about shooting them all down. Although she does not carry out her murderous fantasy, these thoughts let us know how far she could potentially go when pushed.

Under Lecter's regimen of drugs and psychoanalytic therapy, Starling discovers for herself why she is so angry. She is mad at her father for making a stupid mistake that got him killed. Once she taps into this essence of rage, she lets it all loose to her therapist, calling her father a night watchman whose stupidity left her and her mother all alone. These negative feelings, the shadow side to Starling's conscious veneration of her father's memory, have festered over the years to taint Starling's adult interactions with those she includes in the same category as the "town jackasses" who indirectly killed her father by putting him in a dead-end, dangerous job. In a bureaucratic agency full of back-stabbing politicos and career climbers like the FBI, it's now clear the idealistic but angry Starling was doomed from the outset, in spite of her promising beginning as a trainee. She finally takes out her anger on Krendler, a surrogate for the failed father and her own feelings of inferiority, by calling him an oaf who doesn't know anything and is beneath notice. Though the confrontation is personally cathartic, it comes far too late to salvage anything of her professional life.

In fact, by the time *Hannibal* opens, Starling's career is pretty much already done. FBI Director Tunberry provides her professional epitaph to Crawford: "But she's got a smart mouth, Jack, and she got off to the wrong start with certain people."[27] Starling recognizes her own irascibility but nevertheless has difficulty accepting her stagnation. Ironically, she comes to realize her early triumph actually worked against her, making her male contemporaries too jealous of her. Krendler personifies all of her professional obstacles in the patriarchal FBI. In this world of sexist men, she has few allies. One, Jack Crawford, is too old, sick, and close to retirement to help her anymore. Another, Hannibal Lecter, has his own private designs on her. Only her black female roommate, Ardelia Mapp, stands as a rock-solid counterweight between her and the seduction of Lecter. In the end, however, Mapp's loyalty is not enough to save her.

Perhaps the last word on Starling is this: *warrior*. Lecter calls her that in his letter to her following the fish market massacre. She certainly has the warrior's heritage in her Southern blood. She hails from a family that fought in the Civil War and then struggled to survive the generational indignities of Reconstruction. She selects a dangerous profession in which she can take up arms against enemies. She bears the mark of her initiation into the warrior's life—the spot of gunpowder on her cheek from shooting Jame Gumb. She lives a warrior's code of ethics, for instance cherishing as sacred her bond to her fellow warrior John Brigham. In return, he bequeaths to her his weapon, a symbolic transference of power. Acting on her warrior code, she saves the helpless, as she does with Catherine Martin and does again in washing mother's blood off Drumgo's crying baby in the fish market. Her code even compels her to rescue Lecter from Verger: "But she could not abide the thought of Dr. Lecter tortured to death; she shied from it as she had from the slaughter of the lambs and the horses so long ago. . . . With this thought, she made a simple decision. . . . *The world will not be this way within the reach of my arm* [italics in original]."[28] This warrior quality is why the public fell in love with Starling's character and why the loss of her to Lecter hurts so deeply. We have lost the committed warrior who seeks to right the bloody injustices of a world of malice.

## Mason Verger

Truly the most repulsive villain yet created by Harris (no small claim), Mason Verger is the spoiled scion of an *uber*-wealthy family of crooks whose riches accrue to them from the spilled blood of slaughtered animals. As if in fulfillment of this karmic legacy, Verger is a pedophiliac predator who rapes even his own younger sister while growing up. His court-ordered therapy with Dr. Lecter ends with Verger faceless and paralyzed, physically helpless but still in command of a vast empire of corrupt politicians and underworld criminals to carry out his wishes. The plot of *Hannibal* is almost entirely driven by Verger's vendetta against Lecter. So, like Gumb, Verger seems at times little more than a plot device. He is cartoonishly evil, singularly without redeeming virtue.

His background is as ugly as his appearance. Verger is the son of Molson Verger, a man of equal parts vision and corruption who built the Mason meatpacking business into a far-reaching empire. The Vergers, originally based in Chicago, survived intact the muckraking journalists and food industry legislative reforms of the early twentieth century by buying legislative favors and protection. The elder Verger tutored Mason in all aspects of the family slaughter business, including the unsavory tactics by which Molson had prospered.

As Mason grew up, he developed a taste for pedophilia and brutal entertainments, even going to Africa for a time to serve as roving executioner for dictator Idi Amin. In spite of Mason's continuous trouble with the law and the disastrous injuries he sustained in his encounter with Lecter, the younger Verger showed a ruthlessness in business dealings equal to that of his father. Proven worthy of the honor, Mason Verger became the head of the family business with his father's passing. With the entire wealth of a dynasty at his disposal, he has almost unlimited resources to track down Lecter so that he may feed the doctor to the special breed of man-eating swine he has developed.

Verger initially presents himself to Starling as an ally to her. Even though Verger saves Starling from her first professional firing squad, Crawford makes clear to her from the beginning that the man is motivated more by his vengeful quest to find the fugitive Lecter than any altruistic impulse toward her. So we are already primed to mistrust Verger upon our first meeting with him. The man's deformed outer appearance, in Harris's medieval-flavored melodrama, speaks to the inner condition of his soul. He has a lidless eye through which he observes everything, like an omniscient evil god. His long plaited ponytail lies coiled like a serpent on the respirator covering his chest. His voice is radio quality, although lacking plosives and fricatives.[29] Forever harnessed to a respirator and a pan-pipe device in front of his face to control the movement of his bed, he is a viable organism only through the machines his wealth and status afford him. He is a Darth Vader character, the mechanical man as monster. The isolated chamber in which he exists apart from the main Verger mansion is dominated by a large tank containing a vicious, gigantic eel—another serpent image. In looking at his ruined body, we see the symbolic fruit of his corruption.

He demonstrates the folly of giving one's life over to wrath, one of the seven deadly Christian sins. In spite of his surface veneer of born-again religiosity, he is motivated by a wrathful vendetta against Lecter. Whenever Verger's plot goes awry, as it consistently does, he is practically undone by raging temper tantrums until he can get himself back under control. Certainly, Verger's animosity toward Lecter is understandable. Where he crosses the line is his all-consuming quest to capture Lecter and feed him bit by bit to man-eating swine as payback. Verger disingenuously claims to Starling he is not seeking revenge, that he has forgiven Lecter as Christ forgave those who crucified Him. However, Verger's actions leave no doubt he is devoting his physical and intellectual energy, as well as his family fortune, to destroying Lecter in the most gruesome way he can devise.

Verger claims to be a religious man. However, his drive for vengeance belies his claim to piety. The specific shape of Verger's revenge upon Lecter comes to him in a Christmas epiphany shortly after Lecter's escape. Inspired by the Christian miracle of transubstantiation, Verger decides he will have Lecter eaten alive. Verger's plan to have Lecter eaten by swine is certainly a type of poetic justice, but what is most egregious is Verger's hypocritical piety. Ironically, given that his last name means "a church caretaker," Verger masks his sins with bogus testimonials of Christian faith. In Harris's fiction, we must immediately suspect the good motives of any character who often claims to be born again.

In his first meeting with Starling, Verger makes a point of asserting his religious beliefs as he claims to have accepted his fate and asks her if she has faith. He proceeds to tell her the story of his finding Jesus in a childhood Christian camp sponsored by his father, a story less than inspirational given that Verger routinely sexually abused other children at camp. He has no trouble confessing his past sins, he says, because he has been cleansed by his faith and given immunity by Christ (whom he calls "The Riz"). Almost within the same breath, however, he vows to smite his enemies. The monologue reveals him to be the basest kind of hypocrite. He begins by wielding his born-again status as a spiritual get-out-of-jail-free card and finishes by ranting wrathfully about utterly destroying his enemies. His oft-professed belief in Christianity is sometimes hard to swallow, not only for the barbarity of his plans but his underlying lack of true belief. During his Christmas epiphany, for example, he looks beseechingly to the Christmas stars outside his window for some answer to his misery and hears nothing, implying that God is nonexistent or uncaring. Harris uses the Verger character to comment unfavorably on the kind of hypocrisy allowing someone to plead piety while at the same time planning and executing bloodthirsty acts of cruelty, a theme extending back to *Black Sunday*.

What makes Verger particularly loathsome is his history of child molestation. As a youth, he sodomized other youths at his father's church camp in exchange for candy bars, which Verger forever after refers to as "taking the chocolate." His youthful attacks on his sister were so brutal that he ripped her anus and permanently crippled her left arm. Even after his own injuries make it physically impossible for him to act on his perverse sexuality, he continues to torment children psychologically. He uses his wealth and influence to have welfare children from Baltimore bussed in to daycare at Muskrat Farm, where the children play on the expansive grounds and ride ponies. Verger's supplier in Baltimore sometimes roughs up a couple of the children to make them more vulnerable. Verger then traumatizes selected children by showing them his mutilated face and threatening them. For instance, he threatens the black child Franklin with removal from his home and loss of his foster mother and beloved cat. When the cumulative effect of the threats breaks down Franklin into tears, Verger directs his male nurse Cordell to wipe away the child's tears so that Verger may consume them in his martinis—an indirect allusion to the death's-head moth in *Silence* that feeds upon the tears of mammals. He relieves his stress by the only kind of pedophiliac aggression he can now perform.

By the time he meets his end at the snapping jaws of a moray eel, he has undergone no discernable character arc. He is a static, monolithic presence orchestrating events behind the scenes. Not so much a believable character as a necessary evil to advance the plot, his malign influence is everywhere. He is a melodramatic villain whose reprehensible nature makes him a suitable target for the poetic justice that Lecter, in God's absence, metes out.

## Rinaldo Pazzi

Our first sight of Chief Investigator Rinaldo Pazzi of the Questera is in the shadows, an appropriate place for this ambiguous character to be. He is a gifted, ambitious detective whose public disgrace in the high-profile "Monster of Florence" case leads him into a momentous act of betrayal of his professional and personal ethics for money. He is a fascinating villain, more complex than Verger, his motives easier for an audience to relate to.

Pazzi grew up in the city of Florence. His family is an ancient one, with an infamous history. Pazzi's ancestor Francesco de' Pazzi was executed by hanging for taking part in the assassination of Giuliano de Medici and the attempted assassination of Lorenzo the Magnificent in April 1478. A child during the World War II years, Pazzi remembers the Germans blowing up the bridges over the Arno and a German sniper executed against the Madonna of Chains. As an adult, he is an investigator in the Questera. He is married to a beautiful young woman, whom he loves very much. However, he feels great pressure to provide her with a high standard of living. Like many an older man married to a much younger woman, Pazzi feels insecure about her level of commitment to him. So he overcompensates by spending money he doesn't really have on her.

His life changes dramatically when he is promoted to chief investigator at the height of the public and press clamor over the Il Mostro, or Monster of Florence, investigation. Under the kind of intense scrutiny given to high-profile serial murder cases, he is pressured night and day to produce a suspect. When he arrests a man named Tocca, who is later convicted, Pazzi becomes a hero. However, when Tocca's conviction is reversed on appeal, the public and press savagely turn on Pazzi. Disgraced, he waits for his inevitable termination from the Questera. Then fate puts Dr. Lecter in his path.

It is ironic for Pazzi to be so discredited. He is actually a skilled investigator, capable enough of being appointed chief investigator. He is hard-working, putting in the many long hours of legwork necessary to build a case. When he lacks the resources to do his job, he knows how to navigate the bureaucracy to get what he needs. His investigative method is based on sound principles. He has the skill set necessary to be a solid investigator. Above all, he is ravenously ambitious.

He makes inspired imaginative associations between clues, the primary distinguishing characteristic for the profiler-as-artist in Harris's fiction. Pazzi's intuitive leaps, or eurekas, resemble those we have already seen from Graham and Starling. Consider this passage, a description of how the eureka feels to Pazzi: "In that moment when the connection is made, in the synaptic spasm of completion when the thought drives through the red fuse, is our keenest pleasure."[30] Graham, Starling, and Pazzi have the best moments of their lives when they make the critical connections that solve their respective puzzles. These sudden intuitive leaps are the tipping point at which enough clues have been absorbed to suddenly recognize a pattern. Unlike Graham and Starling, however, Pazzi gets it wrong. His epiphany hinges upon a connection between a crime scene and Botticelli's painting *Primavera*. Since Botticelli also painted the hanging of Pazzi's ancestor, Pazzi is already predisposed to think of the painter. Personal bias contaminates Pazzi's epiphany. The cautionary note here for all would-be profilers is to remain as objective as possible when connecting the evidence. Pazzi, unconsciously or consciously, forces the evidence to fit the most satisfying scenario for him.

However, he does get it right next time. He realizes Dr. Fell is really Dr. Lecter. Then Pazzi faces a moral dilemma. Should he arrest Lecter and be restored to good graces, or sell him to Verger and use the reward money to make a better life for his wife and him? Harris puts the dilemma directly to the reader with a series of rhetorical questions, asking if the good opinion of others really matters when conventional honor is a sham. Though Harris does not provide answers, the implication is clear enough. If the good opinion of others does not carry any authority, then acting according to any social code of ethics or morality is difficult if not impossible. From this perspective, it is easier to see why Pazzi as a good investigator makes the final decision he does. His recent disgrace liberates him from caring about the judgments of others to focus only on his own self-interests. Whatever honors he may receive from arresting Lecter will be temporary.

Pazzi is motivated by greed, or avarice. Verger's reward money can make his wife happy. The fact he must sell his honor and soul does not sway him from contacting Verger. Once he commits to the scheme, he applies his considerable investigative gifts in this new solo, illegal direction. On his own, he is willing to let others be hurt if he will profit. The most dramatic example of Pazzi's indifference to others' pain occurs when he prevents his pickpocket accomplice Gnocco from staunching the blood flow from the wound given him by Lecter. Gnocco bleeds out in the street and dies. Avarice has consumed Pazzi's basic humanity. Yet in spite of his greed, he is not a completely unsympathetic character like Verger. Pazzi's drive to please his wife stems from a genuine love for her.

Unfortunately, he allows his insecurity over her need for money to lead him into a terrible mistake.

Under no illusions as to what he is engaged in, Pazzi thinks selling Lecter to Verger is a sin, leading him at one point to think about what good deeds he could do with the money for poor children or donation of medical equipment, by way of personal redemption. He even tries to sanctify his avaricious action by prayer, thanking God for the opportunity to rid the earth of a monster and save many souls from pain. However, the cost of this sin is too high for him to pay. Lecter guts him and then hangs him from the same balcony where Pazzi's ancestor died hundreds of years before. Pazzi can't buy off death with money. All he has done is squander his professional gifts, his honor, and his life in pursuit of the crassest of goals.

## Paul Krendler

Deputy Assistant Inspector Paul Krendler of the Justice Department is a sleazy mixture of misogyny and corruption. Like Freddy Lounds and Dr. Chilton, Krendler can best be called a lout. He is a flat character whose sole purpose in the story is to function as Starling's professional nemesis. We don't learn much about his background other than what has already been established for him in *Silence*. He is a career-climbing bureaucrat who has made Starling's life hell for seven years, ever since she embarrassed him by solving the Buffalo Bill case. She also rebuffed a drunken advance from him, further aggravating his desire to take vengeance on her. In collusion with Mason Verger, Krendler ultimately destroys Starling's FBI career. His karmic debt finally catches up to him when Lecter brings him to dinner.

Krendler is the worst kind of bureaucrat or administrator, lording it over others like a petty tyrant. He exhibits many of the worst traits of the bureaucrat. Surrounding himself with cronies, he is part of a self-protecting network impervious to repercussions from those they harm. Even his language has devolved over the years into bureau-ease, a type of cautious, reveal-nothing rhetoric designed to obfuscate actual meaning and intent rather than clarify. Prone to entering the office spaces of subordinates without knocking, he demonstrates no respect or professional courtesy to those lower down the political ladder than he. In particular, he insults Starling by speaking to her as if she were a child unworthy of trust.

To make matters worse, he has never served as a front-line law enforcement agent. His lack of field experience doesn't sit well with Starling. When he patronizes her by saying she can take her forced administrative leave to have the spot of "dirt" on her cheek removed, she retorts that it's no wonder he doesn't recognize the spot as gunpowder. Like Dr. Chilton without a medical degree trying to run a mental hospital, Krendler is in over his head when working with real cops.

None of his inadequacies stop him from seeking higher office. He aspires to be the congressman from the 27th district, a position for which he is quite willing to sell whatever integrity he may have left. His actions are crafted with an eye toward how they may elevate his public profile. He practices snappy one-liners or sound bites for his future public speaking. Like any politician with great ambition and little moral center, he enters into convenient arrangements with powerful financiers for money in exchange for future votes. Specifically, the relationship between Krendler and Verger exemplifies the corrupt alliance between politics and big business. Krendler shares confidential FBI records with Verger in exchange for the promise of enough campaign money to win political office. In return, Verger asks for opposition to the Humane Slaughter Act, which will save millions of dollars for the Verger syndicate if defeated. As if this shabby arrangement weren't bad enough, Krendler and Verger manufacture evidence to break Starling's career in order to draw Lecter to her in her exposed vulnerability. Like Pazzi, Krendler is a corrupt lawman driven by avarice. Where Krendler differs is his ambition for political, not necessarily financial, gain. In keeping with the book's theme of poetic justice, his drive to become a political big shot is the very trait that dooms him. Under the belief that he is flying to a meeting with a congressman who will make his political future, he is instead lured into a trap. Lecter, in collusion with Margot Verger, exploits Krendler's political aspirations, which ultimately seats him, bound and lobotomized, at Lecter's dinner table.

Krendler possesses many less-than-endearing qualities, all of which combine to create a perfect synergy of loutishness. For one thing, he is quite vengeful. Once insulted, he works behind the scenes to wreck lives. Face-to-face confrontation is not his style. Rather, he goes for the low blow. In retaliation against Starling for her showing him up, he places damaging information in her personnel file at every opportunity and gradually turns the Career Board against her. He sabotages her so sneakily she isn't even aware of it until much later. She thinks of him as a black hole, visible only because of the influence he has on those around him.

His vengefulness is motivated by a deep-seated misogyny, in turn rooted in a tangle of pathological insecurities going back to his adolescence. Though he won't acknowledge it to himself, Starling reminds him of a long-ago female who called him "a queer" for his lack of sexual performance. Haunted by the memory of this ridicule, he is secretly afraid of women and sexual failure. So he overcompensates by seeking out sexual conquests or otherwise exploiting women. His sexual attraction to women is indistinguishable from the hateful desire to hurt them.

One face of his general misogyny is his sexist attitude in the workplace. He thinks of professional women like Starling as office girls. Breaking Starling's career does not bother him as much as it would to destroy a man's, since in Krendler's ultra-traditional view of things a man has a family to provide for. Additionally, his preoccupation with sex leads him to take pleasure in working crude lascivious references into practically any conversation. He enjoys saying the word *dick* around Margot Verger, a lesbian. He wonders aloud if Lecter is into S and M whores and male prostitutes, and if Starling and Mapp are lesbians. These observations are misguided and irrelevant, but bring him a naughty juvenile thrill.

Starling in particular stokes his lust. Obsessed by her, he once drunkenly called her at night to ask her out, but she turned him down. Angered by the rejection, Krendler redirects his lust into slowly but surely wrecking Starling's career. He expresses his animosity toward her in ugly, demeaning insults, such as calling her "cornpone country pussy." Even with a portion of his cerebral cortex removed by Lecter, he retains enough hate-filled mind to repeat this pungent insult. At the dinner party, Starling finally gets the chance to turn the tables on Krendler for his misogynistic behavior toward her. She compares him to the Apostle Paul, saying he hated women too. Krendler has been such a sexist lout to Starling, it's hard to feel much regret when Starling and Lecter put an end to his offensive behavior and language.

## Jack Crawford

The strong, natural leader we first met in *Red Dragon* was subjected to a devastating loss in *Silence*, the long illness and death of his wife. Though still effective at what he did, the Crawford that Starling met was distracted and grieving. Now, seven years later, Starling's FBI mentor is fifty-six, facing mandatory retirement in one more year. His career is over. His once-formidable influence is almost nonexistent. With his protégé Starling in the deepest professional trouble of her life, he is powerless to help her anymore.

The extent to which Crawford's star has descended is clear in the first scene he appears. When Director Tunberry tells him Starling is going to take the fall for the Drumgo shooting, Crawford objects, of course, but Tunberry orders him to stay out of the fight. As a consolation prize, Tunberry informs Crawford he will become a deputy director if he keeps his mouth shut. It's hard to imagine the Crawford we've seen before accept this injustice. Back then he was highly respected, loved by many, and at the height of his career. He moved the right pieces into place to stop the careers of serial killers like Garrett Jacob Hobbs, Hannibal Lecter, Francis Dolarhyde, and Jame Gumb. Now he's old, tired, and nearly done.

*Helpless* is the word best describing Crawford at the end of his career. While still respected as "one of the boys" by his colleagues, they recognize that the FBI Crawford once thrived in is no longer the FBI of the 1990s. Crawford has no real power within the system, only the legacy of his good name. Unable to direct events any longer, he is helpless to directly stop Starling's administrative discharge, resorting to a desperate back-channel ploy by contacting Verger. Even Starling has come to have some doubts about Crawford's range of influence and judgment. Ardelia Mapp does not hesitate to tell Starling that Crawford is finished, even if Starling can't (or won't) see that. One image best captures the bleakness of Crawford's professional status. When Starling goes to his office for what turns out to be the last time, it is empty. A sweater knitted for him by Bella hangs on a coat tree. The "empty sweater" in the empty office is the symbol of his ineffectuality (as well as a harbinger of his imminent death by heart attack).

Crawford's end is ignominious. When Verger releases the FBI to chew up Starling for good, Crawford is professionally impotent. He isn't allowed to stand by Starling's side when she faces her hearing; in fact, he is even prevented from entering the meeting room. Faced with the awful knowledge of his inability to help his favorite pupil, he is stricken with chest pains and hospitalized. A month later, he is dead. The proximity of his literal death and Starling's symbolic one is appropriate, given their professional connectedness. Losing one mentor, Starling surrenders completely to the other.

If he had made more political friends or achieved more promotions, Crawford might have been able to do more for both himself and Starling. He spent too much time working to catch criminals and earning the loyalty of his subordinates, and not enough time trumpeting his own worth to the powers that be. In this sense, Crawford and Starling are alike. Neither is very political. They do what they believe is right in order to fight crimes. It may be this shared quality that first drew Crawford to Graham, then Starling, both of them outsiders to the FBI political structure. Crawford as section chief struggles to provide a safe place for his superstars in a system full of political opportunists and career climbers, but the task is too much. In the end, crippled by grief and disappointments, he loses out to the Krendlers of the world.

## STYLE

Harris's prose style has undergone something of a sea change by the time of *Hannibal*. His minimalist style has morphed into the literary equivalent of the Florid Baroque, the seventeenth-century European artistic style characterized by its dramatic sweep, exquisite detail, elaborate design, and raw emotional appeal. The novel certainly has a grand design, much like Lecter's expansive memory palace. Harris's writing style becomes just as grand to support the structure. The imagistic quality is the richest of any Harris novel so far. The description of Pazzi's return flight from Switzerland, for instance, is dramatically couched in thunder and lightning: "Descending through the ozone smell of lightning, feeling the booms of thunder in the fabric of the plane, Pazzi of the ancient

Pazzi returned to his ancient city with his aims as old as time."[31] The image of Lecter carrying Starling in his arms out of Verger's barn is also grandly theatrical: "Dr. Lecter, erect as a dancer and carrying Starling in his arms, came out from behind the gate, walked barefoot out of the barn, through the pigs. Dr. Lecter walked through the sea of tossing backs and blood spray in the barn."[32] The vivid imagery and rich prose of passages such as these carry the novel along to its Grand Guignol conclusion, which does not seem so far-fetched after 500 pages of dramatic excess involving a faceless villain, a global stage, gore, betrayal at every turn, and man-eating pigs.

In previous books, Harris usually implies violence rather than explicitly presents it. This, too, has changed for the generally excessive *Hannibal*. The gore quotient is considerably higher. The bloody fish market shootout that opens the book sets the stage for what is to come. The pickpocket Gnocco's death is detailed unflinchingly, most graphically in the arterial blood shooting from his trousers all over Pazzi's face and hands. Pazzi is literally drenched in what reads like an ejaculation of blood, the cost he pays for the bracelet bearing Lecter's fingerprint. Then Pazzi himself meets a bloody orgasmic end, hanging from the piazza wall with his bowels swinging beneath him and a death erection sticking out in front of him. It's a startlingly grisly, memorable image: so, too, the Sardinians eaten by pigs, or the hideous death of Verger with a moray eel stuffed into his mouth and blood blowing out of his nose hole. The climax is the spectacle of Lecter carving chunks out of Krendler's brain to sauté them. The violence in the earlier books has been just as extreme but generally kept offstage; here, it's front and center. For all of its excess, however, the violence fits Harris's agenda in trying to present a picture of true wickedness to a readership jaded by ubiquitous portrayals of media violence, ironically including Harris's previous work. Harris slaps us in the "clammy flab of our submissive consciousness hard enough to get our attention."[33]

Harris's dramatic use of point of view certainly calls attention to itself. Though there have been hints of it before, by now the author's voice has become privileged to the point where it becomes a character in its own right—typically acerbic, scathing, and polemical, but sometimes quite lyrical. Directly addressing us as readers, Harris (or his authorial persona, if you prefer) guides us from the streets of Florence into the Capponi Library and from there into Lecter's point of view. Note the use of the second-person voice intertwining with the first-person plural: "Here beside you is the palazzo of the Capponi. . . . Go closer. Rest your head against the cold iron . . . and listen. . . . If you believe you are beyond harm, will you go inside? . . . The alarms cannot see us. . . . Come. . . . The tall double doors of the main salon would squeak and howl if we had to open them. For you, they are open."[34]

This passage reads like the written equivalent of a Steadicam tracking shot, gliding impossibly through walls and doors to peer voyeuristically at what is hidden to all except the invisible audience. At the end of this "Steadicam" shot, we find Lecter playing Bach's *Goldberg Variations*. Then the authorial voice sweeps us from our outside vantage point into Lecter's mind as he contemplates what to do about Pazzi. It's a daring move, since Lecter has remained more or less impervious to outside scrutiny since his introduction to us in *Red Dragon*. Now we begin to find out what the monster thinks about behind the screen of his mocking rhetoric. We follow Lecter's consciousness as it moves through the halls and rooms of the memory palace, a marvelous feat of the imagination.

However, the palace is described as full of pitfalls or oubliettes in the floor. These holes are Harris's metaphor for unconscious repressed memories. Mischa's memory lies interred in these oubliettes but emerges periodically to torment Lecter to the point of screaming. His sudden vulnerability to a past trauma is jarring, considering how

preternaturally self-possessed the doctor has seemed
before. He is abruptly rendered as human as we are. It
seems we do share something in common with Lecter—
our vulnerability to self-betrayal.

This complicated novel asks a lot of us, not the least of
which is identifying with a cannibal. The story asks us to
consider a variety of moral issues. Recognizing the difficul-
ties in navigating them, Harris offers up aphorisms for guid-
ance, again directly addressing the reader in the manner of
the mentors that populate his fiction.[35] Frequently, he
frames moral issues by asking rhetorical questions, such as,
"What do you have when you come from a poor-white
background?"[36] These questions signal to us that a critical
moral dilemma must be considered and a decision made:
Starling must decide whether to rescue Lecter from the pigs,
or Pazzi must decide whether to betray professional ethics
for personal gain. Regardless of what Starling and Pazzi do,
Harris slaps us in our clammy flab once again to force us to
grapple with these weighty issues on our own. What would
*we* do in similar circumstances? Not content to let us
passively follow the story, Harris insists with the ferocity of
a hellfire-and-brimstone preacher that we think about
morality. *Hannibal* is more interactive, a more personal dialogue between author and reader, than any of the previous
novels.

## ALLUSIONS

Research remains an important part of Harris's literary
voice. *Hannibal* takes this trend to an altogether higher
level. In the previous two novels, much of the detail
focused on forensic investigations. This time, while forensic work is still important, the primary focus is on history
(particularly Florentine), literature, and the arts in general. A blow-by-blow recounting of all of Harris's esoter-
ica is not necessary, especially since the Web site
*Dissecting Hannibal* does exactly that in far more detail

than space allows for here. However, the research can be loosely grouped into certain categories.

First, Harris indulges his fondness for showing off his privileged-guest's knowledge of law enforcement facilities, procedures, accoutrement, lore, and "street knowledge." He has also pored over the relevant literature, openly acknowledging his debt to Vernon J. Geberth's textbook, *Practical Homicide Investigation* (1983). With the loving attention to detail of the connoisseur (or the fetishist), Harris points out items of interest to us as he guides us like a modern-day shade of Virgil through the hellish world of *Hannibal*. He often interjects his authorial voice (almost always in the present verb tense) into the narrative flow to tell us that crystal meth is called "ice" or that "Avon calling" refers to a powerful magnum shell used to blow out door locks without harm to the people behind the door. Serving as FBI docent, Harris takes us to the Behavioral Science basement offices and describes convincing details, like the futile attempts in recent years to brighten the space with bright colors. When he's not guiding us around the office space, he helpfully points out for us certain professional accessories worn by the various agents and cops. The Yaqui slide on Starling's hip, for instance, is a holster designed for easy concealment. These details could only be noted by a man quite familiar with the world of police work.

Harris's knowledge extends to the law enforcement apparatus of another country. He takes us inside the Questera, where the fictional Pazzi is the disgraced head of the very-real investigation into the unsolved murders committed by Il Mostro, the so-called "Monster of Florence," who ritually murdered couples in a series of murders that terrorized the city for years. The time Harris spent in Florence researching the case shows in the amount of material that finds its way into the narrative to provide sufficient background for Pazzi. The Questera as seen through Pazzi's eyes contrasts strikingly with the

FBI we already feel we know from earlier Harris fiction. The Italian agency has a single computer, as compared to the FBI's sophisticated cyber systems. The Questera's crime lab is garlanded with garlic to keep out evil spirits, showing another difference between the superstitious Old World agency and the secular technocrats of the FBI. Though Pazzi at the height of his fame dreamed of recreating the Behavioral Science Section in Florence, this dream seems very distant, given the gap between the two worlds. Harris's experience with law enforcement agencies makes both of these worlds vivid.

The book contains far more esoteric research. However, the material, no matter how arcane, is always relevant to the story. *Hannibal* educates us about a grisly Norse method of execution known as the "Bloody Eagle," in which the ribs are broken and spread apart, the lungs pulled out through the back to create the illusion of wings. We learn about the finer points of swine husbandry, including the breeding of two species, the giant forest pig and the European wild boar, to produce the giant hybrids designed to eat Lecter. We are given a mini-lecture on pig dentition and chromosomal structure. Harris even throws in a scholarly reference on the subject, the too-perfectly-named *Harris on the Pig* (1881) by Joseph Harris. Other scientific disciplines play their part in the book. Quantum physics, for one, is introduced in Lecter's fondness for the work of Stephen Hawking, a man even more brilliant than Lecter. Lecter's interest in Hawking's work exists primarily because Lecter believes time can be reversed to bring back Mischa from the dead. Somehow, Harris works in this multidisciplinary knowledge in a reasonably coherent storyline.

Ironically, Harris scorns many academic disciplines. The field of psychiatry in particular comes in for a pasting. The character of Dr. Doemling, the fictional head of the psychology department at Baylor University (Harris's alma mater) and holder of the Verger Chair, is the worst kind of pretentious academic. He pompously lectures

Verger about the psychology of the Lecter/Starling bond and prattles on about Starling's transference of her father fixation to Lecter. By reducing Starling and Lecter's relationship to simplistic Freudian terms in a way that leads Margot Verger to make fun of him and Verger himself to become bored, Doemling embodies the worst kind of pompous academic. The character may represent Harris's artistic slap at critics who apply similar reductive readings to his work.

In addition to academic research, cultural allusions densely populate the story. Harris weaves these allusions into the text to create a baroque tapestry in which the detailed background scenery takes on as much importance as the foreground action. Many times these allusions to high art and culture occur in conjunction with scenes of violence and bloodshed, as when Harris compares drug dealer Drumgo's neck to that of the famous bust of the Egyptian queen Nefertiti or her dead body in repose with her blood-soaked infant to that of the Florentine painter Ciambue's rendition of the Madonna. When Starling snatches the "man-child" infant (probably an indirect reference to the curiously mature aspect of the infant Jesus in many such Madonna paintings) from the dead mother to wash away the blood, she becomes the Madonna herself. Madonna imagery appears again when we see Lecter in the Palazzo Capponi beneath a thirteenth-century tapestry depicting an Ciambue-school Madonna with a head bent like an enormous bird, indicating that Starling's memory looms as large over him in his dark dreams as this tapestry does. This kind of pairing of classical aesthetics and horrific scenes is vintage Harris. His playful combinations of the highest and the lowest in art suggest humanity's capacity for both the sublime and the heinous.

The Florence section of the novel contains the most allusions, as one would expect since the city's artistic legacy informs much of the rest of the story. As Lecter and Pazzi engage in their long courtly dance of death through the city's ancient streets, history unfolds at every turn. Famous places appear as if marked off one by one in a guidebook: the Palazzo Vecchio, the Church of Santa Croce, the Duomo, the Ponte Vecchio, the Uffizi Museum, the Forte di Belvedere. We see the bronze boar, *Il Porcellino*; Donatello's bronze sculpture *Judith and Holofernes* (1460); and Sandro Botticelli's *Primavera* (ca. 1482). Beyond taking us to the usual sight-seeing "musts" like these, Harris struts his intimate local knowledge of the shops along the Florentine streets, such as the fine food store Vera dal 1926 on the Via San Jacopo. Famous names from Florentine history and culture, such as Savonarola, the Medicis, the Pazzis, and Dante Alighieri, populate the story.

The dizzying whirl of history's great names and places certainly establishes the local color of the region, but the details are selected with a keen eye toward their thematic purpose. For instance, when Lecter lectures in the Salon of Lilies within the Palazzo Vecchio to the joint meeting of the Uffizi directors and the Belle Arti Commission, he comments upon Dante's sonnet "La Vita Nuova" and the poet Guido de' Cavalcanti's response to it. What links the two poets together, among other things, is their love for their respective female muses, Beatrice Portinari (Dante) and Giovanna (Cavalcanti). Pazzi and Lecter also love two certain women: Laura (Pazzi) and Starling (Lecter). However, these love affairs are hopeless, even dangerous—capable of annihilating as much as they inspire. Witness what happens to Pazzi out of his desire to give his wife all the material things she expects, or to Lecter in returning to America to save Starling. These two mortal enemies are mirrored in each other.

The scene where Lecter delivers his lecture to the Studiolo, with Pazzi in attendance as a full-circle conclusion of their acquaintance, is full of significant allusions. The lecture spells out the themes of betrayal and avarice to the very man who is about to be punished for them.

The story Lecter relays of Pier della Vigna, the Chancellor to Emperor Frederick II who betrayed the ruler's trust and later hanged himself, foreshadows Pazzi's imminent demise. Pazzi, too, is a betrayer, turning his back on his sworn oath to the law for money (or the possibility of redeeming his good name by the capture of the notorious Lecter) just to keep his young wife happy. Lecter peppers his lecture with allusions to the numerous other betrayers who appear in Dante's *Inferno*, including two Pazzis, one of whom murdered a kinsman and the other who was a traitor to Dante's party, the White Guelphs; Judas Iscariot, who hanged himself after betraying Christ; and Ahithophel, the advisor to David who deserted him during Absalom's revolt and later hanged himself. One cannot help but wonder, with this kind of advance notice and Lecter's known track record, why Pazzi doesn't see it coming when Lecter soon thereafter disembowels him in accord with the image of Judas hanging bowels-out on the door of the Benevento Cathedral and then hangs him from the very balcony where Pazzi's ancestor had met his own fate.

With Pazzi's death, the Florence section concludes, but the allusions continue. Of these, the most significant can be categorized as Biblical, mythological, artistic, architectural, literary, and pop culture. The Biblical references include a couple to Jezebel and Jesus. In his letter to Verger, Lecter parallels Verger to Jezebel. Jezebel, the queen of King Ahab of the Northern Kingdom, is thrown from a window and then eaten by dogs, as described in 2 Kings of the Bible. It is likely that Lecter had this story in mind when he suggests that Verger, high on angel dust, feed his face to the dogs. Also of note are the story's frequent comparisons between Starling and Christ. Starling will be thirty-three, the traditional age of Christ at his death, two days before Christmas. In his memory palace, Lecter places her at the side of Christ leading a parade. The parallel is that Starling, like Christ, is the sacrificial victim of a conspiracy of the powerful elite.

The mythological allusions underscore Lecter's unique nature as something both part of and above common humanity. For example, the driving of the cattle prod into Lecter's eye bears a passing resemblance to Odysseus's blinding of Polyphemos, the cannibalistic Cyclops.[37] Most important to the plot, however, is the story of Leda and the swan, alluded to at least twice. This story serves to link the relationship between Lecter and Starling to the ancient tradition of gods consummating sexual relationships with mortal women. In mythology, Leda is the wife of King Tyndareus of Sparta and the mother of Helen as a result of a union with Zeus, who either seduced or raped her in the physical form of a swan. The story appears (without the rape element) in the Roman poet Ovid's *Metamorphoses* (ca. 8 C.E.) The physical union of the god and the human implies a certain shared commonality in Greek myth, with each aspiring to the other's status; however, the rape aspect in some versions of Leda's story argues for this union being a little one-sided at times. The story has been a popular subject in art over the centuries, including works by Leonardo da Vinci, Michelangelo, and the Irish poet William Butler Yeats. In Harris's book, Lecter's absentee landlord in Maryland displays a collection of four bronzes and eight paintings of Leda's intraspecies coupling. Lecter's favorite is a fairly explicit painting by Anne Shingleton. The Leda story parallels Lecter to Zeus and Starling to Leda. Like Zeus, Lecter forces himself upon Starling, breaking down her resistance and morality through an irresistible combination of hypnosis and powerful drugs.

Harris references the painters Balthus, Vermeer, and William Blake. Balthus is apparently Lecter's cousin, although Lecter perhaps mistakenly sends art show catalogs to him in France. Balthus (1908–2001) was born in France, but within the timeframe designated by *Hannibal* was living in Switzerland. Balthus was friends with a wide variety of famous writers and painters, including

Pablo Picasso, Albert Camus, and Antoine de Saint-Exupéry. Having Balthus in the Lecter pedigree certainly contributes to Lecter's intellectual bona fides, even if by proxy.[38] Balthus, like Lecter, was also dislocated by the Nazis and spent time in Florence. Jan Vermeer (1632–1675) was a Dutch Baroque painter, known for his exquisitely detailed portraits and paintings of everyday life. Vermeer is important to Barney, Lecter's former orderly. As a result of years spent learning culture from Lecter, Barney is embarked on a quest to see every Vermeer painting in the world before he dies—Barney's own "bucket list." In fact, this quest sends him to Buenos Aires, where he sees Lecter and Starling living blissfully in exile. Finally, William Blake, a fixture in Harris's fiction since *Red Dragon*, takes a bow. A print of his *The Ancient of Days* hangs above Verger's couch, its image of God with a pair of calipers suggesting the extent to which Verger controls the events of the plot.

Several scenes allude to famous architecture. To provide the entryway for his memory palace, for example, Lecter chooses the foyer of the Norman Chapel (or Cappella Palatina), which is located in the ground floor of the Palazzo dei Normanni in Palermo, Sicily, dating from the ninth through the twelfth centuries. The chapel combines several different architectural styles, including the Norman, Byzantine, and Arabic. Its fine detail is appropriate not only for the complexity of Lecter's mind but for this most densely allusive of Harris's books. In another example, the smoky mirror in which Lecter shows Starling her makeover is taken from the Château de Vaux-le-Vicomte, an exemplary seventeenth-century house of the French Baroque period that creates a unified space of structure, décor, and landscape. Presumably, Lecter seeks a similar unification for Starling's compartmentalized mind by breaking through her walls of repression.

Harris alludes to many well-known writers, either directly or by cribbing unacknowledged lines from them.

William Blake, *The Ancient of Days Putting a Compass to the Earth*. Photograph © The Trustees of the British Museum.

To give one small instance of an unattributed line, the description of Lecter as "imperially slim" amid the sea of pot-bellied rednecks at the gun show is taken from the poem "Richard Cory" (1897) by Edwin Arlington Robinson (1869–1935). The line in "Richard Cory" reads: "He was a gentleman from sole to crown/Clean favored and imperially slim." Robinson's line is as apt a summary of Lecter's appearance as we could find. Whether Harris also had in mind the Simon and Garfunkel song "Richard Cory" (1966) is an open question.

Among the direct allusions, there is the occasional nod to William Shakespeare; for example, Harris titles Part 5 "A Pound of Flesh," a reference to the price demanded by the moneylender Shylock for a defaulted loan in Shakespeare's *The Merchant of Venice* (ca. 1596). The epigram for Part 6 reads, "Therefore bihoveth hire a ful long spoon/That shal ete with a feend," taken from Geoffrey Chaucer's "The Squire's Tale" in *The Canterbury Tales* (ca. late 1380s), although Harris misattributes it to "The Merchant's Tale." Given that Part 6 contains the notorious dinner party, the epigram cues us to remember something that Starling, under Lecter's hypnotic influence, does not—she sups with a fiend.

Another poet, T. S. Eliot, is referenced. Eliot is apparently a personal favorite of Starling's, since she slightly misquoted some lines from him in *Silence*. During her revisit to the ruins of the mental hospital in *Hannibal*, she repeats to herself some lines from Eliot's "Burnt Norton" (1935) in the *Four Quartets* (1943). *Four Quartets* is a collection of four long poems, each divided into five sections. The setting of the section entitled "Burnt Norton" is a rose garden at a country estate in North Gloucestershire, England. One of its many themes is the relationship of human existence to time. Starling is reminded of the poem while remembering her visits with Lecter seven years before in the now-abandoned hospital. The lines read: "Footfalls echo in the memory/Down the passage which we did not take/Towards the door we never opened/Into the rose garden." She likely thinks of it now because of her meditation upon the passage of time. Its invocation in this setting, however, is ironic. As Starling dryly notes, this spooky deserted building is nothing like a peaceful rose garden in the English countryside.

Though not directly referenced, Eliot's "The Waste Land" (1922) is another likely influence on Harris. Eliot's quintessential modernist poem alludes to high art from a variety of cultures as well as popular entertainment, such as the music hall. Similarly, Harris routinely refers to recognized classics of high art and various artifacts of popular culture, often side by side. One of the more amusing juxtapositions of this type involves Barney and Margot watching football and *The Simpsons*, followed up with the decidedly high-brow public television series *I, Claudius*. One can only imagine the suffering Lecter endures when he must watch an episode of the TV game show *The Price Is Right* in the waiting room of a hospital while waiting for a surgeon he can steal credentials from. Then there is the macabre humor of the scene where Krendler, his mind a shambles from the removal of four slices of his prefrontal lobe, abruptly sings the first two lines from the Bing Crosby song *Swinging on a Star* (1944). The optimistic, child-like innocence inherent in the lines "Would you like to swing from a star/Carry moonbeams home in a jar" contrasts ironically, to say the least, with the horror of Krendler's higher-level brain functioning removed from him one slice at a time.

These allusions serve another useful purpose in deciphering the meaning of the Harrisverse. It is relatively easy to figure out Harris's authorial attitudes toward his characters by the kind of culture, high or low, they embrace. Lecter and to some extent Starling score highest in Harris's regard, as both exhibit more rarefied tastes in art. Barney also comes off relatively well, in that his long stewardship of Lecter's needs in the asylum has cultivated within Barney a desire to see every Vermeer painting in the world before he dies. By contrast, pity poor Inelle Corey, who speaks of her alleged relationship with the missing Dr. Chilton as "a love, a love you don't find everyday," a clear cribbing of the lyrics of "You've Lost That Lovin' Feeling" (1965), a song by The Righteous Brothers. Ms. Corey's embrace of mass culture condemns her to the ranks of the Philistines, as Lecter the pitiless snob would label them. Paradoxically, however, Harris subsumes popular entertainment to create his unique brand of literary thriller.

## SYMBOLS

The symbolic structure of *Hannibal* is the most complex of any Harris book so far, as fits a work that "reaches to a form of poetry, rather than to the police procedural."[39] Moving away from the realism of *Red Dragon* and *Silence*, *Hannibal* takes us to a place where the most mundane objects are fraught with meaning. Just to give one example, consider the orange (the fruit, not the color). In terms of its placement in the story, the humble orange takes on a sinister cast. In the painting *Primavera*, which serves as the catalyst for Pazzi's epiphany about Il Mostro, the mythological figures stand in an orange grove. Once the symbolic association between oranges and death has been created, oranges appear repeatedly. The pickpocket Gnocco selects oranges from a street vendor shortly before his death, just as Marlon Brando's Don Corleone did prior to being gunned down in *The Godfather* (1972). Finally, Lecter puts orange slices into Lillet to serve to Starling prior to dining on Krendler's brains. Having come to associate oranges with death, we now realize the presence of the orange slices at the dinner party prepares us for the death of Starling's soul.

However, the book's animal symbolism is the most pronounced and sustained. In no particular order, here is a partial list of animals mentioned in the story: fish, crickets, spiders, snakes, spider crabs, vultures, hyenas, horses, eels, dogs, doves, roller pigeons, boars, coyotes, moths, lions, tortoises, and owls. The Harris bestiary is larger than ever. With all of these different animals to consider, a few categories stand out by sheer repetition.

For example, fish imagery appears early, in the opening shootout at the Feliciana Fish Market. After Drumgo is killed, Starling washes her baby free of Drumgo's HIV-positive blood on a cutting board normally used for fish. She takes over Drumgo's role as mother to take care of the endangered infant, so their blood mingling together suggests female bonding. The spilled blood's chemical similarity to seawater, where the lifeless fish in the market originated, establishes a symbolic connection between nature and violence, a significant element of Harris's philosophy. The fish market also foreshadows the entrance of Mason Verger, himself resembling a creature of the deep, with his skeletal face and bared teeth. His one mobile hand is often described as resembling another sea creature, a crab, as it moves across his bed sheet. True to the predatory sea creatures he resembles, he kills off Starling's career.

Appropriately for him, Verger keeps a "pet" brutal moray eel in a tank in his private chamber. The eel endlessly circles around its tank, a visual symbol of eternity. The old saying about pets resembling their owners is certainly true here. Verger's face is all teeth, like a moray with its mouth open. But its primary function in the plot is to tell us through association about Verger's violent nature. The brutal moray earns its name because of its voracious predatory nature, on display in the scene where Verger's assistant Cordell feeds the eel crippled ornamental carp until it is gorged. Verger loves to watch the eel feed, which makes sense for his rapacious character. In the end, the eel serves as a means of poetic justice, killing Verger in a fairly hideous fashion, with a little assist from Margot.[40]

Moving from the sea to the land, we find Krendler described frequently as a "hyena." These predatory/

scavenger creatures have a particularly nasty reputation, both among Europeans and Africans, for their tendency to dig up graves to consume corpses and bite the faces off sleeping villagers. The ghoulish "laughter" sounds made by spotted hyena further add to the animals' bad reputations. Hyenas are typically associated with filth and gluttony, and their name comes from a Latin word meaning "pig." All of these associations are invoked whenever Krendler is described as hyena-like, especially when he opportunistically sizes up Starling for vulnerabilities. He is part of a "pack" of other hyena-like men determined to ruin her. For Harris, the function of the hyena image is to portray Krendler and those like him as negatively as possible.

Harris employs serpent imagery for the snake's evil connotations in the Western tradition.[41] Verger's plaited floor-length hair, for instance, is coiled serpent-like on his chest respirator, its plaits described as scales. Starling thinks of Lecter's old cell as a shed snake skin. Certainly, Lecter's mannerisms could be called snake-like, with his hissing voice and darting tongue. Textual allusions frequently compare him to Satan, so linking him to the snake is yet one more instance of this.

Like the snake, the pig serves in the story as a demonic symbol. In appearance, the boars bred by Verger to eat Lecter are downright diabolical. Trained to associate feeding time with tapes of tortured men screaming, their emergence from the woods is a nightmarish spectacle. They run as fast as wolves, their faces described as hellish. When they refuse to eat Lecter, another diabolical figure, it seems as if they have recognized one of their own. The superstitious Tommaso, survivor of the massacre in Verger's barn, claims that the pigs helped the doctor escape. The demonic symbolism of the pigs advances Harris's agenda to create his own vision of the Inferno.

For Harris, birds typically represent female victims.[42] This point is made clear when Barney Matthews retrieves a dead dove from the busy street where it has been run down. The dove's grieving mate refuses to leave the body, following Barney as he takes the dead bird home to eat it. Murder victims are strewn across the landscape in Harris's fiction, most of them leaving behind grief-stricken family—just like the dead dove and its devoted mate. The pigeon retains the same association with vulnerability as it does in *Silence*, but it's more nuanced, even ambiguous. For instance, Barney relates to Starling a conversation he had with Lecter, during which Lecter explained to him the genetics of breeding roller pigeons. A roller pigeon, as the name suggests, rolls backward to the ground as a form of display. A "shallow" roller pulls up from the ground in plenty of time, whereas a "deep" roller plunges almost all the way down before pulling up. If two deep rollers are bred, the offspring will hit the ground and die. Lecter concluded his mini-lecture by saying, "Officer Starling is a deep roller. We'll hope one of her parents was not."[43] Whether she is indeed a "deep roller" or not is debatable. We could say she crashed in one respect, but then again, she survives her time caged with Lecter to become his willing companion. Is the pigeon necessarily doomed? Perhaps not.

## THEMES

*Hannibal* in almost every significant way redefines Harris's thematic approach to his material. The themes are not necessarily new for Harris, but they are more extreme in their implications—more nihilistic, more cynical. Harris has never sounded more over-the-top or downright scornful of the human condition. Whatever optimism *Silence* may have gingerly offered, *Hannibal* blows it all to hell. The affirming coming-of-age story of the previous novel, full of promise for a bright future for Starling, ends here in the profound disillusionment of bitter experience. The book's master theme is corruption in all of its forms—physical, moral, and political. To reference William Blake, the book is the "Tyger" to *Silence*'s "The Lamb."

A primary theme centers on the corruption of the twin demons of politics and capitalism, forces that doom Starling's career and help drive her right into Lecter's arms. This confluence of powerful forces constitutes an economy of cruelty. The representatives of corrupt capitalism and politics are, respectively, Verger and Krendler. Their machinations take place against the backdrop of the national spectacle of the impeachment of President Bill Clinton and the on-going political fallout from the FBI debacles of Waco and Ruby Ridge.[44] The book marks the return of politics as a central concern for Harris, *Black Sunday* being his other overtly political book. This time, however, the political threat is strictly internal.

The first sentence signals the political theme, when Harris states that the landlord of the headquarters of the Bureau of Alcohol, Tobacco, and Firearms is the Reverend Sun Myung Moon of the Unification Church (aka the "Moonies"). The church is financially involved in any number of business, political, and media organizations; it draws controversy for allegations of fraud and the propriety of the Reverend's extravagant lifestyle. The mention of this church introduces the theme of corrupt political and financial alliances. The plot is interspersed with references to real-life allegations of political opportunism at best and abuse of power at worst. For instance, the ill-fated drug raid at the fish market is co-opted in part by the unnamed mayor of Washington (Marion Barry?), who wants to crack down on drugs in order to offset the negative publicity of his own drug conviction. After the raid fails, Starling is selected by the feds as a scapegoat to take the blame, in order to satisfy the media and public demand for accountability after the Waco and Ruby Ridge debacles. Starling's second, and professionally fatal, hearing before the FBI takes place during the media frenzy in the capital over President Clinton's impeachment; Crawford believes the timing of the hearing is deliberate, so that whatever is decided will slide by unnoticed. These real-life figures and events make an otherwise fantastic story more grounded in reality.

The closing of the fictitious Baltimore State Hospital is based on actual governmental trends over the past many years. Like all state institutions, the Baltimore facility is dependent on the vagaries of budget. When the dollars dry up because the budget has been cut or the legislature removes funding, certain institutions are faced with the hard knowledge that they are no longer viable as businesses. The Baltimore asylum is forced into this hard corner when cut off from its funding by a legislature fed up with its on-going waste and mismanagement. The patients are cut loose to wander the streets, often dying there. The sad fate of the hospital's patients is embodied in Sammie, the hebephrenic from *Silence* who wants to go with Jesus. With nowhere else to go and no one in this world willing to help him, Sammie lives in the dark basement of the abandoned building. The hospital's closing parallels the real-life fate of many mental health institutions, shut down in ever greater numbers during the past few decades because of rising costs, reallocation of monies, and deinstitutionalization of patients not yet ready to be released.

Another aspect of Harris's political theme is the crooked partnership between politics, big business, and law enforcement. Like colossal spiders, the book's villains spin webs of deceit that ensnare many victims, including Starling. The primary "spider," or center of all corruption, is Mason Verger, and behind him, his father. The Verger meatpacking dynasty has grown fat from government contracts since the Civil War. The family survived the embalmed beef scandal in the Spanish-American War and the muckraking investigations of Upton Sinclair and others during the 1920s, a feat made possible by greasing the palms of politicians with a never-ending flow of money. Molson Verger, Mason's father, pioneered the economics of cruelty as applied to the meatpacking industry. He fed pigs large amounts of hog hair and manure to cut down on the expense of their feed, and gave them ditch liquor made from fermented animal waste to drink so they would gain more weight. He spent vast sums of money to prevent legislation to make animal slaughter more humane. He treated people little better. Exploiting his connections with organized crime, he intimidated union leadership to keep wages and safety conditions low. Molson Verger represents the worst of the big-industry magnates. Through him, Harris indicts American big business, and capitalism itself, as inherently cruel to the helpless and disadvantaged.

Having learned the art of corruption from his father, Mason Verger uses his family fortune to buy political influence and the powers of federal law enforcement. His money buys him numerous international contacts that keep him ahead of the FBI in the global search for Lecter. He shares information with the FBI in return only when he needs access to its resources. His crooked financial network, made possible by bank secrecy laws in nations such as Switzerland, extends around the world. The world-wide bounty he offers for Lecter poses an overwhelming temptation for the likes of Pazzi, demonstrating Verger's ability to corrupt those around him by appealing to their greed. Avarice, as represented by Pazzi, is the means by which Verger maintains his power, domestically and abroad. If Verger stands in for unchained American capitalism, America's drive to acquire material goods and fortunes comes with a cost—the sacrifice of one's moral principles, including basic human decency. Because of money, a repulsive man like Mason Verger can wield massive global influence. For money, a middle-class working stiff like Pazzi, or a political wanna-be like Krendler, will sell his soul and "make his own house be his gallows," to paraphrase Dante.

Starling, impervious to financial temptations, faces her own unique dangers. In a world dominated by men, she continues her lonely journey as a female professional. The danger posed by gender dynamics is another of the book's themes. Starling's career is in desperate jeopardy, the result of her "smart mouth," early success, and physical attractiveness antagonizing too many powerful men. Her male mentors are essentially gone to her—one is near retirement and the other is a fugitive serial killer who may or may not want to kill her. Continually demeaned as a professional, she endures both hostile comments and ogling daily. Fellow FBI agents and policemen question her ability to fire weapons—doubts they would never express to another man. These glances and doubts are routine annoyances for an attractive professional woman like Starling.

However, many of the men she encounters transcend the aggravation level to actually become dangerous to her. Krendler is her biggest professional danger. His grudge against her, stemming from both her early success and her rejection of his drunken advance toward her, leads him into an alliance with Verger to break her career once and for all. He expresses his hatred for her in ugly expressions like "cornpone country pussy." Harris typically puts language like this into the mouths of misogynistic characters like Krendler in order to demonstrate the extent to which they dehumanize women. By reducing Starling to a female body part, Krendler verbally dismembers her. Starling returns the favor by eating part of his cerebral cortex at Lecter's dinner party. In this novel about revenge, Krendler gets his appropriate comeuppance for misogyny from the woman he victimized the most.

In *Silence*, we've seen that one female response against a misogynistic world is to create a haven away from it. Ardelia Mapp, still Starling's roommate seven years later, represents the possibility of family for the orphan Starling. The two of them have set up their own house together as a place away from the stress of the male workplace. The house is a safe place for Starling. Its washing machine, with its sloshing warm water, represents the safety of the womb. Mapp provides her with the emotional support of a life partner, although the two are not lovers. Even when Starling runs off with Lecter, she still thinks enough of Mapp to send her a note reassuring her she is fine. The relationship between Starling and Mapp is paralleled to another that some of the novel's critics find quite maddening—Margot Verger and her lover Judy. While Harris's fiction has often been lauded for its pro-feminist stance, *Hannibal*'s depiction of Margot Verger as a lesbian is more problematic. The film adaptation of *Silence* drew heat over its supposed homophobia, and *Hannibal* does little to dispel that charge. Margot fits in many ways the "butch" stereotype of a lesbian woman. She is a bodybuilder with a masculinized body. Her steroid use has shriveled her ovaries, rendering her even more masculine. She engages in actions bordering on caricature, including the cracking of walnuts with her fist and her desire to take semen from Mason to impregnate her lover, Judy. The Judy-Margot subplot may be Harris's attempt to address the timely issue of family rights for gay parents. Perhaps Margot functions as a cautionary tale of the wages of unnatural transformations, an ongoing theme in Harris's fiction. Maybe she is one more grotesque in Harris's cast of Southern Gothic characters. What seems most likely, however, is that Margot and Judy constitute another example of the female family, liberated of the dangerous presence of men.[45]

Starling does choose to leave Mapp, however, for Lecter. This plot development speaks to Starling's biggest source of internal conflict—her oedipal neurosis. Implied in *Silence*, this primal conflict emerges openly in *Hannibal* during Lecter's hypnotherapeutic sessions with Starling. Starling confesses to being really mad at her father for being stupid enough to get himself killed and leaving her and her mother in poverty. In a revelation that incenses many readers, Harris demonstrates that, in the words of Stephen M. Fuller, "[Starling's] exaggerated sense of compassion and her obsessive pursuit of justice originate not in any intrinsic national quality, but in the burden of her unresolved oedipal conflict."[46] Once having verbalized this inner tension, Starling's sexual libido is freed to express itself, which she promptly does with Lecter, her benefactor. She no longer views Lecter as a paternal mentor, but as an equal partner. In the strangest of ways, *Hannibal* does prove to have a happy ending after all. Starling is liberated from her oedipal neurosis and the misogynistic tyranny of the FBI.

The Harrisverse is not complete without a few bitter salvos fired at Christianity. *Hannibal*, however, elevates the antireligious theme to new heights. Practically the entire novel is a diatribe against the inhumanity of those who pay lip service to God even as they sin in the most egregious of ways. Sexton points out that the book is structured throughout on "sustained blasphemy."[47] Since the novel focuses a great deal on Lecter, whose animosity toward religion is well established, this blasphemous tone should not be surprising. Paradoxically, however, in the very ferocity of his condemnations of sins such as avarice, hypocrisy, and lust, Harris emerges as an old-fashioned moralist, inveighing against the hedonism and violence of the fallen world as much as any hellfire-and-brimstone preacher. The book inflicts punishments upon its sinners in a manner worthy of Dante, whose *Inferno* is a primary literary influence on Harris.

We've already seen how an avaricious fellow such as Pazzi suffers a grisly judgment because of his sin. However, as a sworn officer of the law and a religious man to boot, he is also guilty of hypocrisy. The devoutly Roman Catholic conspirators who assist Verger are equally hypocritical. One of them, Tommaso, prays with his victims before killing them. However, Verger is the story's prime hypocrite, one who winces at using the Lord's name in vain but doesn't hesitate to abuse children or feed a man to the pigs for the sake of vengeance. He conceives of his scheme at Christmas-time, in defiance of the "peace on earth" sentiment of the season. He believes his born-again acceptance of Christ as savior gives him immunity from punishment for his sins. "Verger" is the name for a lay-person who assists in religious services, so Mason's last name is ironic in the context of his actions, which trans-gress against the principles of Christian theology in prac-tically every way imaginable. Like the book's other sinners, however, he can't elude poetic justice.

Lust, too, takes the full fury of the novel's moral con-demnation. The book is full of perverse sexuality, from Verger's sexual abuse of children to Starling's intercourse with Lecter. Sex is anything but life-affirming in the Har-risverse; more often than not, it is a lethal indulgence. *Hannibal* makes a clear connection between sexuality and violence. For example, snuff films, in which women are sexually brutalized and then killed on-screen, are men-tioned several times. One of Verger's Italian conspirators, Oreste Pini, has made a snuff film; Starling thinks of "snuff-queen style" as a fashion statement. Similarly, the torture-instrument exhibition in Florence draws massive crowds, mostly couples titillated by the graphic descrip-tions of the effect the implements had on the human body. Of these crowds, Harris writes that "excitement leaped like a trout in the public trousers"[48] and "many [couples] were in estrus, rubbing against each other in the crowd at the exit."[49] The connection between sex-uality and death is most grotesquely depicted in Pazzi's death by hanging, with his erect manhood and his blood and viscera falling from his swinging body like a ghastly ejaculation. Linking orgasm and death is nothing new, of course, but *Hannibal* dramatizes it to an extreme.

So the sins of humanity, especially those who claim to be pious, are called to a reckoning. Not content with that, the book frequently assaults the naïve notion of a caring

God, continuing at an epic scale Lecter's habit of collecting stories about church roof collapses. The novel's
images are often mockeries of Christian iconography,
such as the light reflected in the spray from Starling
washing HIV-positive blood from Drumgo's baby: "Water
flying, a mocking rainbow of God's Promise in the spray,
sparkling banner over the work of His blind hammer."[50]
In another example of blasphemous mockery, Verger's
plans to have Lecter eaten alive are explicitly framed in
the language of communion, in which devout Christians
consume the body and blood of Christ. Even the classical
paintings of Christ's crucifixion are mocked, when Harris
describes the Uffizi museum as "that great meat house of
hanging Christs."[51] Most fundamentally, *Hannibal* questions the nature of God. Starling, for one, has given up on
God's direct intervention in human affairs, knowing that
God will not send rain to prevent infants from dying during a drought. Given the evidence of lack of divine intervention, the question then becomes, is God indifferent to
human suffering? Or, if God causes it, why? One of the
most dramatic expressions of embittered despair about
ever understanding the nature of God is found in this
passage: "God's choices in inflicting suffering are not
satisfactory to us, nor are they understandable, unless
innocence offends Him. Clearly He needs some help in
directing the blind fury with which he Flogs the earth."[52]
In a way, Harris as author steps in to direct that blind
fury at the sinners populating the narrative. But God
(assuming such a being exists) remains incomprehensible
to us. If there is an answer to our plight, Harris insists, it
will not come from God.

In the Harrisverse, any answers to the violent miseries
of the human condition lie within our hearts, or more
literally, the complex structure of the brain. Lecter tells us
that the limbic brain is the seat of primal senses and violent emotions, and the cerebral cortex is the home of the
finer emotions, including pity. "Pity has no place at my

table," Lecter asserts, but at the same time he compares the civilized exchanges and ceremonies of dinner to miracles in a church.[53] As Lecter implies, the elements of murder and pity coexist in the biology of the brain. They do not cancel each other out; the virtuous man may murder, and the murderer may dispense mercy. As Barney describes his philosophy of the human heart, the good can coexist with the terrible in one person. His words imply that clear separation between the good and the terrible is not possible. In the contemporary world, categories are not mutually exclusive; boundaries are permeable. In fact, as Fuller argues, Harris "wholly collapses the boundaries, accomplishing this dissolving of distinctions by coupling Clarice with Hannibal Lecter, thereby merging hero with antihero/villain."[54]

No one signifies the collapse of defined boundary more than Lecter. In Barney's words, Lecter "doesn't believe in syllogism, or synthesis, or any absolute. . . . [He believes in] Chaos. And you don't even have to believe in it. It's self-evident."[55] Lecter believes what is true one moment may not be true the next, as he tells Starling. Context determines meaning, he claims, and context is ever changing. Even if personality is formed by early experiences, psychological conditioning can be undone. Seemingly unshakable behaviors deeply rooted in past trauma may be conquered—as Lecter proves by helping Starling heal from her neurosis, and as Starling proves by helping Lecter heal from his. Even hard-wired behavior may be altered through the power of cognition, thus allowing for freedom from the absolutism of genetics. Harris's fiction consistently maintains that to look for absolute meaning is folly, but nowhere has this philosophy been more radically stated than in *Hannibal*.

As a novel, *Hannibal* perplexes, provokes, and even outrages. More of a surrealist's diatribe against all that is ugly or "rude" in human behavior than a police procedural, the novel bears little in common with Harris's previous work but may yet be his truest expression of his signature themes. *Hannibal* also constitutes Harris's taking back his characters from a public expecting the same characters immortalized by Anthony Hopkins and Jodie Foster in Jonathan Demme's version of *Silence*. Harris dares to demystify his most mythic creation, Hannibal Lecter, by giving him a past. The next novel, then, revisits Lecter's past to fill in the gaps.

# 6

# "We'll Call Him a Monster": *Hannibal Rising*

A severely traumatized orphan from a war-ravaged country seeks revenge against the brutal, lawless thugs who not only murdered but ate his younger sister. Admittedly, the vengeance taken upon these cannibals falls into the "extreme" category. But consider the plea for leniency, if not sympathy, such a righteously vengeful individual might enter on his own behalf if ever called to account for his actions. A jury, even in these vindictive times, might well consider that kind of childhood trauma a mitigating factor in a death-penalty murder trial.

In a sense, the readers who have followed the adventures of Hannibal Lecter this far do serve as that jury. The readers of the latest (and as of this writing, the last) Thomas Harris novel, *Hannibal Rising* (2006), are asked to accept Lecter as a hero of almost mythic proportions and understand him as a human being, then reconcile that with what is already known about his grotesque crimes. The backstory partially revealed in *Hannibal* is fully expanded upon in this novel. We see the entirety of what happened to Lecter's sister, Mischa. Further, we see that

Lecter tracked down and killed his sister's butchers. The novel makes the case that while Lecter may have been born with certain physical and psychological predispositions to murder, it took his environment to complete his transformation into a serial-killing cannibal.

Considered by most critics to be the weakest novel in the Lecter series, *Hannibal Rising* may be the victim of its author's insistence on providing some kind of explanation for Lecter's pathology, much against the wishes of the majority of the audience. The story accounts not only for his most notorious trait, that is, his cannibalism, but also his *eideteker* ability, his rarefied taste for the finer things, his genius, and so forth. Harris takes the character as we know him, reverse engineers from those characteristics a second character, and then makes that second character evolve into the first character.

It's a daring artistic gamble on Harris's part, the success of which is debatable. The net effect, at least according to the detractors of the last two novels in the series, is to strip the good doctor of his mythic grandeur, to pluck him from the metaphysical realm of pure evil. These are the readers who rage against the dying of Lecter's dark light. For them, to provide Lecter with something as mundane as an explanation for his evil actions is to dishonor him. In another context, Harris warned us about the dangers of looking too closely at Dr. Lecter: "We can only learn so much and live." But what if the converse were true, that if we learned too much about him he would not live on as our favorite serial-killing superman? What is Lecter without his mystery? To make Lecter a clockwork monster, wound up by past trauma and then set loose upon the world—why, then he would just be another lunatic, afflicted by a troubled childhood, endlessly repeating his mechanistic modus operandi. It's somehow so—ordinary.

Yet what if—just what if—Harris had this diminishment of the Lecter character in mind all along? Or came to it as the character developed from a secondary role to a starring role? What if Harris means to do exactly what many readers cry "foul" for—strip the doctor of his evil glamour? After all, the seventeenth-century poet John Milton does the same thing to Satan over the duration of *Paradise Lost*. As part of Milton's carefully plotted design, Satan at first is a compelling, even tragically heroic figure in his refusal to accept defeat. However, Satan's obsession for revenge against God leads him to adopt a variety of guises (a snake, for example) that render him progressively less attractive and sympathetic in the eyes of Milton's audience. Milton sets up his readers for this disenchantment with evil. Might Harris, having explicitly compared Lecter to Satan at the end of *Silence*, be striving for something of the same character diminishment here?

Lecter's melodramatically awful childhood shouldn't have been a surprise to the experienced and/or perceptive Harris reader. What's surprising is that it took Harris this long to do it. Consider the past history of Michael Lander in *Black Sunday* that led him inexorably to his destiny in the skies above the Super Bowl. Or the brutal refugee past of Dahlia Iyad. Or the abuse suffered by the child Francis Dolarhyde that transformed the adult into a monster. By contrast, little is mentioned of Lecter's childhood in *Red Dragon*. Graham notes in passing that the boy Lecter tortured small animals, but nothing is said about Lecter's Old World origins or what happened to him there. The Lecter of *Red Dragon* is nowhere near as erudite as his later incarnations, nor does he seem of foreign origin. So either Lecter's European past was unknown to Graham and the FBI, which seems unlikely, or Harris just hadn't gotten around yet to giving Lecter much of a past. In *Silence*, Lecter shows an attraction toward European culture, as evidenced by his sketch of the Duomo in Florence, but he still does not seem to be anything other than a very educated, well-traveled intellectual of American origin. Only in *Hannibal* do we learn he is of noble Lithuanian birth and that he is the product of an atrocity inflicted upon his younger sister during World War II on the Eastern Front. When Harris gave his most enduring character a childhood trauma, it was certainly a dramatic one, almost operatic in its scope.

The horrors of war, more than any other root cause, created Hannibal the Cannibal. In this one regard, Lecter is quite similar to Dahlia Iyad, the orphaned survivor of another war in another foreign land in another time. *Hannibal Rising* is populated by characters marked by wartime atrocity and genocide. The interior landscape of the mind can be ravaged and scarred every bit as much as the landscape pitted with bomb craters. The ruins of the hunting lodge the older Lecter returns to in search of Mischa's remains represent the true state of Lecter's twisted subconscious. The lodge is a haunted house to complement the magnificent memory palace Lecter consciously constructs for himself. Lying buried beneath the memory palace floors are the shattered timbers of the hunting lodge where Lecter lost both his sister and his mind and emerged as what we'll call, in the words of his nemesis Inspector Popil, a monster.

Lest one assume Harris excuses Lecter's actions on the basis of his wretched childhood, we must remember Lecter has the power of choice. Offered a home by his widowed Japanese aunt, it seems fleetingly possible for Lecter to choose another destiny in France. Even after his first few murders, he still has the option of accepting Mischa's absence and living with his aunt in relative peace. Like Dolarhyde, Lecter can choose to turn his back on murder and embrace love. However, the imprint of the past is too strong, his psychosis too compelling.

## CRITICAL RECEPTION

As already mentioned, *Hannibal Rising* was not a critical darling upon publication. In fact, it spawned some pretty vociferous rhetoric. A typical reaction was that the Lecter "franchise" had run its course, sapped of its vitality through overexposure, absurd plotting, trite dialogue and characters, purple prose, and superficially described foreign settings. Note, for example, Anthony Lane's complaint: "The failure of 'Hannibal Rising,' which seems to me absolute, is easily explained. It stems from the author's newfound conviction that Hannibal, too, can be easily explained. . . . all we get is influences, beginning with the loss of home and family, plus the implication that these were the making, or the warping, of Hannibal Lecter. . . . we watch the legend sink." Lane concludes, strongly: "Hannibal the Unboreable, thanks to his overzealous creator, has dwindled to less of a monster and grown into more of a bore. He would kill me for saying so, but it's the truth."[1] Stronger still, however, is Will Self's verdict: "*Hannibal Rising* [is] little more than evil twaddle. . . . I rather suspect that Lecter has begun—as he did with the crass Paul Krendler in *Hannibal*—to eat his own creator's brain."[2] Janet Maslin's review drips with contempt, saying that "market forces . . . impelled Mr. Harris to cough up this hairball of a story."[3] Strong words, indeed.

Tina Jordan gives the book a grade of "D," justifying the grade with this: "Harris will rightly be remembered as the creator of Hannibal Lecter. . . . But Harris should have stifled Lecter after *Silence*. *Hannibal* gave me indigestion, and *Hannibal Rising* didn't leave me hungry for more either."[4] Deidre Donahue doesn't pull any punches either, basically calling Harris a bleeding-heart liberal: "Go weep on Oprah's couch, Tom, but stop portraying Lecter as a victim. We like him fine as a monster."[5] She bitterly complains that Harris, a skilled regional writer, is out of his element when trying to describe foreign locales.

Thomas Leitch explains his dislike for the book by comparing it as a prequel to the recent cinematic spate of

"origin" stories of comic book superheroes such as Superman and Batman:

> These prequels, heavy with retrospective knowledge,
> have to load each detail with ironic significance even as
> they're pumping up the story. . . . The result is a demysti-
> fication that leaves heroes looking less heroic and villains
> less villainous, because, after all, they're just reacting to
> the past histories that have been created for them. . . .
> With *Hannibal Rising*, Harris, ever eager to demystify his
> monstrous hero, confirms the promise he showed in *Han-
> nibal* as his own most determined imitator.[6]

Will Cohu calls the book a "stinker," primarily because
of its filmic quality: "The dot-to-dot simplicities of this
book, its fatuous psychology, its sketchy detail and curt
characterisations seem less of a novel than a draft of a
screenplay."[7] John Sutherland tiptoes up to the line of
accusing Harris of plagiarism by drawing dark parallels
between some online Lecter fan fiction written by an
unknown named "Blythebee" and the opening of *Hannibal
Rising*. Sutherland incidentally uses the allegation to
smack Harris for his infamous media silence: "If an
author picks up and uses something from 'his' fanfic is
he plagiarising, collaborating, or merely playing games?
One thing's certain. Harris won't tell us."[8]

Some reviewers do find something of merit in the
book, though they still spend a great deal of time pointing
out its flaws. Steven Poole, for instance, encapsulates his
faint praise and keen disappointment in a short passage:
"But though there are still individual sentences and paragraphs to recall Harris's past mastery, the extremely short
chapters are telling. Mere sequence, as of a film composed
entirely of brief scenes, has replaced rhythm and suspense."[9] Peter Guttridge diagnoses the novel's flaw in
its overly heightened quality, where the plot tips "into
black farce," and otherwise takes it to task for its "ludi-
crous elements," such as the conversation between Lady
Murasaki and Lecter in haiku. Nevertheless, Guttridge

finishes with this left-handed compliment: "This novel may be flawed, but Lecter remains a powerful, iconic creation, especially thanks to Anthony Hopkins's screen incarnation."[10] Tibor Fischer, while acknowledging the story is less than convincing, appreciates Harris's skill even when applied to an inferior project:

> You know the destination, but that doesn't mean the journey isn't bracing. Harris has a great eye for detail, does pithy dialogue, has concocted some imaginative new horrors, and often lavishes loving care on minor figures. It isn't *Silence of the Lambs*, but you're probably only allowed one perfect novel in a career. Fans of Harris will be delighted with *Hannibal Rising*. I was.[11]

In summary, even the kindest reviews acknowledged that *Hannibal Rising* suffered from some major weaknesses.

It probably didn't help that Harris might have felt pressure to publish from Italian producer Dino de Laurentiis. Written in what is for Harris a relatively short span of seven years, its setting far from Harris's normal comfort zone of stark rural settings and FBI crime profiling, the novel seemed rushed. Was this perhaps due to some sort of pressure from producer de Laurentiis for Harris to write the prequel before de Laurentiis himself had someone else do it? Daniel Fierman and others speculate as much when they quote de Laurentiis as saying on the set of the film version of the book: "I own the [movie rights to the] character Hannibal Lecter. . . . I say to Thomas, 'If you don't do [the prequel], I will do it with someone else. . . . I don't want to lose this franchise. And if the audience wants it. . . .' He said, 'No. I'm sorry.' And I said, 'I will do it with somebody else.' And then he said, 'Let me think about it. I will come up with an idea.'"[12]

Whether this bit of grandstanding by the famously outspoken de Laurentiis is literally true or not, *Hannibal Rising* is a unique business venture for Harris in that this was the first time he had adapted one of his books for the screen. In fact, he completed the screenplay before the novel.

Did any of this cross-fertilization between the worlds of the book and movie business negatively skew the perceptions of the waiting critics, or did it perhaps have an adverse effect on Harris's own creativity? Or even more speculative—did Harris sabotage his own creation in order to free himself of the Lecter albatross (and a certain Italian film producer) once and for all? Is this Harris's purest, most authentic vision yet, stripped of the formulaic conventions of the crime thriller? Is Harris now walking freely amid gardens of florid prose, heedless of the critical barbs shot at him? Or is this critical ire a lasting grudge left over from what many considered to be a betrayal of Clarice Starling's character back in 1999 with *Hannibal*? These questions are ultimately unanswerable, but they do speak to the degree to which Harris has fallen from the reviewers' good graces with the last two Lecter novels.

The handful of academic critics who have thus far analyzed *Hannibal Rising* find more merit to the book than most of its initial reviewers. Charles Gramlich, for one, praises the book for daring to depict Lecter as the hero everyone has tacitly accepted him to be already: "When Hannibal experiences the horrors of his childhood, we are rooting for him completely. Even when he begins to kill, we root for him. . . . In *Hannibal Rising* we again hear the word 'monster' used to describe Lecter, but this time it is far from convincing because we have come to know him as a human being who is capable of love and wants to be loved."[13] Gramlich submits for our consideration the rather uncomfortable proposition that we root for Lecter to succeed as much as we do Will Graham or Clarice Starling.

Peter Messent disagrees with the conventional wisdom that the book humanizes Lecter. Rather, Lecter's character arc begins with him as human and concludes with his full-fledged transformation into a murdering Other, or monster. Messent claims exploration of Lecter's past is a prerequisite "for an understanding of Lecter's connection with Clarice as it is represented much later in his life,"[14] when the two are bonded together through an act of cannibalistic/oral communion that repairs Lecter's trauma of losing both mother and sister.

Dispensing with Freudian theory and taking up a more formalist approach, Robert H. Waugh examines the animal and insect imagery in *Hannibal Rising* and its relationship to the theme of transformation. He ultimately faults the novel for "squandering" Lecter as a character by uncovering his past,[15] but his reading does suggest the storyline is more complex than its detractors have generally given it credit for. S. T. Joshi praises the book for its theme of moral responsibility, but does acknowledge its "greatest failing is its author's unwillingness—one can hardly call it an inability, given his past work—to engage in a psychological portrait of Hannibal. . . . Harris is in danger of becoming so enraptured with the figure of Hannibal that he loses his manifest skill as a writer of suspense novels."[16]

Ali S. Karim makes the interesting observation that it made sound commercial sense for Harris to write a book about the young Hannibal's tutelage in the art of murder, as the publishing world and the popular media was then afire with the *Harry Potter* series. So if a boy wizard generated such interest, why not a boy serial killer—especially if that boy serial killer is Hannibal Lecter? Of the book itself, Karim finds much to praise, in spite of what others may say of it: "To be honest, I don't really care what other critics have to say . . . because for me the novel provided such a wonderful opportunity to be back in the embrace of Harris's prose and his dark, witty imagination."[17]

## PLOT DEVELOPMENT

The plot of *Hannibal Rising* is divided into three parts, although Part 3 is really an epilogue. The first part begins with a prologue, taking the reader from Lecter's colossal memory palace back in time to the death of Lecter's family and his odyssey from a state orphanage to his uncle's home in France. In Part 2, Lecter recovers his memory of what happened to his sister and tracks down her killers one by one. Part 3 finds Lecter in Canada, his metamorphosis into a serial killer complete. Unlike Harris's last convoluted book, the plot of *Hannibal Rising* is relatively straightforward, even simple. It's a revenge tragedy told in three acts. As many reviewers commented with varying degrees of snarkiness, the narrative structure and writing style is quite fast paced, almost cinematic.

The short prologue, with Harris taking on the narrative persona of a museum docent, guides the reader into the labyrinthine halls of Lecter's memory palace. The reader's destination is the Hall of the Beginning, where Harris promises to join the reader in watching "as the beast within turns from the teat and, working upwind, enters the world."[18]

Part 1 begins with Lecter at the age of eight, living at his ancestral castle home with his parents and sister. The Lecter family is forced to flee to a hunting lodge to escape the advance of the German armies in World War II. After the death of their parents, Hannibal and his sister Mischa are taken prisoner by a band of Hiwis, or locals who help the German invaders. Desperate and starving, the Hiwis kill and eat Mischa. A bombing raid sets Hannibal free before he, too, can be eaten. His memory of the events at the lodge repressed, he lives in a state orphanage in his old castle until he is thirteen. His uncle, Robert Lecter, brings him to France. At Lecter's chalet, Hannibal's aunt, Lady Murasaki, patiently tutors him. When a local butcher lewdly offends Lady Murasaki, Hannibal kills the butcher. Robert Lecter dies of natural causes under the stress of the situation. Hannibal falls under suspicion for the butcher's murder by the Parisian police inspector, Popil. The section concludes with the revelation that the former Hiwi leader, Grutas, is now a ruthless criminal living in France. The stage is set for Hannibal's revenge in Part 2.

In Part 2, Lecter is now eighteen years old, a brilliant medical student who decides to recover his repressed memories (with help from a self-injection of hypnotic drugs) of what really happened to his sister during the war. Once he remembers her murder and the faces of her murderers, Lecter returns to the ruins of his family's hunting lodge where the atrocity took place and finds the killers' dog tags. Now knowing their names, he tracks them down and kills them, one by one. Lady Murasaki, now forming a romantic bond with Hannibal, pleads with him to stop, but he won't. When she is taken prisoner by Grutas on his houseboat, Hannibal rescues her and kills Grutas in a savage raid on the boat. Lady Murasaki recognizes Hannibal's desire for her has now died and so has any hope for a relationship between them.

Part 3 concludes with Hannibal, now residing in the United States, traveling to a taxidermy shop in Quebec to kill the proprietor, Bronys Grentz, who is also the last Hiwi survivor. Hannibal then takes the train back to his new home in America.

## CHARACTERS

### Hannibal Lecter

This novel, even more than its predecessor, centers exclusively on Hannibal Lecter. It is a book-length character study, answering the question of how Lecter became the way he is. Before *Hannibal*, we had no real backstory for Lecter, aside from a single reference to childhood torture of animals and some sparse knowledge of the murders that brought him to the mental hospital. Now that we know he has a Lithuanian background and his pathology originates in the wartime loss of a beloved sister, this novel's burden is to fill in the gaps in the backstory. The story shows Lecter as we've never seen him before—a relatively innocent child who through a combination of genetic predisposition and horrible circumstance becomes the character we already know.

As the book opens, Hannibal is eight years old. He is the son of a Lithuanian count. His Italian mother is descended from the Sforza on one side and the Visconti on the other. His maroon eyes are inherited from his mother. No mention is made of an extra finger. We learn he essentially taught himself to read at the age of two in the family library. Gifted with a superior mind, he gravitated to the work of Euclid at the age of six, making accurate measurements of the height of the castle's towers using Euclidean geometry principles. Taking note of his son's prodigious intellect, Count Lecter hired a Jewish scholar named Mr. Jakov as the boy's tutor. When Hannibal was six, his sister Mischa was born. On his seventh birthday, Mr. Jakov showed him a non-mathematical proof of the Pythagorean theorem using tiles on a bed of sand. When Hannibal turned eight, Mr. Jakov began to tutor him in the construction of a "memory palace" so he could, as Mr. Jakov put it, "learn everything." Then the world war threw their lives into upheaval.

Hannibal has a proud but ambiguous family legacy. His remote ancestor is Hannibal the Grim, who built Lecter Castle using slave labor captured in war. However, this same Hannibal the Grim promised his captives freedom on the day of the castle's completion. The former captives were so grateful that they stayed on with the castle. Hannibal the Grim is capable both of casting his enemies to die forgotten in oubliettes and of turning enemies into steadfast allies. Our own Hannibal's birthright is perfectly positioned between two potentialities—the capacity for both good and evil.

At first, we see only what is endearing about young Hannibal, which makes his fall all the more poignant. His bond with smaller children is one characteristic. He shows his love for his younger sister Mischa by being her constant companion and playmate. She, in turn, loves him with the complete devotion of the innocent. When we first see the two of them, Hannibal is helping her feed bread to the black swans in the moat. Hannibal scares away one of the more aggressive swans, establishing his protectiveness of Mischa. Although frustrated by her inability to read as he did at an early age, Hannibal tries to help her by writing the first letter of her name upon her palm and repeating the mantra, "M for Mischa." When their parents are killed, Hannibal by default becomes Mischa's guardian and sole protector, a duty that he does his best to uphold. One of the most powerful examples of this is when he softens hard food in his mouth in order to give it up to Mischa to chew, in one case even transferring it to her mouth to mouth. Even after the horror of the lodge, his generosity toward smaller children remains, as illustrated by his sharing of treats with younger orphans at the state institution. These kinds of protective, loving gestures on behalf of helpless or weaker children establish Hannibal as not only sympathetic but heroic.

We already have been primed to see Hannibal as a romantic hero of sorts in his relationship with Starling. Here, his first love for Lady Murasaki establishes his bona fides as a chivalric leading man, another attractive trait to an audience. When Hannibal first sets eyes on Lady Murasaki, it's a magical moment, clearly offering the possibility of a normal life for him if he chooses wisely. She tutors him in the nuances of Japanese culture and art. In doing so, she helps him refine his good manners, thus fulfilling our audience expectation to see just how Hannibal became so emphatic about courtesy.

As he matures, his love for her turns toward the physical. He uses his growing artistic skill to draw her naked in the chateau bath, illustrating his desire for her. He displays an intuitive knack for giving just the right gift at the right time, such as his purchase of a suzumushi cricket to ease her seasonal pining for her Japanese home. The gift creates a magical space of transcendent time for the war-crippled boy and the older woman, where they can dwell together without painful memories. The relationship remains chaste, but marked by simmering passion. His unconsummated desire expresses itself through extreme (and violent) acts of devotion. He kills for her when her honor is insulted by the butcher. When she is abducted by Grutas in order to draw Hannibal into surrender in exchange for her life, Hannibal charges to her rescue. Their relationship, while not overtly sexual, is violently physical. However extreme Hannibal's reactions, he nevertheless earns audience points for his devotion.

Our sympathy for Hannibal only intensifies with the depth of his grief for Mischa's loss. In fact, he is so scarred by the hideous nature of her death and his own part in it that he blocks the entire period of time, from the moment of Mischa's death until his emergence from the forest, from his conscious recollection. He does not often cross the grounds of his memory palace to retrieve the few scraps of recollection he does store there. For a boy whose conscious memory is otherwise phenomenal, this gap is testament to the power his subconscious holds over him.

However, when he sleeps, those buried memories resurface in nightmares that make him scream or act out in other spectacular, frightening ways. As the story progresses, each one of Hannibal's nightmares reveals slightly more of what happened. During the first nightmare that we experience from Hannibal's point of view, as he sleeps in the orphanage dormitory, we discover that the men sang a verse from an 1891 opera entitled *Hansel und Gretel* to Mischa while taking her outside to the slaughter: "*Ein Mannlein steht im Walde ganz still und stumm.*" Hannibal, in trying to save her, has his arm broken. The second nightmare, occurring on Hannibal's first night in Robert Lecter's chateau, reveals that Hannibal bit Grutas on the cheek during the fracas. (Hannibal often goes for the cheeks in his assaults.) This nightmare image is so vivid that Hannibal tears apart his feather pillow with his teeth. In Paris, Hannibal's third nightmare shows Mischa dragged outside by men carrying an axe and a bowl. Since we already know what happened to Mischa, our anticipation is built solely upon when Hannibal is going to remember and what he will do when he does.

Inevitably, Hannibal's nightmares cross the boundary of his waking life to inflict vivid flashbacks upon him in response to certain stimuli. For example, when he hears the water in Lady Murasaki's tea vessel boil, he involuntarily remembers the sound and sight of the horned deer skull rattling inside the boiling water in Mischa's tub. The flashback is so strong that he cuts his hand with the knife he is using to cut flowers. Dr. Rufin, in the first of Hannibal's experiences within the mental health field, elicits another memory from him—Mischa's baby teeth in the stool pit (a false memory, as it turns out). The dreams somewhat ease their tyrannical hold upon Hannibal only after he begins to kill, which alleviates the pressure within. However, he still cannot access the primal trauma causing the dreams in the first place, no matter how hard he tries. He knows the subconscious contains the answers he seeks, but he cannot "think" his way down to them. His subconscious emerges only when his higher brain is somehow bypassed, be it through dreaming or drawing or hypnotic drugs.

When he discovers the identity of his tormentors, he sets about his vengeance in his cold, methodical way. His capacity for violence has definitely been set in motion by what happened to him as a child at the hunting lodge. Whether Hannibal is violent by nature or if events made him so is open to question. Who knows if Hannibal would ever have come to kill anyone without the victimization of him and his sister? However, Harris's statement about the "beast" in the prologue suggests a basis in human instinct for what Hannibal becomes. Specifically, the beast is a metaphor for those base urges within Hannibal beyond the reach of civilized thought. "The world" the beast must make its way into is shorthand for the pain of Hannibal's experience, the severity of which inflames bestial urges already present and creates a tyrannical matrix of learned associations that drive Hannibal to act out violently. The "beast" metaphor resurfaces when Hannibal as an adolescent realizes his past is not distant from him, but rather structures the here and now: "Hannibal . . . knows the past was not the past at all; the beast that panted its hot stench on his and Mischa's skins continues to breathe, is breathing now. . . . He is growing and changing, or perhaps emerging as what he has always been."[19] Harris leaves it ambiguous as to whether Hannibal was destined to be a serial killer or became so as a result of his experience on the Eastern Front.

Hannibal's capacity for violence becomes evident five years after the hunting lodge ordeal, when Hannibal is thirteen years old. Tormented by another boy named Fedor, Hannibal strikes back at the bully by pummeling and nearly drowning him. Hannibal next lashes out at the abusive First Monitor Petrov, impaling the older boy's hand with a fork. These are not isolated incidents but rather a pattern of behavior, a foreshadowing of the poetic justice the adult Lecter loves to exact for all forms of rudeness. The orphanage headmaster cautions Robert Lecter about the boy's violence to older boys, particularly bullies. Hannibal acts out again at the village school, when he breaks the coccyx and nose of an older boy who spat in the hair of a first-grader. By beating up bullies, Hannibal confronts by proxy his primary nemesis, Grutas. Over the span of four novels, then, Hannibal's childhood expressions of violence have morphed so that he now tortures bullies, not helpless animals (as Will Graham said of him). This revision is in accord with Harris's agenda to make Hannibal a tragic hero, a man whose mind divided against itself falls.

A remarkable scene during Hannibal's student days in Paris suggests just how divided Hannibal's mind is, or could potentially be. In his capacity as procurer of anatomical specimens for the dissection lab, he interviews the prisoner Louis Ferrat as a potential "donor" shortly before the man's date with the guillotine. Ferrat, under enormous stress as his execution approaches, seeks refuge in an alternate personality—a lawyer representing the condemned man. In response to Hannibal's questions, Ferrat as the "lawyer" often addresses himself as the "prisoner" and relays the prisoner's answers back to Hannibal. To Ferrat, Hannibal implies he, too, is a divided person. The bifurcated mind is an apt metaphor for the contraries in Hannibal's character. On one side of the division, he is a refined man of culture—on the other, a beast.

The man and the beast unite when Hannibal uses his formidable intellect to stalk his victims, immobilize them, address them with equal measures of courtesy and cruel humor in a ritual prelude to murder, kill them in progressively more creative ways, and in some cases eat parts of them. We've seen Hannibal do this in the other novels, as when he ambushes Pazzi, trusses him up, taunts him, and finally eviscerates him and kicks him off a balcony. The first time he engages in this MO, as we learn in this novel, is his murder of the butcher. He slashes the butcher from side to side with the samurai sword while reminding the butcher about his lewd comment to Lady Murasaki about whether "Japanese pussy" runs sideways.

During his second murder, he courteously—but with unmistakable intent—thanks Enrikas Dortlich for the opportunity to speak with him about his eating Hannibal's sister. He then forces Dortlich to sing Mischa's song in order to be spared, all the while knowing that he will kill Dortlich. He eats Dortlich's cheeks postmortem, re-enacting the most horrific element of the primal crime that so warped his childhood. Before drowning his third victim (Zigmas Milko) in a vat of formalin and preserved corpses, Hannibal tells him one of the corpses in the tank with him is of a child, partly cooked like Mischa. The man dies surrounded by floating corpses symbolically standing in for his wartime victims, yet another illustration of Hannibal's taste for poetic justice. He follows up this act with a bad pun about Milko arriving at a solution.

When confronting Petras Kolnas, the man who carried the bowl to catch the blood of his sister, Hannibal implies he has the butchered remains of Kolnas's children with him in a bag and presents Mischa's bracelet to him as reminder. In Canada, Hannibal puns to Grentz, now a taxidermist, that he has come to collect a head (Grentz's, of course). Since much humor is fundamentally cruel at some level, based on the misfortune or pain of others, it's appropriate that Hannibal in his growing inhumanity displays glee in punning as his victims suffer. For all of his wit and intellect, Hannibal is slave to the matrix of associations formed during his time at the hunting lodge. His desire to punish his tormentors as he believes they have injured him is deliberate, while his signature mode of expression in doing so is determined by his past.

Trapped as he is by his past, he nevertheless exhibits great skill and planning in carrying out his revenge. To find and defeat such a formidable enemy as Grutas, Hannibal needs all of his cunning. He anticipates the different possible scenarios and creates contingency plans accordingly. For instance, in his first adult confrontation with Grutas, Hannibal skews the odds into his favor by rigging up an improvised time bomb in Grutas's basement. The device detonates just in time to save Hannibal from Grutas's henchmen. In another example of Hannibal's meticulous planning, the tanto knife that Hannibal straps to his back deflects the bullet Grutas fires point-blank at his spine.

Many times in the narrative, Hannibal has the choice to continue down this path of violence, or take another path toward a positive, fulfilling life. Lady Murasaki symbolizes the path Lecter can take toward love. In a telling moment, in front of the samurai armor in the attic of Robert Lecter's chateau, Murasaki says to Hannibal he "can leave the land of nightmare" to join her on "the bridge of dreams."[20] She tells him the bridge passes through the doctor's office and the schoolroom—in other words, placing before him the specific strategies he can undertake to heal his body and mind in order to leave his nightmarish past behind him. Later, she pleads with Hannibal to turn over the names of the men who killed his sister to Popil, rather than risk imprisonment or death. She offers him a home in Japan, where he can practice in the country and live the remainder of his life in healing peace. Though rebuffed, Murasaki persists in her determination to save Hannibal from himself. As Hannibal prepares to kill Grutas, she pleads with Hannibal to turn the war criminal over to Popil and come with her. After he savagely kills Grutas, she finally rejects him by telling him there is nothing left in him to love. Hannibal's last, best chance to move forward with his life leaves with her. Harris makes it clear that whatever genetic and environmental baggage Hannibal is burdened with, the boy still has opportunities in his journey to turn aside if he truly wants to do so.

The paradox of human nature, returned to repeatedly in Harris's fiction, is its bestial quality hand-in-hand with its higher beauty. Hannibal is the ultimate embodiment of that paradox. Many qualities combine to make Hannibal an extraordinarily attractive character. As a precocious youngster with a wonderful tutor, for example, he embraces the study of all academic disciplines and learns the memory chapel technique to store his acquired knowledge. A true polymath, he is as adept with science and math as he is with art, history, literature, philosophy, and language. He is admitted into medical school as the youngest person ever to do so in France. He is the talk of Paris for his ability to read his textbooks once and memorize them (while then returning the textbooks within the week for a full refund). He displays a talent for anatomical dissections, an ironic touch in light of his evolution into a serial killer. Jakov's gift to him of the memory palace technique is key to Hannibal's scholastic success. His memory palace contains a Hall of Mathematics (one of the oldest parts of the palace, there since age seven), of

Chemistry, of the Cranium—halls through which he can wander and retrieve any information he has stored there.

Additionally, his genetic gift of artistry enables him to excel in drawing, painting, calligraphy, origami, flower arranging, lute playing, poetry, and other assorted art forms. Of these, music is dominant. He has an inherent grasp of music, seeing musical notes in such disparate phenomena as the bursts of flak in the sky or Murasaki's alto voice. Music's rhythmic beats come naturally to Hannibal, given that he is obsessed with the marking of time. He finds meaning in the mathematical progression of musical chords because he is concerned with all matters related to time and its passage, as we have seen before in his fixation on time pieces, actuarial tables, the time reversals theoretically possible through quantum physics, and the like. When he is stressed, he seeks comfort in the syncopated beats of time; for instance, when Popil presses him uncomfortably about his lack of memory about what happened to his sister, he wishes he could hear a clock.

Poetry as another kind of music also appeals to him in many forms, such as his love for the Japanese tradition of Heian, or communication through verse. His dialogue with Murasaki is usually distinguished by its poetic imagery, beginning with a note from her to him saying to meet him at the "Hour of the Goat," or in other words, 10 A.M. in France. They often converse in this highly formulaic, imagistic way. Though these exchanges are ritual in nature, true passion drives them to select verse appropriate to their feelings. In fact, we can chart the rise and fall of their relationship through poetry. After Hannibal's fall has driven an irrevocable wedge between them, Murasaki, reciting a poem from her ancestor, calls him troubled water, "frozen fast." Though Hannibal replies to her in verse as required, he is only going through the motions. He is truly ice, as Murasaki points out. However frozen Hannibal's waters may be, he forever after retains his fondness for poetic imagery, which comes alive again when he calls Starling such things as "the honey in the lion."

He is equally adept at painting and drawing. Under the tutelage of Robert Lecter and Lady Murasaki, his innate artistic skill blossoms. During his medical studies in Paris, he becomes good enough at art to capitalize on the vogue for Japanese art by selling his inks and watercolors of birds, signed with the symbol of Eternity in Eight Strokes, to art galleries. Interestingly, the elder Lecter believes that the impulse to create art has the potential to offset Hannibal's core darkness. Count Lecter directs Hannibal to draw for relief from the inner demons. Art as therapy only goes so far for Hannibal. Following the Count's death, Hannibal attempts to seek relief by drawing in the studio, but it no longer works. The demons take him over. This failure immediately precedes Hannibal's first murder. Art may be Hannibal's aspiration, an expression of his higher self that he cultivates the rest of his life, but murder comes just as easily and naturally to him.

Keen senses are another of Lecter's well-established traits in the earlier novels. Here we see those senses in their early development. The most pronounced one is his sense of smell. As an adolescent, he plays the Aroma Identification Game as a pleasant diversion. However, the power of his senses quickly takes on a more sinister cast as the plot unfolds. In the dark, he can detect the aroma of his first victim lying on the slab when Popil brings him in for questioning. During his violent episodes, his sensory powers become even more heightened. His sight, always sharp, becomes clearer as he prepares to kill, with his peripheral vision going red. The acuity of his senses marks him as different from normal human beings.

He maintains remarkable self-possession in the face of stress or pain. We've grown accustomed to seeing how unflappable Hannibal is, no matter what is going on around him or how he's being threatened. His lack of reaction is due to his ability to distance himself from external stimuli by concentrating on ideas and images. For example, he can sit still, with nary a flinch, while Murasaki stitches up his hand. To take his mind off the pain, he thinks of the arc of the needle's eye as a function of the diameter of the hairpin. This degree of self-control allows him to respond calmly to Popil's relentless interrogations, pass a polygraph exam with no rise in blood pressure, or kill Kolnas with a pulse rate of only seventy-two. When Popil shows him the butcher's headless body and asks Hannibal how he feels seeing it, Hannibal says only that he feels detached. *Detached* is the perfect word to describe him. His mental discipline allows him to kill without conscience, remorse, or fear of apprehension. In the other novels, this detachment allows him to endure the hell of years of captivity in the asylum, or the cattle prod to the eye and the searing touch of the red-hot poker during his brief imprisonment at Verger's estate.

Another marker of Hannibal's extraordinary nature is his bond with animals, a trait that we have seen spare him from Verger's herd of man-eating pigs. Already remote from the majority of humanity, Hannibal understands animals at a primal level. Many examples abound. He knows that the proper way to face down the aggressive swans that frighten Mischa is to spread out his arms to create a more intimidating "wingspan." Introduced to his uncle's mastiff, Hannibal quickly wins over the dog's initial wariness toward him. The draft horse, Cesar, forms a bond with him that endures even after years of separation. In a way, Cesar and Hannibal collaborate in Hannibal's murder of Dortlich. Cesar first alerts Hannibal to Dortlich's approach. At Hannibal's command, Cesar in harness pulls the rope that decapitates Dortlich. Thus, Hannibal's alliance with animals even extends to a shared act of murder. The beast within Hannibal finds kinship with other beasts.

Some human beings see the beast behind Hannibal's eyes. Whether this "beast" is natural instinct or metaphysical evil is uncertain; there may not be a single answer, as Harris likes to say. For example, a sexton in the dark of Notre Dame mistakes Hannibal's red eyes glowing in the firelight as those of an animal or perhaps a devil, which explains why the sexton makes the sign of the cross. In a none-too-subtle scene in the Paris Opera, Hannibal roots for Mephistopheles over Faust, reinforcing the association of Hannibal with the devil. As Hannibal's humanity diminishes in direct proportion to his victim toll, his face is described as demonic as the ones that haunt his dreams. Whatever innocence he may have once possessed, by the end of the novel he is embracing his destiny as serial killer. He no longer suffers from a divided mind. His anger and nightmares disappear. He becomes an entity both human and Other, one that ordinary men and women cannot describe in words. Popil, Hannibal's first policeman nemesis, comes to the same conclusion about Hannibal as many more will in the future: "The little boy Hannibal died in 1945 out there in the snow trying to save his sister. His heart died with Mischa. What is he now? There's not a word for it yet. For lack of a better word, we'll call him a monster."[21] Hannibal's fall is complete.

## Pascal Popil

A handsome man of forty, Popil is a police inspector from Paris. Popil bedevils Hannibal immediately after the murder of the butcher and does not let up until Hannibal leaves for America. Popil becomes an impediment to Hannibal's quest for revenge. The handsome Parisian inspector is also a rival for Murasaki's love. He is a man of integrity, with many admirable traits. Unlike the corrupt Pazzi or Krendler, Popil is in the same league as Crawford and Graham—flawed, certainly, but sympathetic.

Part of what makes Popil a complex, even flawed, character is his wartime history. Like every other character in the novel, World War II has left permanent scars on him and a lasting desire for revenge. During the course of the war, he progressed from Vichy policeman to Resistance fighter. He served as a police officer in the Vichy government under Marshal Henri-Philippe Petain, in part because his father and uncles fought under Petain in World War I. Charged with helping to keep the peace until the Germans could be overthrown, Popil does so until one day he sees a train leaving with Jewish deportees, destined for the Nazi death camps. He deserts to join the Resistance. To prove his loyalty, he kills a Gestapo officer. In retaliation, the Germans kill eight civilians, which makes Popil feel directly responsible for their deaths. When the Allied armies come in from the beachheads at Normandy, Popil and other members of the Resistance come to their assistance. Following the war, he serves as an investigator for the Nuremberg trials.

By virtue of his wartime experience, Popil serves as dramatic foil to Hannibal. Just like Hannibal, Popil knows what it is like to lose family in the war—some died on the Eastern front, others in the camps. Like Hannibal, he spends his postwar life in tracking down war criminals. Both men take satisfaction in the death of those who committed wartime atrocities. Popil, for instance, always attends the executions of those he brings to justice. Unlike Hannibal, Popil funnels his righteous anger and desire for vengeance into a more socially approved channel: the legal investigation of war crimes. Popil works for the system, while Hannibal is a vigilante crusader. Popil's violence is carried out by a guillotine blade carrying the weight of society's judgment upon it; Hannibal carries out judgments for no greater cause than himself and Mischa's violated memory.

Popil at first seems inclined to grant some degree of sympathy or at least understanding to Hannibal, even though Popil is convinced from the start that Hannibal is a murderer. During his first interview with Hannibal in reference to the butcher's murder, Popil says he understands Hannibal's situation as a survivor of a war crime. He speaks of Hannibal being an orphan and how the beauty of Lady Murasaki cleanses the boy of wartime memories. Though using the time-tested cop's technique of expressing understanding to a suspect in an attempt to get him to open up, it's still likely Popil understands all too well the long-term effect of wartime atrocity on the survivor.

Reinforcing the idea that Hannibal and Popil share a real, if reluctant, bond, the two become temporary allies in an investigation of stolen artwork from Lecter Castle. The pairing is more the result of a convergence of interests than any acknowledged kinship, but it does compel them to work together in spite of their differences. To discover who is trafficking the artwork, Popil uses Hannibal to verify that one of the paintings in the Jeu de Paume museum is genuine. This seemingly tangential episode actually puts Hannibal back in contact, however indirectly, with the men who killed his sister. It begins the chain of events leading to Hannibal's murder campaign. In a way, then, Popil unwittingly assists Hannibal in his revenge. This assistance later becomes more direct when Popil agrees to let Hannibal continue in his hunt for Grutas if Hannibal promises to share everything he learns about the man's whereabouts. Popil is just as interested in taking down Grutas, albeit without the personal motivations Hannibal has. Hannibal and Popil form an unlikely partnership, though Popil's integrity in doing so is never in question. It's the beginning of Hannibal's lifelong pattern of forming unlikely partnerships with cops to solve crimes.

While committed to stopping Hannibal, Popil gives him any number of opportunities to walk away from prosecution. For instance, he warns Murasaki that if Hannibal kills in France, Popil will see him beheaded. The intent is to scare Hannibal away, which of course doesn't work. Admittedly, Popil as a policeman is not as interested in Hannibal's welfare as Murasaki is, but he does want to preserve his life, if possible. To an assistant, Popil states he does not want to convict Hannibal, but rather have him committed to an asylum where he can be studied to determine what he is. It is easy to imagine Popil's dismay when the weight of public sympathy for Hannibal's tragic past compels the public prosecutor and the court to free Hannibal from jail. If Popil's wish to con-fine Hannibal for further study had been heeded, perhaps Hannibal's serial killings in the United States would never have happened. So we know Popil has good instincts, even if he ultimately is unsuccessful in stopping Hannibal. In the Harrisverse, the mere fact that he sur-vives the narrative is a testament to his good-cop status. (Think of Pazzi's fate for contrast.)

To Hannibal, Popil is much more of a threat than an ally. A big part of Hannibal's hostility toward Popil is the inspector's romantic interest in Murasaki. After their first meeting, Popil thinks that the lovely Murasaki may need company if the boy were removed to an institution. He calls upon her with the gift of a plant and bag of sweets, which leads an irritated Hannibal to tell Murasaki she will find the inspector to be tedious. Disregarding Hannibal's words, Murasaki occasionally takes lunch with Popil, although she declines his dinner invitations. Increasingly jealous, Hannibal fantasizes about the inspector's death. He becomes even more annoyed when Murasaki com-pares Popil favorably to the handsome actor Louis Jordan.

All of this is a minor aggravation compared to the real threat that Popil, as a superb criminal investigator, poses to Hannibal. As with any of Harris's law enforcement agents, Popil is a hunter or predator. He always seems poised to strike, his intensity contained but immediately at the ready. Murasaki thinks of him as a spider (albeit a handsome one), ready to pounce. However, he does not wait for his prey to come to him. Like any predatory animal, his senses are acute. His sense of smell, like

Hannibal's, is highly developed. Murasaki observes a minute change in his eyes and nostrils when he smells her faint fragrance at a distance. It's a moment reminiscent of Lecter sniffing Starling's skin cream through the vents in his cell. Since we already know that in the Harrisverse it takes a predator to catch a predator, details like these establish Popil's bona fides as a worthy adversary for Hannibal.

Popil is typical of Harris's cops in another way. He revels in the thrill of the hunt. When he realizes that Hannibal is a killer directly in his sights, he experiences a rush of exhilaration. He lives for the thrill of the hunt. Like Starling and Graham, his professional counterparts across the sea in another time, he finds a savage joy in solving the puzzles left for him in blood by killers—the more intelligent his nemesis, the sweeter the victory. Even if he fails, as he does here, the thrill of the hunt itself drives him.

Whatever predatory instincts he possesses, he rationalizes them with his higher intellect. He says to Hannibal that he believes in execution as a consequence for war crimes. For this reason, he threatens Hannibal with professional ruin in France if Hannibal gives laudanum to Ferrat. Popil wants Ferrat aware of what is about to happen to him. Hannibal in turn implies that Popil is a sadist who enjoys the spectacle of execution. Be that as it may, Popil's intelligence is what makes him one of Hannibal's more effective adversaries. As a hunter, Popil is relentlessly methodical. He draws upon a reservoir of interrogation techniques depending on the situation. His technique, like his demeanor, is alternately smooth and rough. At first, Popil tries sympathetic understanding. He pleads with Hannibal to open up to him after the butcher's murder and offers to help discover what happened to Mischa, a wily stratagem indeed when dealing with Hannibal. When sympathy fails, he accuses Hannibal of murder and threatens to have him arrested and Murasaki deported. Whenever Popil hears anything even slightly incriminating in Hannibal's words or tone, he springs verbal traps to monitor Hannibal's reactions. When all else fails, he uses the brute force legally afforded him. After Hannibal blows up Grutas's mansion, Popil arrests him and then beats him with a sap. Through sympathy and coercion and threats, Popil uses every investigatory weapon in his arsenal to confirm Hannibal's guilt.

Of course, we know from the beginning that Popil will fail to stop Hannibal's career in murder. However, Popil fares better than any other policeman ever has against Hannibal. Like Kabakov and Graham and Starling, Popil enjoys the thrill of the hunt and the ecstasy of solving a puzzle. In this last of the Hannibal novels so far, he stands both at the beginning and the end of Lecter's story as a representative of the law.

## Vladis Grutas

Harris's narrative need to create villains even more dastardly than Lecter in order to valorize him shows some real deficiencies by this novel. A problem confronts Harris here—how to create a villain to top Mason Verger for readers familiar with the previous novel. After all, Verger is a hideously mutilated pedophile and crime lord of a multinational syndicate. What kind of man, then, would commit deeds so traumatic as to create a cannibalistic serial killer? Harris comes up with the character of a brigand and thug who leads a Hiwi gang through the ashes of the Eastern Front in World War II to become a trafficker in stolen goods, drugs, and prostitutes in postwar Europe.

Part of the problem with Grutas as villain is that he is more of a plot necessity than a rounded character. We don't know a lot about him, other than what the immediate plot contingencies demand. We learn nothing about his past; the war is all we are given by way of explanation of Grutas's character. In a plot full of characters motivated by past trauma, Grutas is the unmoved mover of all the action. Nor does he seem to evolve or change much through the course of the story, except possibly to become even more depraved. He is static and flat, which is often a problem for Harris's secondary characters. Grutas is not filled in, so to speak.

We first see him as a looter of other people's goods. We may best think of Grutas as a vulture, preying upon (and occasionally creating) the carcasses left behind by war. Edgar Allen Poe described a man with a pale blue eye as a vulture in his short story "The Tell-Tale Heart" (1843), and this ocular imagery is almost the first physical detail we are given about Grutas. He has pale blue eyes, a detail repeated more than once. His motive in entering the courtyard of the Lecter Castle is both to loot and feel a sexual thrill in violating another's home. Like Verger, then, Grutas is a thief and sexual deviate. Equal parts fetishist and opportunist, Grutas proceeds to violate the Lecter family's den in the most egregious of ways: killing the household staff in collaboration with the SS, stealing the family's priceless art collection, killing and eating the youngest daughter, and last, but certainly not least, turning the eldest son from innocent into many-times-over killer.

Like a vulture, Grutas is an opportunistic creature. Lecter Castle is in his path, so he raids it. The artwork is hidden in the concealed room behind the wine cellar, so he steals it. He kills the cook because an SS officer challenges him to do it in order to prove his worth to the organization. He later deserts and, with the aid of his newly formed gang in the guise of Red Cross personnel, kills SS men in order to strip them of their belongings. He imprisons Hannibal, Mischa, and a couple of other local children at the hunting lodge in order to keep them as food stores in case of necessity. In his postwar career, he is the same opportunist, except on a grander scale. Headquartered on his houseboat, he cruises up and down the canal system like a pirate, collecting treasure from his illicit activities. For Grutas, the war has not been a colossal human tragedy; it has been a windfall.

He is ruthless in his opportunism, killing any and all who threaten his survival or freedom. During the war, his drive to survive leads him to prey upon helpless children for nourishment. Years later, he tells Hannibal he loves himself so much he was willing to eat Mischa to survive. Because Grutas loves himself to the exclusion of any human sympathy, he kills anyone without any inconvenient feelings of remorse. He engages in any activity, no matter how morally reprehensible, to acquire money. After the war, he has no qualms about dealing in SS medical-grade morphine or selling desperate boy and female deportees into prostitution. Of these spoils, he selects various women to beat and violate in whatever way satisfies him.

Grutas and Hannibal share some of the same tastes. Like Hannibal, Grutas seeks out the finest merchandise available to fit his aesthetics. For example, he commands one of his flunkies to bring him the best piano, a Bösendorfer, from Paris. He wants only the most superior appliances from America. When momentarily held at gunpoint by Hannibal, Grutas points out how alike the two of them are. These similarities raise the possibility that, metaphorically, some of Grutas's evil has been transferred into Hannibal through the trauma Hannibal suffers at the hunting lodge. Indeed, Grutas the ruthless businessman and opportunist, and Hannibal the trauma-scarred killer, are the New Men of the postwar twentieth century.

## Lady Murasaki Shikibu

Stepmother and aunt to Hannibal, she is also the wife of renowned painter Robert Lecter. She represents the possibility of love, family, and a normal life for Hannibal if he turns aside from the path of revenge. Because she loves Hannibal, she covers for him. However, she also tries to turn him back from the moral precipice he walks upon. When Hannibal continues to kill against all of her wishes, she is heartbroken. She gives up on him to return home to Japan.

She is an interesting addition to the Harrisverse. Her character may well be patterned after Countess Setsuko Klossowska de Rola, the young Japanese wife of the Polish painter Balthus. Within the story structure, she forms the template (or matrix, if you will) for the kind of attractive, strong, intelligent woman that Lecter obviously prefers. She helps shape his aesthetic tastes during a critical formative period for the boy, much like Lecter in a future decade will shape Starling's tastes as her tutor. The simmering, but never consummated, relationship between Lady Murasaki and Hannibal also establishes the dynamic for the sexual undercurrent developed in the first phase of the relationship between Starling and Lecter.

Murasaki, like Hannibal, is born into a prestigious family. Her ancestral namesake is the author of what is arguably the world's first novel, *The Tale of Genji*, in the eleventh century. Another of her ancestors is Lord Date Masamune, a samurai during the turbulent Sengoku period. As a young girl, she meets Robert Lecter at an exhibition of his artwork in Tokyo in 1921. Fifteen years after their first meeting, she comes to Paris with her father when he is appointed ambassador to France. In spite of the ambassador's disapproval, the count and Murasaki marry. Their life is idyllic until the Nazis come to Paris. The count is arrested as a subversive, his paintings confiscated for Goering's and Hitler's private collections. Murasaki manages to hide from the Germans the samurai commander armor worn by her great-great-great grandfather, Lord Date Masamune. When the count is freed by the Allies, he and Murasaki return to their chateau and put their lives back together. The end of the war comes at great cost, however, as one of its final horrors rises on the atomic mushroom cloud above Hiroshima, Lady Murasaki's home. Some years go by. Then their nephew Hannibal comes to live with them.

Murasaki loves the finer things in life: poetry, music, literature, and other arts. She instructs Hannibal and her attendant, Chiyoh, in many of them, including origami (which he later uses to infuriate police interrogators), calligraphy, flower arranging, and communication through verse. Of these, poetry holds a special place in her heart. Upon her husband's return from travel, she murmurs to him a passionate love poem written by her ancestor Ono no Komachi a millennia ago. The deepening of her love for Hannibal, complicated by her knowledge of what he is becoming, also finds expression in verse. Upon sight of the drawing Hannibal made of her naked in the bath at the chateau, for example, she thinks of a poem by Yosano Akiko: "Amid the notes of my koto is another/Deep mysterious tone,/A sound that comes from/Within my own breast."

She is a pious woman with a great sense of familial honor and duty. Because family is sacred to her, she offers Hannibal a place in a family to replace the one he lost. In the attic of the chateau, she has created a God shelf or altar to create a link between her world and family and that of her deceased ancestors. The ancestral samurai armor stands guard over the altar. This tableau is one of the first things she introduces Hannibal to when he comes to live with her. At this altar, she makes her first plea to Hannibal to leave behind his troubled past to join her on "the bridge of dreams."

These are no mere or idle words for Lady Murasaki. She too has to make her peace with what war has done to her. It stole her home city of Hiroshima from her. But unlike Hannibal, she can move forward from this terrible loss. While acknowledging the pain of her memories, she shows Hannibal a way out of the grip of the past by constructing new worlds in the present moment. She is sympathetic to all who suffer the aftereffects of the war. For her attendant Chiyoh's cousin Sadako, dying of radiation poisoning in Hiroshima, she folds paper cranes to ease Sadako's mind. At a critical moment in Hannibal's fall, she reminds him again of their mutual losses in the war and that the remedy is to create new worlds and new relationships. Just as Sadako is dying of radiation poisoning, Hannibal's soul is dying of moral poisoning caused by that same war. All of the touches promised by Lady Murasaki, or all the paper cranes folded by her in his name, cannot change that.

Of course, as with any Harris character, the Lady is a study in dualities and contradictions. As gentle and refined as she is, she is also a hunter. Not one to flush game from the bushes, she patiently waits for her prey to come to her. She knows she can exploit Popil's attraction to her if she chooses to. Knowing Hannibal's freedom is at stake, she uses her hunter's wiles to gain advantage over Popil. As the daughter of a diplomat trained in the art of masking one's emotions, she has a more passive hunting style.

The moral dilemma she faces compromises her. When presented with pretty clear evidence of Hannibal's first murder (the butcher's head in front of her attic altar), Lady Murasaki must make a choice. Will she give him up to the authorities? She is horrified by what Hannibal has done but then has to decide immediately whether to surrender Hannibal to Popil. Her decision made, she leaves the butcher's head in the village square to draw suspicion away from Hannibal. Keeping one's mouth shut is one thing, but misdirecting a police investigation is a whole other level of criminal complicity. Though she tells Popil she would do anything to help Hannibal, that's not entirely true. Were it only one murder of a foul-mouthed butcher shared as a guilty lover's secret, it is likely that Lady Murasaki and Hannibal could have had a life together. However, when Hannibal commits his life to murder, Lady Murasaki cannot walk over that bridge of nightmare with him. Hannibal must walk it alone.

## STYLE

Harris's prose has always been a bit on the lean side, which on the whole has been an admirable thing. His well-chosen detail conveys a richness of texture few other popular writers can match. Rather than belabor the scene or the description, he deftly captures its essence, or implies just enough that the reader's imagination can take over, and moves on. The prose style in this novel, however, seems a bit spare even for Harris. Spareness is indeed its distinguishing mark. Its chapters are short. Its characters are quickly sketched in. Its descriptions are brief. The plot is almost cinematically linear. Perhaps the rushed (for him) circumstances of the book's composition explain its rather skeletal feel. Perhaps Harris, working on a screenplay at the same time as writing the novel, essentially created a film novelization. Whatever the case, the book is a surprisingly quick read, considering the epic aspirations contained therein. The timeframe covered in *Hannibal Rising* is the longest of any of them so far, yet the novel is the thinnest.

Harris crams a lot of action into few words. For example, consider this line, when Lady Murasaki definitively rejects Hannibal's love: "'What is left in you to love?' she said and ran from the companionway and over the rail in a clean dive into the canal."[22] Now, that's a fairly dramatic moment in the narrative. Hannibal has just saved her from Grutas, but he's also just demonstrated the utter savagery of his soul in the most violent way, so she decides she's had enough. She flings herself away from his embrace and throws herself into the canal. Harris compresses all of that drama and action in one sentence—not even the two or three arguably deserved for carrying the dramatic weight of the moment.

Harris's descriptions are always sparse, but here they seem more vague than before. Deidre Donahue has a theory as to why: "The problem? Foreign locales. . . .

Harris falls into positively purple prose vapors trying to capture the world of European and Asian sophisticates."[23] She implores Harris to "come home" to the rural America he captures so vividly in *The Silence of the Lambs*. She may have a point. Let's take a look at Hannibal's stroll down the Boulevard Saint-Germain: "The outdoor tables at the cafes were full and the sidewalk clowns were badgering passersby for the amusement of the crowd at the Café de Flore. In the small streets nearer the river, the Rue Saint-Benoit and the Rue de l'Abbaye, the jazz clubs were still shut tight, but the restaurants were open."[24] The tables are full, the clowns are amusing the crowd, the jazz clubs aren't open, and the restaurants are. That's it as far as the local color goes. The description is abstract, lacking the stark poetry of Harris's previous work. That being said, he still captures images that are especially vivid or striking, such as this one: "The swan stood over her mate hissing, hitting the tank with the hard blows of her wings at the last, and the tank rolled over them, oblivious, in its whirring treads a mush of flesh and feathers."[25] This jarring, graphic tableaux captures in a few words the mindless destruction wrought upon the Lecter household by the engines of war.

The novel's dialogue is relentlessly formal. Lecter's urbane dialogue always works pretty well when it contrasts with the earthier dialects of others around him, usually working stiffs like orderlies and middle-class professionals like Starling and Graham. However, in this novel, nearly all the people are sophisticates and European swells. Even most of the Hiwis who eat Mischa Lecter turn into professionals and/or urbanites (albeit corrupt ones) in the postwar years. Consequently, the vast majority of the dialogue is upper-crust in diction and tone. After awhile, the dialogue threatens to descend into caricature. A good example is found in the scene where the commandant of the gendarmes momentarily locks Hannibal in a jail cell to "scare him straight" after

Hannibal has hit the butcher in the face with a leg of lamb. The village commandant lectures Hannibal, at first improbably sounding like an upper-class Yoda and quickly falling apart into parody: "Temper is a useful but dangerous gift. Use judgment and you will never occupy a cell like this. I never give but one pass. This is yours. But don't do it again. Flog no one else with meat."[26] It's a funny last line, but probably not intended to be.

Probably the most over-inflated, downright unrealistic dialogue involves the courtly exchanges between Lady Murasaki and Hannibal. It's an ambitious narrative conceit to have this attractive, sophisticated couple speak in poetry to each other much of the time. Sometimes it works, such as the "bridge of dreams" imagery. Sometimes the conceit doesn't work. It doesn't get off to a promising start with Murasaki's "meet me at the Hour of the Goat" invitation. Hannibal's first protestation of love to her, given that he has just eviscerated and decapitated the butcher, falls a little flat as well: "You are in perfect possession of yourself, but you are trembling like a bird. I would not have approached you without flowers. I love you, Lady Murasaki."[27] Since there is a severed human head leaking blood nearby, Hannibal's flowery speech is just incongruous enough to be funny. Undoubtedly the funniest such exchange, which is too bad because it's supposed to be romantic, is Lady Murasaki's expression of gratitude for the thoughtful gift of the cricket: "I see you and the cricket sings in concert with my heart." Hannibal replies, "My heart hops at the sight of you, who taught my heart to sing."[28] Jarringly, the symbolic creature for Lady Murasaki and Hannibal's emergent love is a cricket. Or perhaps the hop of Hannibal's heart is that of a frog? A rabbit? It's enough to make one wonder if Harris is having a good laugh at the expense of all those readers who take Lecter so seriously. Indeed, it's this very scene that drives Anthony Lane over the edge in his review of the book: "What the hell is going on here? Where is the damn SWAT team when you need it?"[29]

A number of critics, no matter how favorably or unfavorably inclined toward the book, take note of its unusual brevity and its stylistic shortcomings. Steven Poole describes Harris's style in this book thusly: "But though there are still individual sentences and paragraphs to recall Harris's past mastery, the extremely short chapters are telling. Mere sequence, as of a film composed entirely of brief scenes, has replaced rhythm and suspense."[30] Will Cohu says "the dot-to-dot simplicities of this book, its fatuous psychology, the sketchy detail and curt characterisations seem less of a novel than a draft of a screenplay."[31] Tibor Fischer, more kindly, calls the style "workmanlike."[32] As these examples show, the proximate release of the book and the movie invite critical comment about the book's cinematic style.

A Harris book would not be complete without its shifting verb tenses. Generally speaking, when the narrative breaks from the past tense to the present, the tense shift flags those passages significant to the readers' understanding of Hannibal's development into a killer. For instance, the prologue taking us back in time to see how he became a serial killer is written in this same authorial, present-tense voice. It's the voice of the guide who, like Virgil, will show us the "hot darkness" of Lecter's mind all the way back to his childhood. This same guide also assumes authority for filling in the gaps in Lecter's memory with material taken from historical records, Robert Lecter's letters, forensic reconstructions, interviews, and the like. In passing, the guide blithely reconciles any apparent contradictions between this story and previous Lecter stories by stating that the doctor freely altered details about his past to throw people off his trail. It's a sly metatextual move: Harris the writer assumes an authorial persona in order to discount the previous work of Harris the writer. These preliminary matters settled, the authorial voice then retreats into background invisibility as the story unfolds in the past verb tense.

However, this voice continues to interrupt the narrative flow from time to time to coach us to think about certain plot developments or themes in a certain way. One of the most significant is a declaration of why the courteous Hannibal and Lady Murasaki get along so famously: "Good manners from every culture mesh, having a common aim."[33] Sometimes Harris uses the plural first-person pronoun to connect reader and author, such as saying of Hannibal's would-be assassin, Milko, that he "made the slight adjustment of the heart that we make before we kill."[34] With this phrase, Harris observes matter-of-factly, but disturbingly, that we are all potential killers. These interjections serve as Harris's way of connecting his exotic characters to the common, shared emotions and experiences of his readers.

Other times, the shift to present tense alerts us to a change from the linear flow of plot into the eternal present of Hannibal's hellish nightmares, the precursors to his murder campaign. Other shifts to the present tense occur during scenes of mayhem, linking those scenes to Hannibal's present-tense nightmares as well as indicating on the written page the same kind of temporal rupture, that paradoxical accelerated/slowed pace, depicted during cinematic action sequences. The almost balletic murder of Paul Momund, the butcher, is the first and most extended, particularly when the dying man is given the coup de grace: "Paul's vision is darkening around the edges. Hannibal swings the sword and for Paul everything is sideways for an instant, before blood pressure is lost and there is the dark."[35] The present tense marks those passages describing key stages in Hannibal's transformation into unrepentant serial killer.

In other words, for Hannibal the past still holds him in its grasp. The injuries done to him still move him to take murderous action. By the time he murders Grutas, his transformation is all but permanent. He is troubled no more by nightmares, purged of anxiety by murder, and transformed into a remorseless killer.

## ALLUSIONS

Harris supercharges his revenge tale with many allusions from all fields of study, some of them quite esoteric. As always, the book is meticulously researched in the interests of verisimilitude. The forensic detail is not so pronounced here, however. Like *Hannibal* before it, this book is built more upon cultural and historic research (much of it related to the Eastern Front of World War II and postwar Europe) than Harris's earlier detective/profiler stories are. We learn a great deal about Hiwis, Vichy France, the Eastern Front, and so forth. Harris continues to showcase his knowledge of cityscapes. At times, for example, the sections dealing with Hannibal's student days read like a travel guide to Paris, though not so exhaustively detailed as the Florence material in *Hannibal* and prone to factual errors.

For a critic like Will Self, this literary idiosyncrasy of Harris's is outstaying its welcome. Self writes: "In *Hannibal Rising*, we have the fruits of seven more years' dilettantism. This time, Harris shows us he knows a great deal about Japanese flower arranging, Lithuanian aristocracy, Paris in the aftermath of World War II and, naturally, enormous viscous heaps of anatomy. I won't trouble you with the rest of his murderous search for authenticity, save to say that, even when it's going well, Harris manages to hamstring your suspension of disbelief."[36] Without giving up on Harris's fiction entirely, as Self appears to, we can still focus on the most thematically relevant allusions.

Of interest here is the children's song *"Ein Männlein steht im Walde,"* first introduced in the book when Mischa asks her brother to sing to her about "the mysterious little man in the woods." Hannibal later forces the terrified Dortlich to sing it with him just before Hannibal kills him. The song was written by August Heinrich Hoffmann von Fallersleben (1798–1894) and used in the opera *Hansel und Gretel* (1893) by Engelbert Humperdinck, based upon the Brothers Grimm's tale of Hansel and Gretel. The song is quite fitting, since Hannibal and Mischa, like Hansel and Gretel, are held captive in a house in the dark woods under threat of being eaten. Furthermore, the simple little song, loosely translated, is about a quiet little man wearing a purple coat standing in the woods all alone. This isolation foreshadows Hannibal's fate, because he will be left standing alone, a mysterious figure in the woods, without his sister. Once again, Harris has carefully chosen a seemingly innocuous detail to add richness to his tale.

It wouldn't be a Harris book without its intellectual pretensions. For example, the young Hannibal is fascinated with Christiaan Huyghens's *Treatise on Light* (1690) and Euclid's *Elements* (ca. 300 B.C.E.). Huyghens (1629–1695) was a Dutch mathematician who argued that light was a wave. His intellectual endeavors were many, including the invention of the pendulum clock. Given Lecter's established interest in timepieces, reversing the flow of time, and advanced physics, who better as an intellectual role model for the young Hannibal than Huyghens? As for Euclid, his thirteen books of the *Elements* became a textbook used as part of university curricula for many centuries. This mathematical treatise is the foundational work for plane and spatial geometry, ratios, and proportions. Euclid is another fitting role model for Hannibal, who is always fascinated by math and geometry.

Art history plays its part in the narrative. When Hannibal becomes involved in his bit of intrigue involving art theft in Paris, the names of famous painters like Turner and Caravaggio and Guardi and Bellotto inevitably follow. Bernardo Bellotto and Francesco Guardi are linked by being students of the eighteenth-century Venetian painter Canaletto, famous for his paintings of the Grand Canal, a Venetian landmark. Furthermore, Bellotto was Canaletto's nephew and pupil, not above using his uncle's name for the benefit of his own career. Of the specific paintings cited in the text, Bellotto's *Bridge of Sighs*, paired with Canaletto's painting of the same name (ca. 1740), provides a visual parallel to Murasaki's invitation to Hannibal to join her on the "bridge of dreams." Michelangelo Merisi da Caravaggio's painting *Judith Beheading Holofernes* (1599), also has a cameo, appearing in the background as a sinister visual commentary on Hannibal and Murasaki's meeting in the Jeu de Paume.

Harris works in many literary allusions. The epigraph to Part 1 is a poem by Philip Larkin, from his 1951 collection, *The North Ship*: "This is the first thing/I have understood:/Time is the echo of an axe/Within a wood." This linking of primal consciousness to the blow of an axe is both a foreshadowing of Mischa's fate and the annunciation of the formerly innocent boy Hannibal Lecter reborn as a monster or "beast." The epigraph that opens Part 2 is taken from Lawrence P. Spingarn's poem "Definition": "When I said that Mercy stood/Within the borders of the wood,/I meant the lenient beast with claws/And bloody swift-dispatching jaws." Interestingly, the science-fiction writer Fredric Brown used this same epigraph in his novel *The Lenient Beast* (1956), also about what would today be called a serial killer. Whether Harris intends the use of this same epigraph to be an acknowledgement of an obscure genre predecessor is an open question.

Other literary references appear. First, there's Hannibal's French medical school professor and mentor, Dumas. The name is a nod to Alexandre Dumas, whose cookbook Hannibal is reading when we first meet him in *Red Dragon*. Coyly, Harris challenges his readers in his acknowledgements to find exactly where it is in the text he borrows Coleridge's dog. For the record, "Coleridge's dog" makes its appearance in the line "The mastiff bitch in her kennel stirs, and with thirteen short howls she makes her answer to the clock." Sutherland points out that the line is "a remote allusion to 'what can ail the mastiff bitch' in Coleridge's gothic poem, Christabel. It doesn't end there. The boat on which the arch-villain, Grutas, gets his comeuppance is called the 'Christabel.'"[37] Samuel Taylor Coleridge (1772–1834), the English Romantic poet, explores issues of forbidden sexuality between the innocent Christabel and the vampiric Geraldine in his long poem "Christabel," composed between 1798 and 1801 but never finished. Since the poem is often interpreted as metaphor for the conflict between innocence and spell-binding evil, it is appropriate Grutas's floating lair shares the same name as the poem.

In a bit of a departure for Harris's usual focus on Western culture, Japanese history, literature, and other art forms are well represented in the text through the character of Lady Murasaki. She claims ancestry to a number of famous Japanese figures, just as Hannibal is the descendant of some pretty important people. First, she is related to Date Masamune, a samurai (1567–1636) of the Azuchi-Momoyama period who founded the city of Sendai. He was also known as the "one-eyed dragon," his presence in this book thus paying a subtle homage to Red Dragon. Murasaki's namesake is the author of what is arguably the world's first novel, The Tale of Genji, in the eleventh century. Another of Lady Murasaki's ancestors is Ono no Komachi, a beautiful and renowned Japanese poet (ca. 825–900 C.E.) who lived during the early Heian period (794–1185 C.E.) of classical Japanese history. Komachi is remembered for her erotic love poetry, which Murasaki quotes from the night she makes love to Robert Lecter in their master bedroom. She is also fond of the poetry of Yosano Akiko (1878–1942), a female poet known for her feminism and condemnation of Japan's part in the Russo-Japanese War.

Murasaki is versed in many cultural forms other than poetry, such as music. She can play the koto, a stringed instrument similar to the zither and associated with romance. She plays for Hannibal the song "The Sea in Spring," or "Haru no Umi" (1929), composed by Miyagi Michio (1894–1956). The song is influenced by Western musical style; given the relationship between the Japanese Lady Murasaki and the Lithuanian Hannibal, it is the perfect background music. Finally, she is adept in the art of flower arranging. Through her, we learn about the *mori-bana*, or slanting style, which is a less rules-bound form and appropriate for Hannibal's untutored efforts.[38]

## SYMBOLS

As always, Harris loads his scenes with symbolic imagery to reinforce the themes, but three general categories are of note: fruit and flowers, ice and snow, and animals. First, many of the most important preliminary scenes, and the final scene, take place in winter. If this story is about Hannibal entering his heart's long winter, as Harris says, it is symbolically appropriate for a snowy landscape to signify this psychological journey. As the snow banks higher against the outer walls of the hunting lodge, Mischa's fate draws ever closer, which in turn seals Hannibal's fate in ice.

Dr. Rufin predicts the dire possibility that, if pushed too far to remember what happened, Hannibal could freeze his emotions forever to escape the pain of his memories. Much later, Murasaki sadly confirms to Dr. Rufin his prediction has come true—no warmth remains in Hannibal. From Hannibal's point of view, he experiences the act of murder itself as a type of freezing. When he confronts the butcher, he sees red, compared to color refracting through ice on a window. The last scene in the book comes full circle, meteorologically speaking, to the winter at the lodge. It is snowing in Canada, where

Hannibal beheads Grentz, the last of the men who killed Mischa. Then Hannibal enters America in a train that must be blasted with steam to de-ice it. He won't warm up again until a certain young female FBI agent enters his life.

Second, the flowers and fruit in the story tend to symbolize (rather conventionally, of course) passion, life, and love. Significantly, they most often appear in conjunction with Murasaki, who often reclines in a fragrant bath surrounded by floating gardenias and oranges. She represents the possibility of life-affirming love for Hannibal if he will only choose her instead of his vengeance. He compares his first glimpse of her bathing at the chateau to the water flowers of the castle moat. From this point forward, flowers symbolize the subtext of eroticism in Hannibal and Lady Murasaki's relationship. The next morning, Hannibal joins her for a lesson in flower arranging. He is quite aware of the sensuous nature of the lesson, paying particularly close attention to the sight and sound of her kimono as she moves. However, the pleasant interlude is quickly interrupted by a waking nightmare of Mischa, ending in Hannibal accidentally slashing open his own hand with the knife he is using to arrange flowers. Hannibal's "de-flowering" therefore ends rather badly, as such initiatory moments often can.

The consummation of the couple's attraction is forever deferred, though not for lack of invitations by Murasaki. In the scene where she promises to be "warm rain" for Hannibal's "scorched earth," she suggestively cuts into an orange with her fingernails and then presses her hand to Hannibal's lips. She rolls the orange, symbol of her passion, into the waiting bath water. The invitation could not be clearer; however, he rejects her living presence for dead Mischa's memory. Not easily discouraged, she buys more oranges at the market for Hannibal a few scenes later. Their relationship is just not meant to be: whereas Lady Murasaki places flowers on her God shelf,

Hannibal places a severed head. That kind of thing is a difference not too many couples could overcome. (Popil, incidentally, "gets it": when he comes a-courting to Lady Murasaki, he brings her a plant.) Murasaki's warmth, represented by her flowers and fruit, contrasts the wintry hell of Hannibal's near-death experience at the hunting lodge.

Harris pulls out all the stops this time in regard to animal imagery, as Waugh explains. We may add to Waugh's work with some other observations. It only takes Harris one-and-a-half paragraphs to introduce one of his very favorite animal symbols: birds. The black swans in the moat of Lecter Castle are associated with the innocence of Hannibal and Mischa's childhoods. Hannibal delights in protecting Mischa from the ferocious charges of the alpha swan. However, when the black swans attempt to flee the German juggernaut, the lead swan and his mate fall to the ground helpless before the advance of the panzer tank. The treads grind them both to a bloody mush, symbolizing the destructive effect of the war on Hannibal and Mischa. Clearly, the memory of the swans stays with Hannibal after the war. For example, upon sighting from afar Lady Murasaki in her bath, Hannibal silently spreads his arms wide like he did with the swans. He immediately associates her with the graceful swans of his childhood.

Since any pleasant memories of Hannibal's childhood are later poisoned for him, the bird imagery is also as evocative of death as it is life. When he suffers from a nightmare in which he relives events leading up to Mischa's death, for instance, he rips apart his pillow with his teeth so that he is covered in feathers, like a bird. It's an image reminiscent of Grutas tearing into the bloody bird skin. In reaction to his nightmare, Hannibal shivers and then becomes still, like a dying bird. Additionally, when he kills the butcher, he has a momentary flashback to Mischa and the swan. Another important symbolic bird is the pigeon. Hannibal delights in outlining the letter "M" of Mischa's name in grain on the ground of the courtyard so that the pigeons flock to it and form the letter, much to Mischa's delight. The pigeons represent vulnerability here, as they did in *Silence*. Many other birds appear throughout the story, including swallows, night herons, owls, and parrots. Significantly, Kolnas keeps caged ortolans on his restaurant premises in order to serve them on the menu, which evokes the memory of what happened to Mischa. On and on it goes . . . Harris's literary aviary is nothing if not extensive.

He includes a menagerie of other animals, each carrying a different symbolic weight. One general category of animals includes predators. The Lecter hunting lodge, for example, stands upon the stones of a Dark Ages altar built by a people who worshipped the grass snake. Hannibal's sighting of a snake at the lodge implies a link between the boy and the serpent. The snake connotes diabolism and a dark future for Hannibal as a result of his coming to the lodge. The lodge is a gathering point for beasts, each representing the primal forces that create the monster Hannibal. The lodge is besieged by scavenging wolves following the death of Hannibal's parents, presaging the imminent assault by Grutas's gang of looters. Following the events at the lodge, animals recognize some shared instinctual trait within Hannibal. His gradual transition from innocent child (a "lamb" in William Blake's lexicon) to predator (the "tyger" of Blake's poem) as a result of his victimization is signified when the count's mastiff, initially suspicious of Hannibal, quickly warms up to him and greets him with thumps of her tail. We have already seen how Hannibal has the mystic ability to bond with animals (like Verger's swine) that might otherwise eat him; the mastiff's reaction is an early instance of it. These dangerous animals recognize a kindred spirit.

Several other animals take on metaphoric significance. For example, the scavenging Hiwis shoot a deer with an arrow. The dying deer's vulnerability foreshadows Mischa's fate. Another example: Hannibal thinks of horses as good-luck charms. The horse is a divine symbol in Japan, so Cesar's prominence in the story may link Hannibal's past to the role Murasaki plays in Hannibal's development. Another animal symbol with a Japanese connection is the monkey or gibbon, both prominently mentioned at key points in Hannibal's journey. An organ grinder and his monkey are present when Hannibal has his fateful first fight with the butcher. The monkey is described as having wise eyes, which fits the traditional Chinese and Japanese association of the monkey with the heart, the mind, and the seat of consciousness. Supporting this interpretation, a gibbon skull is present in Hannibal's garret room, seemingly watching him as he enters the depths of his own mind to find his repressed memories. Finally, frogs make their first appearance in Harris's bestiary. Hannibal uses frogs as his dissection subjects in the medical school lab, thus associating him with frogs. Lady Murasaki also uses the poetic line "if beset by frogs" in her reply to Hannibal, reinforcing the metaphoric connection between him and the frogs. Typically for Harris, the frog is an ambiguous symbol. One interesting Japanese tradition holds frogs as good luck talismans. A more compelling possibility is the medieval association of the frog with the devil, a legacy of the Catholic Church's designation of the animal as a witch's familiar.

## THEMES

*Hannibal Rising* is really about the danger of growing up. As such, it includes many elements of what is called a *bildungsroman*, literally "novel of formation" in German, but in simpler terms, a straightforward coming-of-age tale. Stories of this kind follow the harrowing journey of a child's development into an adult. The child begins in a state of innocence, but some significant or often catastrophic event propels him or her into the dangerous world at large to begin a reluctant maturation. Along the way, the growing child encounters a number of obstacles, each of increasing difficulty. Success or failure at each of these critical junctures provides further insight or learning for the child's developmental process. Eventually, the new adult either becomes a contributing member to the social order or turns aside to enter exile. Whether the fictional journey is a success or a failure for the main character, the outcome provides critical lessons for its readers. The similarities between coming-of-age stories to Freudian theories of psychosexual development and the pitfalls of each stage are striking. So too are the parallels to the Jungian-influenced work of Joseph Campbell, most famously the hero's journey as described in his *The Hero with a Thousand Faces*. *Hannibal Rising* lends itself to such Freudian or Jungian interpretations.

From a Freudian perspective, Hannibal cannot outgrow what happened to him as a child, most spectacularly between the ages of eight and twelve. Even before that, he has difficulty resolving jealousy of his sister for taking parental attention away from him. The hideous deaths of his family, especially Mischa's, and the part he may have played in eating her scar him to such an extent he is incapable of moving past that time. The trauma is so severe he cannot consciously recall it, but it manifests itself anyway in his nightmares. He can only recall what happened to him through drug-mediated self-therapy. Even then he is not healed. Rather, he ritually re-enacts the formative trauma of his life each time he kills, trying to somehow conquer it through the act of repetition. In Harris's simple Freudian schema, Hannibal becomes a cannibal killer because he survived the attack of another such killer but only at the cost of sharing in his sister's consumption. Given his earlier resentment of his sister, witnessing her death and likely partaking of her earthly remains produces a nuclear meltdown of the mind. When Starling offers her breast to Lecter in *Hannibal*, she alone recognizes in him long-repressed conflicted feelings about Mischa and his mother. He has not dared to acknowledge these resentments in light of the tragic deaths of both of them.

Joseph Campbell's cultural analysis provides a fitting template for the general arc of Hannibal's tortured journey. First, according to Campbell, there is the call to adventure that takes the protagonist far from the comforts of home into a strange, dangerous land.[39] For Hannibal, this call is the exodus to the hunting lodge, necessitated by the onset of Hitler's Operation Barbarossa. Then his family is taken from him and he confronts a number of dangerous characters, Grutas the most dangerous of all. As his journey continues, he confronts a number of other obstacles to be overcome: the Stalin-era state orphanage and its bullies, his own debilitating nightmares, Popil's threat to his liberty, and over them all, his nemesis, Grutas. Before he can continue his journey, he must enter what Campbell calls "the belly of the whale."[40] Hannibal passes through the threshold between reality and the world of dreams to undergo a type of death in order to be reborn with valuable information allowing him to continue his journey. The means he uses to do this involves injecting himself with truth serum to get his memory back. Having done this, he embarks on his quest for vengeance. According to Campbell, the hero's journey requires mentors and guardians at critical developmental points. Hannibal has two guardians, first in kindly Mr. Jakov and second in Robert Lecter, both of whom die, leaving Hannibal to press forward alone but armed with critical knowledge they have imparted to him. A helper along the way is required; Lady Murasaki fits that description. She offers Hannibal the real possibility of love and healing if he will only turn aside from his self-destructive path.

But more than any of these formulaic benchmarks, Hannibal's journey is really about the impossibility of his redemption. Many times, Hannibal has the opportunity to turn away from murder. But he continually fails key moral choices. The result, as Murasaki diagnoses, is having nothing left in him to love. His story is a cautionary morality play hinging upon the question of free will versus predestination. Is Hannibal destined to be a killer because of his "beast within"? Is he really, as Graham says, a monster from birth? Or did he become one, as Popil believes? In Harris's fiction, being human means to struggle constantly against the hard-wired instinct to plunder and kill without remorse. In that sense, then, we are all destined to harbor within our collective breast primal desires, including the will to murder when we have been wronged and/or victimized. We are all balanced on a knife's edge, where it is all too easy to give in to our violent potential and become increasingly desensitized to the pain we inflict on others. But Harris's fiction also insists we have the ability to inoculate ourselves against uncivilized urges—a critical test of humanity some not only fail but deliberately turn aside from. Hannibal's tragedy is rooted in a complex interplay of environmental pressures and birth inheritance, the exact balance of which Harris leaves ambiguous. For what it's worth, Popil is given the final word on the matter when he says Hannibal's heart died when he failed to save his sister. But one thing is not ambiguous. By the time he is a teen, Hannibal kills easily; murder is the therapy by which he ends his nightmares, and he suffers no remorse for it.

By far the largest environmental factor impacting Hannibal or anyone else in the novel is World War II. Arguably, the war is the story's ultimate villain, killing some 40 million people and inflicting lasting harm on countless others. The novel invokes the memory of the Nazi deportations and genocide, the slaughter of civilians caught up in the relentless advance of the German armies, and the displacement of untold millions from their homes—a catalog of atrocity on a scale that all of the serial killers of the world could never match. The large-scale human suffering inflicted by the war is particularized in the book's characters, all of whom have been profoundly affected by their experiences in one way or another. Hannibal is the most melodramatically transformed character, but others suffer, too. Lady Murasaki's home, Hiroshima, was destroyed. Popil lost family in the war and feels residual guilt for serving as a policeman in the Vichy government. Grutas and his Hiwis, while serving their role as the narrative "heavies," nevertheless did what they believed they had to do to survive the Nazi occupation of Lithuania. Through their shared criminality, the Hiwis illustrate the dehumanizing aspect of war and the extremes to which it forces people. In addition to people's lives, the war devastates Europe's culture, as the subplot of the artwork looted from Castle Lecter dramatizes. The rapacious looting of treasured artworks from occupied territory, as carried out on a grand scale by Hitler and a lesser one by Grutas, is an act of cultural violence. The epic violence of the war and its reverberating shockwaves manifest in practically every scene. While some readers may find it objectionable that the very real horrors of World War II are used as a plot device to provide some justification for Hannibal's pathology, the war does suit Harris's controlling theme of the violence in the human heart, here metastasized to a global level.

In Harris's fiction, the trigger for the cancer of violence is the influence of past injury. The scar remaining on Hannibal's neck from the chain Grutas looped around it in the bitter cold symbolizes the staying power of the past. With his tormented childhood memory, Hannibal is an embodiment of the theme. In much the same way as the bitter memory of the humiliation of the Treaty of Versailles at the end of World War I provided Hitler and the Nazis with nationalist justification for the rearmament of Germany, Hannibal's memories frame the terms of his revenge. In a critical epiphany in Notre Dame Cathedral, Hannibal remembers the fire consuming his mother as he watches candlelight flicker on the marble face of a bust of

Joan of Arc. Then, as the church sexton tells him it's time to leave, Hannibal replies it is past time. In this scene, as he connects his knowledge of St. Joan's martyrdom by fire to his personal memory of his mother's immolation, he recognizes that memory inextricably binds the historical past to the present moment, painful memory even more so. His words to the sexton have at least three levels of meaning. The first level is a simple acknowledgement to the sexton that it's time to lock up the church doors. The second is an articulation of Hannibal's epiphany that present time and past time co-exist. The third is a consecration, uttered on hallowed ground, of his own renewed purpose to find out what happened to Mischa once and for all so he can pass poetic justice on those who wronged her. As he walks through nighttime Paris, the word *time* keeps echoing in his mind, reinforcing the point for him. From this time forward, Hannibal seeks the means to recover the gaps in his memory in order to act upon them. He dedicates himself to this purpose with the single-minded drive of a penitent atoning for past sins so as to enter Heaven.

However, for Hannibal there is no heaven, only an empty cosmos and the oblivion of death. There are no metaphysical answers for all those who cry out to an uncaring universe (like the long-ago dying prisoner in the oubliette in Lecter Castle who scratched the word *Pourquoi?* or *Why?* on the wall). Religion, which attempts to supply the answer to "why" we suffer, takes a number of hits in the story. Hannibal is disgusted by what he perceives to be the Christian obsession with the bloody spectacle of Christ's crucifixion, represented by the number of bloody paintings hanging in the Jeu de Paume. In one scene, Kolnas takes communion with his family beneath an especially bloody painting of the Crucifixion. Because he ate Mischa in a broth in a bathing vessel, this communion scene is a none-too-subtle equation of cannibalism to the Christian belief in transubstantiation.

Whatever Christian spirituality Hannibal possesses dies with Mischa, leaving behind only a mocking distaste for the religious rituals of his youth. Certainly, he is not above using Christian trappings to comfort the condemned Ferrat or disingenuously swear to Popil to share what he knows about Grutas. Personally, however, he has no use for God. For example, when confronted with the death of his patron Robert Lecter at the age of thirteen, Hannibal is appalled by "the whining and bleating of the hymns and the droning nonsense of the funeral."[41] Also of note is his graveside prayer not to God, but to Mischa's memory: "Mischa, we take comfort in knowing there is no God. That you are not enslaved in a Heaven, made to kiss God's ass forever. What you have is better than Paradise. You have blessed oblivion. I miss you every day."[42] Because the older Lecter puts Christian iconography to sacrilegious use and recreationally collects clippings of church collapses, the prequel must establish the origin of Hannibal's distaste for religious ceremony. When Hannibal looks at the stars, he sees many things, including the promise of a new life in America, but Heaven is not one of those things.

## CONCLUSION

The fiction of Thomas Harris offers a bleak assessment of the human plight. He proposes that human beings suffer from a radical dualism in their natures, that murder originates in the primitive limbic brain, while the drive to create order and civilization comes from the cerebral cortex. All people are born with the potential to kill, Harris insists, but the cumulative effect of their experiences determines the likelihood of whether they will cross that line. Painful formative experience increases the chances one will commit murder. In the Harrisverse, the murderers—Michael Lander, Francis Dolarhyde, Jame Gumb, and even the elegant Hannibal Lecter—share one commonality: their egos were brutalized during childhood. As adults, they seek to restore their sense of self through the complete destruction of other lives. Killing gives them power to redress the wrongs they believe have been inflicted upon them. Once they become dedicated murderers, they are finally at peace with themselves. Their sense of powerlessness has been relieved, their primitive and higher brains now fully in harmony with one another. They use their intellectual gifts in the service of their killing. Though they hide behind masks of normality, they are in actuality dangerous outsiders, alienated from civilized rules of conduct. Yet the murdering outsider is only a more extreme manifestation of the murder in all our hearts. As Graham knows, we are all haunted by the past, both our personal histories and the cultural and genetic legacy of the human species. We make murder. *We* are the monster.

# Notes

## CHAPTER ONE

1. Thomas Harris, *Red Dragon* (New York: Bantam, 1987), 354.

2. Ibid.

3. Phoebe Hoban, "The Silence of the Writer," *New York*, April 15, 1991, 49.

4. David Sexton, *The Strange World of Thomas Harris* (London: Short Books, 2001), 24.

5. Ibid., 31–32.

6. Meg Laughlin, "The Silence of the Author," *Tulsa World*, August 15, 1999, Final Home Edition.

7. Sexton, *Strange World*, 37.

8. Hoban, "Silence," 50.

9. Quoted in Sexton, *Strange World*, 45.

10. Hoban, "Silence," 50.

11. Sexton, *Strange World*, 45.

12. Ibid., 46.

13. Quoted in Hoban, "Silence," 50.

14. Ibid.

15. Daniel O'Brien, *The Hannibal Files: The Unauthorized Guide to the Hannibal Lecter Trilogy* (London: Reynolds & Hearns, 2001), 21–23.

16. Sexton, *Strange World*, 58.

17. Philip Jenkins, "Myth and Murder: The Serial Killer Panic of 1983–5," *Criminal Justice Research Bulletin* 3, no. 11 (1988), 1–7.

18. John Douglas and Mark Olshaker, *Journey into Darkness* (New York: Pocket Star Books, 1997), 25.

19. Robert K. Ressler and Tom Shachtman, *Whoever Fights Monsters* (New York: St. Martin's Paperbacks, 1993), 273.

20. Thomas Harris, "Foreword to a Fatal Interview," *Red Dragon* (New York: Dell, 2000), ix.

21. Quoted in Sexton, *Strange World*, 57.

22. Ressler and Shachtman, *Whoever Fights*, 272.

23. Ibid., 272–273.

24. Ibid., 273.

25. Chris Nashawaty, "The Hunger." *Entertainment Weekly* May 7, 1999, http://web.ebscohost.com.

26. Douglas Preston with Mario Spezi, *The Monster of Florence* (New York: Grand Central Publishing, 2008), 134.

27. Ibid., 57.

28. O'Brien, *Hannibal Files*, 153.

29. Preston with Spezi, *Monster*, 185.

30. Harris, "Foreword," xiii.

31. Preston with Spezi, *Monster*, 182.

32. Brian Hiatt, "Enter the Dragon," *Entertainment Weekly*, March 7, 2002, http://www.ew.com/ew/report/0,6115,214933~10~0~,00.html.

33. Scott Bowles, "'Red Dragon' vs. 'Manhunter': The Gloves Come Off," *USA Today*, October 7, 2002, http://www.search.ebscohost.com.

34. Ibid.

35. Ibid.

36. Ibid.

37. Comingsoon.net. "Interviews: Production on *Red Dragon*," http://www.comingsoon.net.

38. Daniel Fierman et al., "Lecter Loses His Bite," *Entertainment Weekly*, February 23, 2007, http://search.ebscohost.com.

39. Motoko Rich, "Hannibal Lecter to Drop By for Holiday Helpings," *New York Times*, September 19, 2006, http://www.nytimes.com/2006/09/19/books/19harr.html.

40. One audio review chided Harris for taking a "light and friendly" tone while reading his story of blood and revenge. In *Publishers Weekly*, January 29, 2007, http://web.ebscohost.com.

41. Fierman et al., "Lecter Loses."

42. Davide Mana, "This Is the Blind Leading the Blind: Noir, Horror, and Reality in Thomas Harris's *Red Dragon*," in

*Dissecting Hannibal Lecter: Essays on the Novels of Thomas Harris*, ed. Benjamin Szumskyj (Jefferson, NC: McFarland, 2008), 90.

43. Philip L. Simpson, *Psycho Paths: Tracking the Serial Killer through Contemporary Film and Fiction* (Carbondale, IL: Southern Illinois University Press, 2000), 70–73.

44. Peter Messent, "American Gothic: Liminality in Thomas Harris's Hannibal Lecter Novels," in *Dissecting Hannibal Lecter: Essays on the Novels of Thomas Harris*, ed. Benjamin Szumskyj (Jefferson, NC: McFarland, 2008), 31.

45. Tony Magistrale, "Transmogrified Gothic: The Novels of Thomas Harris," in *A Dark Night's Dreaming: Contemporary American Horror Fiction*, eds. Tony Magistrale and Michael A. Morrison (Columbia, SC: University of South Carolina Press, 1996), 31.

46. Ibid., 39.

47. Sexton, *Strange World*, 153.

48. Ibid., 154–155.

49. Mana, "This Is the Blind," 91.

50. Ibid., 93.

51. S. T. Joshi, "Suspense vs. Horror: The Case of Thomas Harris," in *Dissecting Hannibal Lecter: Essays on the Novels of Thomas Harris*, ed. Benjamin Szumskyj (Jefferson, NC: McFarland, 2008), 120.

52. Charles Gramlich, "Afterword: Mythmaker," in *Dissecting Hannibal Lecter: Essays on the Novels of Thomas Harris*, ed. Benjamin Szumskyj (Jefferson, NC: McFarland, 2008), 213.

53. Ibid., 216.

54. Slavoj Zizek, *Looking Awry: An Introduction to Jacques Lacan through Popular Culture* (Cambridge: MIT Press, 1995), 48.

55. Pietra Palazzolo, "Thomas Harris' *The Silence of the Lambs* and Jonathan Demme's Film Adaptation: The Representation of Cannibalism in the Contemporary World," in *Atti del XVIII Covegno A1A, Genova, 30 Settembre–2 Ottobre 1996: Vol. I Transiti Letterari e Culturali*, eds. Guiseppe Sertoli e Goffredo Miglietta (Trieste: E.U.T., 1999), 361.

56. Phillip A. Ellis, "Before Her Lambs Were Silent: Reading Gender and the Feminine in *Red Dragon*," in *Dissecting Hannibal Lecter: Essays on the Novels of Thomas Harris*, ed. Benjamin Szumskyj (Jefferson, NC: McFarland, 2008), 161.

57. Harriett Hawkins, "Maidens and Monsters in Modern Popular Culture: *The Silence of the Lambs* and *Beauty and the Beast*," *Textual Practice* 7 no. 2 (Summer 1993), 260–261.

58. Greg Garrett, "Objecting to Objectification: Re-Viewing the Feminine in *The Silence of the Lambs*," *Journal of Popular Culture* 27, no. 4 (Spring 1994), 1.

59. Ibid., 3.

60. Ibid., 4.

61. Thomas A. Van, "The Dionysian Horrific in Thomas Harris's Novel, *The Silence of the Lambs*," *Kentucky Philological Review: Annual Meeting of the Kentucky Philological Association* 13 (1998), 44.

62. Ellis, "Before Her Lambs," 165.

63. Ibid., 170.

64. Stephanie Reich, "Paperback Pulp: *The Pirate, Black Sunday, Dubai*," *MERIP Reports* 54 (February 1977), 24.

65. Barney, Lecter's courteous orderly, is presumed by many readers to be black. Certainly, he is portrayed by African American actor Frankie Faison in three film adaptations of Harris's work. Yet the textual evidence for Barney's actually being black in Harris's novels *Silence* and *Hannibal* is not there. His hoarse voice reminds Starling of Aldo Ray (1926–1991), a *white* actor known for his tough-guy roles. Barney is physically described as massive in frame, but his race is not specified. He could be black, but he could also be white.

66. Intriguingly, for the marriage-less Starling, Mapp's enduring domestic presence in her life suggests an "alternative" lifestyle free of patriarchal imprisonment, with a covert hint of lesbianism thrown in for spice. Note, for example, the "A.M.-C.S." ring that Starling sends to Mapp while on the lam with Lecter, suggestive of betrothal.

67. Robert Plunket, "Eating Our Own," *Advocate* 31 (August 1999), 74.

## CHAPTER TWO

1. There's another resemblance to take note of here, as Alex Diaz-Granados points out. The plot of Tom Clancy's novel *The Sum of All Fears* (1991) also features an attack against

the Super Bowl by Palestinian terrorists. In Clancy's novel, the terrorists are aided by an American, who facilitates their placement of a nuclear bomb at the Denver stadium where the game is taking place. Diaz-Granados concludes that Clancy's novel is "clearly inspired" by Harris's thriller. In "*Black Sunday*: A Look at a Pre-9-11 Novel about Terrorism in the U.S.," http://www.associatedcontent.com/article/12831/black_sunday_a_look_at_a_pre911_novel.html?cat=38.

2. Christopher Lehmann-Haupt, "Steelers, Vikings, and Arabs," *New York Times*. January 9, 1975, 33.

3. Newgate Callendar, "Terror at the Super Bowl," *New York Times Book Review*, February 2, 1975, 4.

4. Stephanie Reich, "Paperback Pulp: The Pirate, Black Sunday, Dubai." *MERIP Reports* no. 54 (February 1977), 24.

5. S. T. Joshi, *The Modern Weird Tale* (Jefferson, NC: McFarland, 2001), 181.

6. David Sexton, *The Strange World of Thomas Harris* (London: Short Books, 2001), 47.

7. Stephen King, "Hannibal the Cannibal," *New York Times Book Review*, June 13, 1999, 4.

8. Diaz-Granados, "*Black Sunday*: A Look at a Pre-9-11 Novel about Terrorism in the U.S."

9. Scott D. Briggs, "*Black Sunday*, Black September: Thomas Harris's Thriller, from Novel to Film, and the Terror of Reality," in *Dissecting Hannibal Lecter: Essays on the Novels of Thomas Harris*, ed. Benjamin Szumskyj (Jefferson, NC: McFarland, 2008), 188.

10. Ibid., 198.

11. Ibid., 188.

12. Thomas Harris, *Black Sunday* (New York: Bantam, 1977), 61.

13. Ibid., 63.

14. Briggs, "*Black Sunday*, Black September," 191.

15. Harris, *Black Sunday*, 82.

16. Briggs, "*Black Sunday*, Black September," 189.

17. Harris, *Black Sunday*, 26.

18. Ibid., 221.

19. Ibid., 47.

20. Harris himself makes this point: "I had always liked the character of Dahlia Iyad in *Black Sunday* and wanted to do

a novel with a strong woman as the central character." In "Foreword to a Fatal Interview," *Red Dragon* (New York: Dell, 2000), xii.

21. Harris, *Black Sunday*, 55.

22. Ibid., 263.

23. Ibid., 155.

24. Ibid., 200.

25. Ibid., 158.

26. Ibid., 131.

27. Ibid., 154.

28. Ibid., 19.

29. Briggs, "*Black Sunday*, Black September," 190.

30. Harris, *Black Sunday*, 310.

31. Ibid., 2.

32. Ibid., 59.

33. Ibid., 127.

34. Ibid., 140.

35. Mark Seltzer, *Serial Killers: Death and Life in America's Wound Culture* (New York: Routledge, 1998), 1.

36. Harris, *Black Sunday*, 82.

37. Reich, "Paperback Pulp," 25.

## CHAPTER THREE

1. Stephen King, "The Cannibal and the Cop," *Washington Post Book World*, November 1, 1981, 1–3.

2. Joseph Amiel, Review of *Red Dragon*, by Thomas Harris, *Saturday Review*, November 1981, 77.

3. Christopher Lehmann-Haupt, Review of *Red Dragon*, by Thomas Harris, *New York Times*, November 10, 1981, C11.

4. Jean Strouse, "Such a Cut-Up," *Newsweek*, November 9, 1981, 105–106.

5. Thomas Fleming, "Hunting Monsters," *New York Times Book Review*, November 15, 1981, 14.

6. David Sexton, *The Strange World of Thomas Harris* (London: Short Books, 2001), 58.

7. Daniel O'Brien, *The Hannibal Files: The Unauthorized Guide to the Hannibal Lecter Trilogy* (London: Reynolds & Hearns, 2001), 14–15.

8. John Goodrich, "Hannibal at the Lectern: A Textual Analysis of Dr. Hannibal Lecter's Character and Motivations in Thomas Harris's *Red Dragon* and *The Silence of the Lambs*," in *Dissecting Hannibal Lecter: Essays on the Novels of Thomas Harris*, ed. Benjamin Szumskyj (Jefferson, NC: McFarland, 2008), 39.

9. Robert H. Waugh, "The Butterfly and the Beast: The Imprisoned Soul in Thomas Harris's Lecter Trilogy," in *Dissecting Hannibal Lecter: Essays on the Novels of Thomas Harris*, ed. Benjamin Szumskyj (Jefferson, NC: McFarland, 2008), 84–85.

10. Tony Williams, "From *Red Dragon* to *Manhunter*," in *Dissecting Hannibal Lecter: Essays on the Novels of Thomas Harris*, ed. Benjamin Szumskyj (Jefferson, NC: McFarland, 2008), 102.

11. Davide Mana, "This Is the Blind Leading the Blind: Noir, Horror, and Reality in Thomas Harris's Red Dragon," in *Dissecting Hannibal Lecter: Essays on the Novels of Thomas Harris*, ed. Benjamin Szumskyj (Jefferson, NC: McFarland, 2008), 88.

12. Philip Simpson, "The Contagion of Murder: Thomas Harris's *Red Dragon*," *Notes on Contemporary Literature* 25, no. 1 (January 1995), 8.

13. S. T. Joshi, "Suspense vs. Horror: The Case of Thomas Harris," in *Dissecting Hannibal Lecter: Essays on the Novels of Thomas Harris*, ed. Benjamin Szumskyj (Jefferson, NC: McFarland, 2008), 124.

14. Tony Magistrale, "Transmogrified Gothic: The Novels of Thomas Harris," in *A Dark Night's Dreaming: Contemporary American Horror Fiction*, eds. Tony Magistrale and Michael A. Morrison (Columbia, SC: University of South Carolina Press, 1996), 31.

15. Phillip A. Ellis, "Before Her Lambs Were Silent: Reading Gender and the Feminine in *Red Dragon*," in *Dissecting Hannibal Lecter: Essays on the Novels of Thomas Harris*, ed. Benjamin Szumskyj (Jefferson, NC: McFarland, 2008), 160.

16. Nicholas M. Williams, "Eating Blake, or an Essay on Taste: The Case of Thomas Harris's *Red Dragon*," *Cultural Critique* no. 42 (Spring 1999), 137.

17. In many ways, Graham seems to be an amalgamation of Robert Ressler and John Douglas, two of the FBI profilers Harris met at Quantico.

18. Davide Mana writes that Graham's "course will bring him . . . on a head-on collision with those same traumas he is trying to avoid, forget, exorcise." In "This Is the Blind," 93.

19. Thomas Harris, *Red Dragon* (New York: Bantam, 1987), 2.

20. Ibid., 15.

21. Ibid., 174.

22. Harris discards this aspect of Lecter's childhood behavior in the later novels; possibly it would make Lecter all too common.

23. Harris, *Red Dragon*, 54.

24. Ibid., 270–271.

25. Ibid., 349.

26. Ibid., 184.

27. Ibid., 163.

28. Ibid., 11.

29. Ibid., 346.

30. Ibid., 262.

31. Ibid., 11.

32. Ibid., 63.

33. There seems to be ample confusion among critics and the general public about the exact title of this painting. A Blake painting housed in the National Gallery of Art in Washington, D.C., is officially titled *The Great Red Dragon and the Woman Clothed with the Sun,* and a painting in the Brooklyn Museum is also officially titled *The Great Red Dragon and the Woman Clothed with the Sun.* The two paintings, while depicting similar subject matter, are clearly different from one another. The Brooklyn Museum painting seems to fit the brief description given in the book, yet this same painting is often called by others *The Great Red Dragon and the Woman Clothed in Sun.* The Brooklyn Museum is also the place where Dolarhyde goes to eat the original Blake painting. Just to make matters more confusing, the *Manhunter* film adaptation shows the National Gallery painting, whereas the *Red Dragon* film shows the Brooklyn Museum painting. For the sake of consistency, let's agree to favor the title the Brooklyn Museum gives to its own painting.

34. Robert H. Waugh, "The Butterfly and the Beast," 72.

35. Harris, *Red Dragon*, 39.

36. Waugh, "The Butterfly and the Beast," 73.

37. Philip L. Simpson, *Psycho Paths: Tracking the Serial Killer through Contemporary Film and Fiction* (Carbondale, IL: 2000), 87.

38. The goggles' red color symbolizes aggression. They also resemble the night-vision goggles worn by Jame Gumb in *Silence*.

39. Robert H. Waugh calls her blindness "a grace; she is relieved from the control that comes from too great a reliance on the sense of sight." "The Butterfly and the Beast," 73.

40. The "guest star" of 1054 was first observed by Chinese astronomers. Present-day theory holds that the guest star was in fact a supernova, creating the Crab Nebula. Of course, Dolarhyde thinks of himself as a "comet plunging through the Crab Nebula." Harris, *Red Dragon*, 76.

41. Tony Williams elaborates: "[Graham] finally accepts Lecter's philosophy that an inhumane universe governs the whole of human existence, a fact he previously attempted to deny." "From *Red Dragon* to *Manhunter*," 111.

## CHAPTER FOUR

1. Douglas Winter, "Anatomy of a Murderer," *Washington Post Book World*, August 23, 1988, http://www.newsbank.com.

2. Christopher Lehmann-Haupt, "The Return of Hannibal the Cannibal," *New York Times*, August 15, 1988, C16, http://www.galenet.galegroup.com.

3. William Leith, "Terror Couple Kill Colonel," *Books* 3, no. 5 (August 1989), 11.

4. John Lanchester, "Strangers," *London Review of Books*, July 11, 1991, 5.

5. John Katzenbach, "She Hunts for a Killer with a Killer at Her Side," *Chicago Tribune Books*, August 14, 1988, 7.

6. David Sexton, *The Strange World of Thomas Harris* (London: Short Books, 2001), 99.

7. Daniel O'Brien, *The Hannibal Files: The Unauthorized Guide to the Hannibal Lecter Trilogy* (London: Reynolds & Hearns, 2001), 69.

8. Joe Sanders, "At the Frontiers of the Fantastic: Thomas Harris's *The Silence of the Lambs*," *The New York Review of Science Fiction*, no. 39 (November 1991), 1.

9. Tony Magistrale, "Transmogrified Gothic: The Novels of Thomas Harris," in *A Dark Night's Dreaming: Contemporary American Horror Fiction*, eds. Tony Magistrale and Michael A. Morrison (Columbia, SC: University of South Carolina Press, 1996), 28.

10. Peter Messent, "American Gothic: Liminality in Thomas Harris's Hannibal Lecter Novels," in *Dissecting Hannibal Lecter: Essays on the Novels of Thomas Harris*, ed. Benjamin Szumskyj (Jefferson, NC: McFarland, 2008), 15.

11. S. T. Joshi, "Suspense vs. Horror: The Case of Thomas Harris," in *Dissecting Hannibal Lecter: Essays on the Novels of Thomas Harris*, ed. Benjamin Szumskyj (Jefferson, NC: McFarland, 2008), 127.

12. Linda Mizejewski, *Hardboiled & High Heeled: The Woman Detective in Popular Culture* (New York: Routledge, 2004), 174.

13. Ibid., 185–186.

14. Harriett Hawkins, "Maidens and Monsters in Modern Popular Culture: *The Silence of the Lambs* and *Beauty and the Beast*," *Textual Practice* 7, no. 2 (Summer 1993), 259.

15. Bruce Robbins, "Murder and Mentorship in *The Silence of the Lambs*," *boundary 2* 23, no. 1 (1996), 88.

16. John Goodrich, "Hannibal at the Lectern: A Textual Analysis of Dr. Hannibal Lecter's Character and Motivations in Thomas Harris's *Red Dragon* and *The Silence of the Lambs*," in *Dissecting Hannibal Lecter: Essays on the Novels of Thomas Harris*, ed. Benjamin Szumskyj (Jefferson, NC: McFarland, 2008), 46–47.

17. Edith Borchardt, "Criminal Artists and Artisans in Mysteries by E. T. A. Hoffman, Dorothy Sayers, Ernesto Sabato, Patrick Suskind, and Thomas Harris," in *Functions of the Fantastic: Selected Essays from the Thirteenth International Conference on the Fantastic in the Arts*, ed. Joe Sanders (Westport, CT: Greenwood Press, 1995), 125.

18. Robert H. Waugh, "The Butterfly and the Beast: The Imprisoned Soul in Thomas Harris's Lecter Trilogy," in *Dissecting Hannibal Lecter: Essays on the Novels of Thomas Harris*, ed. Benjamin Szumskyj (Jefferson, NC: McFarland, 2008), 75.

19. Robert Ziegler, "Incorporation and Rebirth in *The Silence of the Lambs*," *Notes on Contemporary Literature* 23, no. 2 (March 1993), 8–9.

20. O'Brien, *Hannibal Files*, 69.

21. Brigham even bestows a special benediction or blessing upon her as she leaves to investigate the murder in West Virginia, which indicates the degree to which her teachers believe in her exceptionality.

22. Thomas Harris, *The Silence of the Lambs* (New York: St. Martin's Press, 1989), 117.

23. Ibid., 142.

24. Ibid., 274.

25. Either Graham doesn't really take notice of this detail about Lecter, which seems unlikely for someone with a near-photographic memory, or Harris just hadn't thought of it yet at the time of *Red Dragon*.

26. Harris, *Silence*, 224.

27. Ibid., 20.

28. Ibid., 76.

29. Ibid., 280.

30. Interestingly, when it came time for Ted Tally to adapt the novel for the screen, most of this background material was omitted, other than Lecter's throwaway reference to Buffalo Bill having been made into a monster rather than born one.

31. Harris, *Silence*, 302.

32. Ed Gein was a rural Wisconsin man arrested in 1957 for two murders of women. Following his arrest, investigators searched his isolated farmhouse where he lived alone. They found gruesome evidence of murders and grave-robbing. A gutted woman hung in a shed on the property. In the house were human skulls, chairs upholstered with human skin, female genitalia, and many other disturbing finds. Gein confessed to digging up the graves of middle-aged women who reminded him of his dead mother. He also wanted to have a sex-change operation, but in lieu of that donned the tanned skins of the dead women he dug up. Gein's mother fixation and macabre transvestitism not only shaped the character of Jame Gumb, but also Norman Bates in Robert Bloch's novel *Psycho* (1959). Tobe Hooper's film *The Texas Chainsaw Massacre*

(1974) is also influenced by the Gein case. The farmhouse in Hooper's film is decorated in similar grisly fashion to Gein's house, and "Leatherface," the chainsaw-wielding maniac, wears a mask of human skin similar to the one found during the police search of Gein's house.

33. Harris, *Silence*, 348.
34. Ibid., 70.
35. Ibid., 235.
36. Ibid., 144.
37. Ibid., 224.
38. Ibid., 171.
39. Ibid., 347.
40. Ibid., 4.
41. It's information like this that really makes one wonder exactly what kind of sources Harris consults while writing his novels.
42. Waugh, "The Butterfly and the Beast," 73.
43. Sexton, *Strange World*, 85.
44. Ibid., 87.
45. Starling references another classic of children's literature (or possibly the film version), *The Wonderful Wizard of Oz* (1900) by L. Frank Baum, when she says to herself in the storage unit after finding the head in the jar, "Well, Toto, we're not in Kansas anymore." Just as Dorothy finds herself in the strange new land of Oz, Starling is now in a place where she has never been before, and she must rely upon her own internal resources to navigate it. We see her determination immediately afterward, when she faces down the television crew with a jack handle.
46. Harris, *Silence*, 226–227.
47. *Dissecting Hannibal with a Blunt Little Tool*, http://www. hannotations.com.
48. Waugh, "The Butterfly and the Beast," 75.
49. Hannah is spared from the slaughterhouse, going with Starling to the orphanage. It's possible Starling drives a Pinto because its name reminds her of Hannah. The movie version removes Hannah entirely from the story, substituting a favored lamb that Starling attempts to rescue from the spring slaughter. The lamb is killed when Starling is brought back to

the ranch. It's an even bleaker story of childhood loss than that mentioned in the novel. Interestingly, the young Hannibal has a family draught horse named Cesar that survives the war to be stabled at the state orphanage with Hannibal. It seems Starling and Lecter live parallel early lives.

50. Harris, *Silence*, 230.

51. Ibid., 367.

52. This scene is handled powerfully in Jonathan Demme's film version, when a visibly uncomfortable Starling is left alone within a circle of men much larger than her. The men stare at her with varying degrees of lust, contempt, and curiosity clearly etched on their faces.

53. Dr. Noble Pilcher also hits on Starling during their professional meetings, but she accepts his advances. Why? First, he is described as having "witchy eyes," which symbolically feminizes him. Second, he is a nonthreatening male from a profession other than the patriarchal worlds of law enforcement and psychiatry. Entomology, as an academic discipline not dependent upon intrusive force, apparently has the Harris seal of approval.

54. Harris, *Silence*, 37.

55. Ibid., 121.

56. Ibid., 122.

57. In *Hannibal*, even Lecter possesses transcendental aspirations. He substitutes quantum physics for magical thinking and belief in God. He thinks he can somehow find a way to reverse time and bring Mischa back by putting Starling in her place.

58. Ibid., 21.

## CHAPTER FIVE

1. Lewis Grossberger, "Give Him a Hand," *MediaWeek*, July 5, 1999, 38.

2. Jeff Giles, "Guess Who's Coming to Dinner? Lecter Returns," *Newsweek*, June 21, 1999, 75.

3. Robert Plunket, "Eating Our Own," *Advocate*, August 31, 1999, 74.

4. Terry Teachout, "Feel His Pain," *National Review*, July 12, 1999, 53.

5. Robert Winder, "A Contemporary Dracula," *New States-man*, June 21, 1999, http://search.ebscohost.com.

6. Mark Dery, "Brain Food," *Village Voice*, June 22, 1999, http://search.ebscohost.com.

7. Christopher Lehmann-Haupt, "Lecter Returns, and One of His Victims Is Out for Revenge," *New York Times (Late Edition)*, Thursday, June 10, 1999, E1.

8. David Edelstein, "Caveat Hannibal Lecter," *Slate*, June 17, 1999, http://www.slate.com.

9. Richard Alleva, "'Hannibal': Nearly Indigestible." *Commonweal*, March 9, 2001, 25.

10. Annie Gottlieb, "'Free-Range Rude.'" *The Nation*, July 19, 1999, 30.

11. Paul Gray, "Dessert, Anyone?" *Time*, June 21, 1999, 72. Apparently Gray does not consider Dolarhyde's biting off the lips of Freddy Lounds and then setting him on fire sadistic, but that's another discussion.

12. Michelle West, Review of *Hannibal*, by Thomas Harris, *Fantasy and Science Fiction* 98, no. 2 (February 2000), 30.

13. Stephen King, "Hannibal the Cannibal," *New York Times Book Review*, June 13, 1999, 4.

14. S. T. Joshi, "Suspense vs. Horror: The Case of Thomas Harris," in *Dissecting Hannibal Lecter: Essays on the Novels of Thomas Harris*, ed. Benjamin Szumskyj (Jefferson, NC: McFarland, 2008), 128.

15. Robert H. Waugh, "The Butterfly and the Beast: The Imprisoned Soul in Thomas Harris's Lecter Trilogy," in *Dissecting Hannibal Lecter: Essays on the Novels of Thomas Harris*, ed. Benjamin Szumskyj (Jefferson, NC: McFarland, 2008), 76.

16. Daniel O'Brien, *The Hannibal Files: The Unauthorized Guide to the Hannibal Lecter Trilogy* (London: Reynolds & Hearns, 2001), 133.

17. Benjamin Szumskyj, "Morbidity of the Soul: An Appreciation of *Hannibal*," in *Dissecting Hannibal Lecter: Essays on the Novels of Thomas Harris*, ed. Benjamin Szumskyj (Jefferson, NC: McFarland, 2008), 210.

18. David Sexton, *The Strange World of Thomas Harris* (London: Short Books, 2001), 140.

19. Charles Gramlich, "Afterword: Mythmaker," in *Dissecting Hannibal Lecter: Essays on the Novels of Thomas Harris*, ed. Benjamin Szumskyj (Jefferson, NC: McFarland, 2008), 215.

20. Peter Messent, "American Gothic: Liminality in Thomas Harris's Hannibal Lecter Novels," in *Dissecting Hannibal Lecter: Essays on the Novels of Thomas Harris*, ed. Benjamin Szumskyj (Jefferson, NC: McFarland, 2008), 27–28.

21. Philip L. Simpson, "Gothic Romance and Killer Couples in *Black Sunday* and *Hannibal*," in *Dissecting Hannibal Lecter: Essays on the Novels of Thomas Harris*, ed. Benjamin Szumskyj (Jefferson, NC: McFarland, 2008), 65.

22. O'Brien, *Hannibal Files*, 137.

23. As we know from *Silence*, Lecter drew a picture of Florence and kept it on display in his cell. Why did the authorities not think to look for him in Florence? *Hannibal* is full of narrative illogicalities like this. However, with the novel's overall surreal tone, they don't really matter.

24. Harris, *Hannibal* (New York: Dell, 2000), 214.

25. Ibid., 291.

26. Ibid., 536.

27. Ibid., 28.

28. Ibid., 448.

29. This detail continues the unsettling tendency of Harris's fiction to associate speech impediments with killers.

30. Ibid., 132.

31. Ibid., 200.

32. Ibid., 477.

33. Ibid., 144.

34. Ibid., 151–152.

35. David Sexton calls these aphorisms "oracular . . . [standing] free from the flow of the narrative . . . and [showing] how far back from the scene of the action the text is being delivered." In *Strange World*, 143.

36. Harris, *Hannibal*, 31.

37. *Dissecting Hannibal with a Blunt Little Tool*, http://www.hannotations.com.

38. It should be noted that Balthus's ancestry is the subject of much debate. The painter claimed an extravagant lineage while denying any Jewish heritage in spite of evidence to the

contrary. The Web site *Dissecting Hannibal* discusses Balthus's self-embellished background in some detail at http://www.hannotations.com.

39. Sexton, *Strange World*, 148.

40. Ridley Scott's film adaptation alters Verger's death in two key elements. In the film, the eel is shown in only one brief early shot, never to be seen again. Margot's character does not even exist, so it is up to Verger's long-suffering assistant to kill Verger. Cordell shoves him, wheelchair and all, down into the barn, where the pigs consume him.

41. The snake is also a molting reptile, fitting the theme of transformation.

42. One exception to this is the owl, which symbolizes both the wisdom and rapaciousness of Dr. Lecter.

43. Harris, *Hannibal*, 105.

44. President Clinton was impeached during the winter of 1998–1999, on charges of perjury, obstruction of justice, and abuse of power as a result of the Monica Lewinsky scandal and the sexual harassment lawsuit of Paula Jones. The "Waco Siege" was a disastrous fifty-one-day standoff near Waco, Texas, in 1993 between the Bureau of Alcohol, Tobacco, and Firearms and the so-called Branch Davidians, a religious cult under the leadership of David Koresh. The standoff ended in the deaths of seventy-six men, women, and children. "Ruby Ridge" refers to another tragic siege in Idaho in 1992 between the Randy Weaver family and the FBI and U.S. federal marshals. During the twelve-day standoff, Weaver's wife and son, plus a federal marshal, were killed.

45. The film version of *Hannibal* excises both Ardelia Mapp and Margot Verger, thus entirely removing the theme of the female alternative to the nuclear family in favor of a safe re-integration of Starling back into mainstream society by the end of the film.

46. Stephen M. Fuller, "Deposing an American Cultural Totem: Clarice Starling and Postmodern Heroism in Thomas Harris's *Red Dragon*, *The Silence of the Lambs*, and *Hannibal*," *Journal of Popular Culture* 38, no. 5 (August 2005), 822–823.

47. Sexton, *Strange World*, 149.

48. Harris, *Hannibal*, 144.

49. Ibid., 146.

50. Ibid., 17.

51. Ibid., 150.

52. Ibid., 111.

53. Ibid., 523.

54. Fuller, "Deposing," 822.

55. Harris, *Hannibal*, 101–102.

## CHAPTER SIX

1. Anthony Lane, "First Bite: What's Eating Hannibal Lecter?" *New Yorker*, December 18, 2006, http://search.ebscohost.com.

2. Will Self, "Senseless Evil," *New Statesman*, January 8, 2007, 49.

3. Janet Maslin, "From Soup to Guts, the Making of a Foodie." *New York Times (Late Edition-Final)*, December 8, 2006, L/WD 31.

4. Tina Jordan, "Hannibal Lesser." *Entertainment Weekly*, December 15, 2006, 89.

5. Deidre Donahue, "'Hannibal' Prequel Doesn't Go Down Well," *USA Today*, December 7, 2006, 5D.

6. Thomas Leitch, "Getting to Know Dr. Lecter," *Kirkus Reviews*, January 1, 2007, 2.

7. Will Cohu, "Portrait of the Cannibal as a Young Man," *Telegraph*, January 7, 2007, http://www.telegraph.co.uk.

8. John Sutherland, "Into the Lists," *Telegraph*, December 24, 2006, http://www.telegraph.co.uk.

9. Steve Poole, "Portrait of the Monster as a Young Boy," *Guardian*, December 16, 2006, http://www.books.guardian.co.uk.

10. Peter Guttridge, "So That's Why Hannibal Eats People," *Guardian*, December 10, 2006, http://www.books.guardian.co.uk.

11. Tibor Fischer, "A Taste for Cannibalism Acquired Young," *Telegraph*, December 24, 2006, http://www.telegraph.co.uk.

12. Daniel Fierman et al., "Lecter Loses His Bite," *Entertainment Weekly*, February 23, 2007, http://search.ebscohost.com.

13. Charles Gramlich, "Afterword: Mythmaker," in *Dissecting Hannibal Lecter: Essays on the Novels of Thomas Harris*, ed. Benjamin Szumskyj (Jefferson, NC: McFarland, 2008), 216.

14. Peter Messent, "American Gothic: Liminality in Thomas Harris's Hannibal Lecter Novels," in *Dissecting Hannibal Lecter: Essays on the Novels of Thomas Harris*, ed. Benjamin Szumskyj (Jefferson, NC: McFarland, 2008), 26.

15. Robert H. Waugh, "The Butterfly and the Beast: The Imprisoned Soul in Thomas Harris's Lecter Trilogy," in *Dissecting Hannibal Lecter: Essays on the Novels of Thomas Harris*, ed. Benjamin Szumskyj (Jefferson, NC: McFarland, 2008), 84.

16. S. T. Joshi, "Suspense vs. Horror: The Case of Thomas Harris," in *Dissecting Hannibal Lecter: Essays on the Novels of Thomas Harris*, ed. Benjamin Szumskyj (Jefferson, NC: McFarland, 2008), 131.

17. Ali S. Karim, "*Hannibal Rising*: Look Back in Anger," in *Dissecting Hannibal Lecter: Essays on the Novels of Thomas Harris*, ed. Benjamin Szumskyj (Jefferson, NC: McFarland, 2008), 152.

18. Thomas Harris, *Hannibal Rising* (New York: Dell, 2007), 2.

19. Ibid., 187.

20. Ibid., 94.

21. Ibid., 324.

22. Ibid., 347.

23. Donahue, "'Hannibal' Prequel."

24. Harris, *Hannibal Rising*, 163.

25. Ibid., 23.

26. Ibid., 113.

27. Ibid., 132.

28. Ibid., 160.

29. Lane, "First Bite."

30. Poole, "Portrait of the Monster."

31. Cohu, "Portrait of the Cannibal."

32. Fischer, "A Taste for Cannibalism."

33. Harris, *Hannibal Rising*, 88.

34. Ibid., 293.

35. Ibid., 123.

36. Self, "Senseless Evil," 49.

37. Sutherland, "Into the Lists."

38. A side note: Lady Murasaki allows Harris to do more entomological name-dropping. Through her, we learn about the suzumushi, a Japanese bell cricket known for its clear, "sleigh-bell" song. The suzumushi apparently loves slices of

cucumber, which is exactly the kind of delightfully obscure factoid we have come to expect from Harris. This cricket is also mentioned in Chapter 38 of the *Tale of Genji*, making it a particularly apt gift for Lady Murasaki whenever she is nostalgic for her homeland.

39. Joseph Campbell, *The Hero with a Thousand Faces* (1949; rpt., New York: Barnes and Noble Books, n.d.), 58.

40. Ibid., 90.

41. Harris, *Hannibal Rising*, 115.

42. Ibid., 255.

# Index

# About the Author

PHILIP L. SIMPSON is associate provost at the Palm Bay campus of Brevard Community College in Florida. He has served as president of the Popular Culture Association and area chair of horror for the association. He received the association's Felicia Campbell Area Chair Award in 2006. He sits on the editorial board of the *Journal of Popular Culture*. His book *Psycho Paths: Tracking the Serial Killer through Contemporary American Film and Fiction* was published in 2000. He is the author of numerous other essays on film, literature, popular culture, and horror.